Rock Concert Performance from ABBA to ZZ Top

FOR THE RECORD:
LEXINGTON STUDIES IN ROCK AND POPULAR MUSIC

Series Editors:
Scott D. Calhoun, Cedarville University
Christopher Endrinal, Florida Gulf Coast University

For the Record: Lexington Studies in Rock and Popular Music features monographs and edited collections that examine topics relevant to the composition, consumption, and influence of the rock and popular music genres which have arisen starting in the 20th century in all nations and cultures. In the series, scholars approach these genres from music studies, cultural studies, and sociological studies frameworks, and may incorporate theories and methods from literary, philosophical, performance, and religious studies, in order to examine the wider significance of particular artists, subgenres, fandoms, or other music-related phenomena. Books in the series use as a starting point the understanding that as both products of our larger culture and driving forces within that wider culture, rock and popular music are worthy of critical study.

Advisory Board

Joshua Duchan, Wayne State University; David Easley, Oklahoma City University; Bryn Hughes, University of Miami; Greg McCandless, Full Sail University; Ann van der Merwe, Miami University; Meg Wilhoite

Titles in the Series

Rock Concert Performance from ABBA to ZZ Top, by Peter Smith with Laura Smith

Portraying Performer Image in Record Album Cover Art, by Ken Bielen

Rock and Roll, Social Protest, and Authenticity: Historical, Philosophical, and Cultural Explorations, by Kurt Torell

"We Didn't Start the Fire": Billy Joel and Popular Music Studies, edited by Joshua S. Duchan and Ryan Raul Bañagale

The Rock Music Imagination, by Robert McParland

From Factory Girls to K-Pop Idol Girls: Cultural Politics of Developmentalism, Patriarchy, and Neoliberalism in South Korea's Popular Music Industry, by Gooyong Kim

Rock and Romanticism: Blake, Wordsworth, and Rock from Dylan to U2, edited by James Rovira

The Beatles, Sgt. Pepper, and the Summer of Love: Roll Up for the Mystery Tour! edited by Kenneth Womack and Katheryn Cox

U2 Above, Across, and Beyond: Interdisciplinary Assessments, edited by Scott D. Calhoun

Rock Concert Performance from ABBA to ZZ Top

Peter Smith
With Laura Smith

LEXINGTON BOOKS
Lanham • Boulder • New York • London

Short dedication—14/16

Lengthy dedication—Text size

Bring down to align with top of copyright.

Published by Lexington Books
An imprint of The Rowman & Littlefield Publishing Group, Inc.
4501 Forbes Boulevard, Suite 200, Lanham, Maryland 20706
www.rowman.com

86-90 Paul Street, London EC2A 4NE

Copyright © 2022 The Rowman & Littlefield Publishing Group, Inc.

All rights reserved. No part of this book may be reproduced in any form or by any electronic or mechanical means, including information storage and retrieval systems, without written permission from the publisher, except by a reviewer who may quote passages in a review.

British Library Cataloguing in Publication Information Available

Library of Congress Cataloging-in-Publication Data Available

Names: Smith, Peter, 1956- author. | Smith, Laura (Singer) author.
Title: Rock concert performance from ABBA to ZZ Top / Peter Smith, with Laura Smith.
Description: Lanham : Lexington, 2021. | Series: For the record: Lexington studies in rock and popular music | Includes bibliographical references and index. | Summary: "This book presents an analysis of 100 rock concert performances and answers the question 'What makes a truly great rock performance?' Peter Smith delves into his own recollections of experiencing rock performances and covers themes of icons, persona, energy, fandom, venues, communities, politics, art-rock, authenticity and maturity" —Provided by publisher.
Identifiers: LCCN 2021046920 (print) | LCCN 2021046921 (ebook) | ISBN 9781793618566 (cloth) | ISBN 9781793618580 (paper) | ISBN 9781793618573 (epub)
Subjects: LCSH: Rock concerts. | Rock music—History and criticism.
Classification: LCC ML3534 .S579 2021 (print) | LCC ML3534 (ebook) | DDC 781.66078—dc23
LC record available at https://lccn.loc.gov/2021046920
LC ebook record available at https://lccn.loc.gov/2021046921

This book is dedicated to the memory of my lovely wife, Marie, who sadly passed away, yet dances, skips and meanders her way through these pages and accounts. She wanders with me through the dark fields of Knebworth, past the smoking campfires, while the Rolling Stones perform "Jumpin' Jack Flash"; she pogos in front of the Sex Pistols in Scarborough; she drinks with Elvis Costello, Captain Sensible and me in Newcastle Polytechnic student bar; she marvels at the wonder of Kate Bush in Sunderland Empire and many years later in Hammersmith Apollo, London; she dances crazily to Muse in Wembley Stadium and at the Pyramid stage at Glastonbury; she twirls hand-in-hand with Yoko Ono in Liverpool; she shakes hands with Burt Bacharach in Edinburgh Playhouse; she ignores the steward who points a torch in her face telling her to come down from a tower as she watches David Bowie at the Point, Dublin; she runs to the stage and stands in front of Jack Bruce at the Albert Hall, London during the encore at the Cream Reunion; she returns home from Manchester after losing her shoe in a mad crush at an Oasis concert in Bolton Stadium (which she did not enjoy at all); and she manages to blag all of the family good seats after refusing to stand during the massively oversubscribed Led Zeppelin reunion gig at the O2 Arena, London. I think about her always; and I miss her every day.

Contents

Acknowledgments ix

Introduction 1

1 Methodological Approach 5
2 Icons 21
3 Persona 37
4 Energy 51
5 Fandom 71
6 Venues 89
7 Communities 103
8 Politics 121
9 Art-rock 135
10 Authenticity 151
11 Maturity 167

Conclusion 185

References 189

Index 205

About the Authors 217

Acknowledgments

I would like to acknowledge the help and support of many people without whom this book would not have been possible. Firstly, my children, Ashleigh, David, and Laura, and my sister-in-law, Elaine, who accompanied me to many of the gigs written about within this text and especially to Laura for supporting me in the writing of the book. I would also like to thank (in no particular order): Norm, John (who now lives in the United States, remains in touch, and is a good friend), Gilly, Willy, Terry, Tony, Nicky (who I met on the train to and from Newcastle when we were both young and then we accompanied each other to many gigs after that), the late, sadly missed, Clive who introduced me to "the boys," Davey and his brother Pete, Ian F., Ian M., Geoff Doherty for promoting so many gigs in the North East that I attended, Pauline (who Marie and I chatted with at many early punk gigs), Colin, and too many others to mention; all of whom accompanied me to many concerts and/or I ran into at concerts. Apologies if I have missed anyone; I am lucky enough to have had many friends over the years and continue to do so. I will blame old age and my poor memory if I have missed you. I would also like to thank my group of carers, Alison, Chris, Elaine, Hannah, Jackie, Joanne, Laura, Lisa, Naomi, and Vikki, who supported me throughout the period of writing the book and some of whom accompanied me to concerts and continue to do so. Finally, I would like to thank Courtney and Scott who supported me throughout the long period it has taken me to complete this book.

Introduction

This book presents an analysis of the phenomenon of rock in concert. It uses a blended methodology which draws from published and recognised methodologies of Auslander (1998, 2004, 2008) and Vallack (2010) for analysing performance and applies this to a series of concerts and genres, discussing what makes live performance such a special and unique experience. The authors draw from the primary author's (Peter's) own experience of attending over 2,000 concerts since the late 1960s to the present day, and from published academic research on the phenomenon of live performance (Smith, 2013; 2015a; 2016a; 2016b; 2017; 2018). The book concludes by drawing new perspectives on what factors are important in defining a "good" rock performance. I (Peter) believe that my richness, depth and breadth of experience in attending rock concerts can draw new light upon the phenomenon of rock performance.

I have always been fascinated by rock music, and, in particular, rock concerts. This started in 1969 when, as a twelve-year-old, I attended my first pop concert which featured the Bonzo Dog band, a new progressive rock band, Yes and protest singer Roy Harper. From that day I was hooked. I started to go to as many concerts as I possibly could, as a teenager following the rock bands of the time including Led Zeppelin, Deep Purple, Black Sabbath, the Who and the Rolling Stones. Over the next forty-plus years I attended over 2,000 concerts, covering a range of genres including pop, heavy metal, punk, new wave and progressive rock.

I decided to start recording my concert experiences as a blog (www.Vintagerock.WordPress.com). This was soon extended to cover every concert that I have attended, along with images of tickets and programmes which I have collected and archived over the years. Soon I began to write about popular music and my work was published in edited collections and journals (see for example, Smith 2013). I also presented my blog at a series of conferences (Smith 2014a, Smith 2014b, Smith 2015a) and began to look for ways to analyse the performances I have attended to answer the question "what makes a good rock concert performance?"

I then suffered a life-changing accident; I fell down the stairs in my own home and broke my neck leaving me paralysed from the neck downwards. This devastating experience has given me the time and space to reflect upon many things, including my concert experiences, and it is this, along with my academic training and curiosity, which has led me to write this text.

This short introduction summarises the content of the book for the reader. The book starts with the methodological approach to be followed and the research questions to be addressed. Then, through a series of ten chapters I discuss 100 live performances which I have personally attended. These are grouped according to themes. Each chapter discusses one theme and considers 10 performances, each of which are analysed to draw out the important characteristics which go to make up a live performance. The final chapter draws all the characteristics together in order to address my research questions.

Chapter 1 Methodological Approach. This chapter discusses the methodological approach which is based on that of Auslander (2004) and Vallack (2010) and has been applied by Smith (2013; 2015a) to analyse rock performance. I use Vallack's methodology for valid, first-person research located within phenomenology (2010), alongside Auslander's schema for performance analysis (2004). I also use elements of autoethnography (Ellis et al., 2011) and reflection (Gibbs, 1988).

First, I reflected upon the body of concerts I had attended, drawing out themes from the body of work, which I felt were important in characterising rock performance. The 10 themes I arrived at were:

- Icons. Those bands that define rock 'n' roll and rock performance; classic bands like Led Zeppelin, the Rolling Stones and the Who. Bands that I have followed throughout their careers.
- Persona. The way in which artists take on a new persona in performance such as David Bowie as Ziggy Stardust and Alice Cooper as Alice.
- Energy. The raw energy that drew me to exciting bands, particularly those of punk and new wave such as the Sex Pistols, the Clash and the Damned.
- Fandom. Those bands that drew and created massive fan bases including pop bands and artists such as Madonna, Prince and ABBA.
- Venues. The importance of venues in the concert experience: ranging from folk clubs through to arenas and stadiums.
- Communities. The importance of community in rock music. How festivals such as Knebworth and Glastonbury form their own important community.

- Politics. Those bands and artists who use music to give political messages including Pete Seeger, Bob Dylan and Crass. The theme also encapsulates events set up to address political and charitable issues including massive concerts such as Live Aid.
- Art-rock. This theme covers artists who blend art with rock, including performances by David Bowie and Yoko Ono.
- Authenticity. The importance of being "real" and authentic, covering artists such as Bruce Springsteen, Nick Cave and Patti Smith.
- Maturity. How rock music has reached a stage of maturity where elderly bands such as the Rolling Stones and the Who perform to audiences of all ages.

The approach I followed was: First, I wrote largely descriptive narrative accounts of my memories of the live performances, recalling as much detail as I could. These narrative accounts then formed the basis of my analysis. I immersed myself in the literature relating to the period, setting the performance in the context of the sociological and political climate of the time. I also watched videos of similar live performances and read reviews of the band/artist at the time. In doing so, this enabled me to inform my discussion and analysis of the live performance. I then updated and reread the accounts and performed an analysis of the performance using the approach based on the schema of Auslander (2004). Having immersed myself in the accounts I then stepped back from the material, as recommended by Vallack (2010), waiting for meaning and themes to emerge. After a short period of quiet reflection, I completed my analysis, drawing out final conclusions which addressed the following research questions:

- What constitutes a "good" live performance?
- What are the crucial elements of a live performance?

The chapters which follow use the above methodology to address those research questions. Ratner (2002) explores the role of subjectivity and its relationship to objectivity in qualitative research. The late Melanie Jasper (2011) taught me the importance of reflection as an approach to qualitative research. Ellis, Adams and Bochner (2011) have established the validity of autoethnography in research. In this text I blend these techniques to produce a critical analysis of rock music in performance.

Chapter 2. Icons. This chapter discusses the phenomenon of the rock "icon": the bands and artists who define rock music for their generation and beyond.

Chapter 3. Persona. This chapter explores the way in which certain artists take on alternative persona as part of their performance, for example David Bowie as Ziggy Stardust, Kiss, the Damned as Gothic pioneers, Alice Cooper and Captain Beefheart.

Chapter 4. Energy. This chapter focuses upon the growth of punk rock, from its infancy in pub rock to its metamorphosis into new wave.

Chapter 5. Fandom. This chapter explores the role of fandom, particularly in relationship to pop music.

Chapter 6. Venues. This chapter discusses the important role that venues play in the concert experience.

Chapter 7. Communities. In this chapter I discuss the importance of coming together at large rock music gatherings such as pop festivals (Anderton, 2018).

Chapter 8. Politics. This chapter discusses the role of rock in discussing and supporting social causes, politics and charity.

Chapter 9. Art-rock. In this chapter I discuss the interface between art and rock music, focusing upon the concept of performance art.

Chapter 10. Authenticity. This chapter discusses the role of authenticity in live performance (Tetzlaff, 1994; Albrecht, 2008).

Chapter 11. Maturity. This chapter discusses the concept of "elderly rock," both in terms of older bands and artists such as the Rolling Stones, the Who, Bob Dylan, the Hollies and Status Quo, alongside the concept of the elderly rock fan (including me).

Conclusion. This chapter draws conclusions about the importance and future of rock in performance, drawing from the analyses in the previous chapters. It addresses the initial research questions and draws together the new themes which have been derived in each of the preceding chapters. These include: the relationship between the audience and the performer as termed "the fifth wall" by Smith (2017), the concept of "epiphany" and life-changing concert performances (Guerra & Bennett, 2015) and rock music as "church" (Finnegan, 2003).

Chapter One

Methodological Approach

This chapter discusses the methodological approach taken, which is a blended approach based on that of Auslander (2004) and Vallack (2010), along with elements of autoethnography (Ellis et al., 2011) and reflection (Gibbs, 1988). This approach has been used in previous published work to analyse concert performances by the Rolling Stones (Smith, 2013), the Who (Smith, 2016b), the Sex Pistols (Smith, 2015b; Smith, 2018), and the Clash (Smith, 2017).

The methodological approach was developed over six phases, as shown in Figure 1.1, starting with the development of a blog of concerts, which was collected as narrative accounts, and moving gradually into an approach which was tested and published in a series of conference, book chapters, and a journal paper. The development took place over a period of nine years. Each phase of the development is discussed in detail below.

PHASE 1. CREATING THE BLOG; DEVELOPING THE NARRATIVES (2010–2016)

I have always enjoyed going to rock concerts. I first started going to see bands in 1969 when I was twelve years old. My first concert experience was at my local theatre, the Sunderland Empire, when I went to see the Bonzo Dog Band supported by Yes and Roy Harper. I sat, wide-eyed, alone in the front row mesmerised by the loud music and the bright, strange guys performing just a few feet in front of me. From that point I was totally hooked on going to see rock bands and started going to as many concerts as I could.

Throughout the 1970s, 1980s, and to the present day, I continued (and continue) to attend rock concerts; my favourite bands being traditional classic rock bands such as the Rolling Stones, Led Zeppelin, the Who, David Bowie,

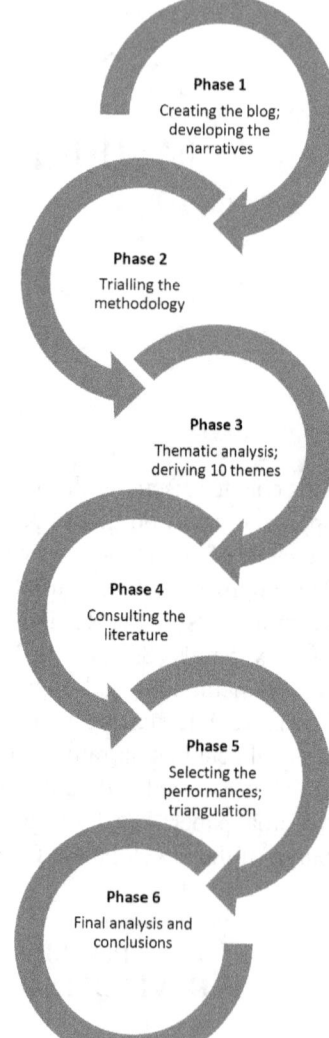

Figure 1.1. Methodological Approach

and Bob Dylan. Over the years I attended over 2,000 concerts by over 1,000 artists and bands. My musical taste broadened, and I went to see bands from many different genres including ABBA, Barbra Streisand, Michael Jackson, Madonna, Prince, Bob Marley, Oasis, Queen, Ravi Shankar, Bruce Springsteen, Burt Bacharach, and many others.

In 2010, I decided to start blogging about my concert experiences. At first, I would write about concerts as I attended them, making notes about the performance, including images of my ticket and my programme, and including a review of the performance and the setlist. I introduced my blog to the world as below:

> Hi, I have finally come clean and admitted to myself that I am totally addicted to going to rock concerts. I have also realised that all attempts at treatment are futile, and anyway I don't want to be cured! This blog is part of my treatment, in creating a permanent record of the gigs that I go to. So far, I have just succeeded in listing the gigs I have been to over the past two or three years.

My blog can be found at www.Vintagerock.WordPress.com.

At the end of 2011, I made a New Year's resolution to begin to write a blog each day, in order to catalogue all my concert experiences. My approach was this. Each day I would select a concert that I had attended and write a narrative account of the event, trying to remember as much detail as I could about the performance, the venue, the interaction between the artist and the audience, and personal details such as who I attended the concert with and how I felt at the time. This was a challenge at times and in order to refresh my memory and provide a more authentic account, I would consult my friends who came to the concert with me, and also scan the internet for reviews of the time and published setlists of that particular concert or from the tour.

This task took me back to concerts from the late 1960s and early 1970s including artists such as the Who, Eric Clapton, the Rolling Stones, Pink Floyd, Led Zeppelin, T Rex, the Sex Pistols, the Clash, Kate Bush, and festivals such as the Reading Rock Festival, Donington Monsters of Rock, Live Aid and Live 8, and significant recent reunion concerts such as the Led Zeppelin reunion at the London O2 arena and the Cream reunion at the Royal Albert Hall.

I have collected and catalogued my ticket stubs and programmes from the concerts (I always bought a programme when one was available) and I scanned these in and included them within my narrative accounts. I had over 1,000 ticket stubs and over 500 programmes in my collection. The programmes also included important and useful data which informed my narrative accounts. I started my project on 1 January 2012, aiming to write 365 blogs in 365 days. I commenced the process by selecting significant concerts and writing accounts of those; however, I soon realised that I needed to be more systematic, and I began to follow an alphabetical process, working through my concerts from the letter A and the band ABBA towards the end of my blog with the letter Z and the band ZZ Top.

When I attended a new concert, that would be my blog for the next day. In that way I was cataloguing my previous concert attendance, but also keeping an up-to-date account of my numerous current concert attendances. I also had to take account of a significant number of gigs for which I did not have a ticket stub or a programme, such as club gigs where the ticket was given up at the door, or gigs for which there was no ticket. There were many of these, when I had attended concerts in nightclubs, ballrooms, and University student unions; nonetheless these were important narratives to include.

For some bands, who I had seen many times, such as, for example, Status Quo who I had seen over forty times, I would write narratives which spanned several performances. For other bands and artists, who I deemed to be significant such as, for example, Bob Dylan, I would write very detailed narrative accounts of each performance that I had attended by that artist. In this way, I constructed a rich dataset of narratives which formed a picture of concert performances of many genres over a fifty-year period.

My original academic training was in mathematics, so my methodological approach had always been quantitative. However, I was now leading a professional doctorate programme at the University of Sunderland (Fulton et al., 2013), and supervising students who came from a business studies and social science background, which led me to qualitative methodologies and methods such as narrative accounts, thematic analysis (Janowski, 2013), autoethnography (Ellis et al., 2011), and reflection (Gibbs, 1988).

In writing my narrative accounts, I was guided by the work of Baumeister and Newman (1994) who discuss how autobiographical narratives can be used to make sense of personal experience, and De Fina and Georgakopoulou's *Handbook of Narrative Analysis* (2019), which gives a comprehensive coverage of the use of narrative accounts and storytelling in qualitative analysis. I also drew from some of my own previous work on storytelling (Smith et al., 2013) in which I used storytelling, along with colleagues, to support police officers in learning from their own personal experiences as part of a management development programme.

This mammoth exercise took me over three years to complete. By 2012 I reached the band ZZ Top, which completed my journey through my ticket and programme collection, and my memories of past concert experiences. At that point I had covered over 2,000 concerts and over 1,300 artists/bands. I also gained almost 500 followers who often commented on my blog, sometimes correcting mistakes in setlists or reminding me who the support act was!

My blog had become a resource for others, and I was receiving comments on a daily basis from followers around the world. Each year, WordPress would provide me with an annual report and some highlights. In 2014, the annual report stated:

> The Louvre Museum has 8.5 million visitors per year. This blog was viewed about 94,000 times in 2014. If it were an exhibit at the Louvre Museum, it would take about 4 days for that many people to see it. There were 819 pictures uploaded, taking up a total of 247 MB. That's about 2 pictures per day. The busiest

day of the year was January 21st with 1,176 views. The most popular post that day was David Bowie Roker Park Glass Spider Tour 23 June 1987.

Typical comments included:

Hi there Peter! Came across your blog, good stuff! In fact, brilliant, to be exact :)! I am too young to have seen bands from the seventies live, but I love the era nonetheless, I collect tickets from back then, and I saw you have a lot of them (or at least scans of them). Is there any chance you'd consider selling any? I would be an easy target for you if so LOL. The Bon Scott era tickets are pieces of rock history. Thanks anyway and wish for happy days to come for both you and your blog! Best wishes from Norway. (Posted by Levi on March 4, 2013)

Hello Peter just discovered your blog after doing a search on Kiki Dee. I am very impressed with your record of musical history and the fact that you have kept all of those concert tickets in such good condition over the years. Visiting this site was like taking a stroll through a Museum of Music. Excellent blog; I will visit this site again. Well done! (Posted by Michael Quinlyn-Nixon on October 1, 2014)

PHASE 2. TRIALLING THE METHODOLOGY (2013–2018)

In 2013 I began to consider my blogging as a longer-term research project and started to utilise my narrative accounts as a dataset for qualitative analysis. I was interested in using my experiences to assess what makes live performance so important to so many people, and the reasons that drew me to it in the first place.

I immersed myself in the literature of popular music and musicology, starting with Simon Frith's seminal text (Frith, 1998). I was lucky enough to attend a lecture by Frith at my own University (Frith, 2011) and one by Brian Eno at the Edinburgh Festival (Eno, 2013). I began to attend conferences on popular music and took my first steps into presenting my blog and my approaches to the analysis of rock performance (Smith, 2014a; 2014b; 2015a).

Auslander (2004) gave me a useful schema for the analysis of performance which distinguishes between the performer, persona, character, means of expression, and the audience. I used this schema as my initial approach to analysing concert performances. In his book *Liveness* Auslander (2008) addresses the question "what is the status of live performance in a culture dominated by mass media?" In this seminal text, Auslander examines specific instances of live performance including theatre, rock music, sport, and courtroom testimony. His analysis includes exploration of the themes of authenticity and memory; themes which begin to play out within my own analysis of the phenomenon of rock concert performance.

Vallack (2010) argues that "it is possible to do rigorous research using subjective, first-person data," and I use her theoretical framework as a basis for my thematic analysis. I also use elements of autoethnography (Ellis et al., 2011) and reflection (Gibbs, 1988). Autoethnography is "an approach to research and writing that seeks to describe and systematically analyse personal experience in order to understand cultural experience" (Ellis et al., 2011). Ellis's work provided me with a means of analysing my own personal experiences of rock performances. However, as this analysis was undertaken sometime after my actual attendance at the performance it can be argued that the approach is one of reflection (as exemplified by, for example, Gibbs, 1988) rather than autoethnography.

The research questions which I wished to address are:

- What constitutes a "good" live performance?
- What are the crucial elements of a live performance?

My peer-reviewed essay "Ladies and Gentlemen, the Greatest Rock 'n' Roll Band in the World: Reflections of the Rolling Stones in Concert" explored the transition of the Rolling Stones from an outsider, rebellious force to becoming members of the rock establishment, the longevity of the band, and the arguments for them deserving the title "the Greatest Rock 'n' Roll Band in the World." This chapter appeared in the collection *The Rolling Stones: Sociological Perspectives* (Staubmann, 2013).

I presented at the International Festival for Artistic Innovation at Leeds College of Music (Smith, 2014a), leading a discussion around the question "How might we analyse popular music performance?" At the Changing Face of Popular Music Performance conference, University of Northampton, I presented my blog as a resource for exploring popular music performance from the 1970s onward (Smith, 2014b). In my paper "Making Private Experiences Public: Creating a Blog of Rock Performance" (Smith, 2015a), presented at the Popular Music Fandom and the Public Sphere conference, Chester University, I discussed the process of creating personal narratives and making them public, thus creating a resource for reference, comment, and critique.

My paper "Holidays in the Sun: The Sex Pistols at the Seaside" (Smith, 2015b), which was published in the journal *Popular Music and Society*, contrasted two performances that I attended by the Sex Pistols. The first, in a small public house in the Yorkshire fishing village of Whitby, saw the band perform a short set before a shocked and incredulous crowd attending a Saturday disco. At this point in their career, the Sex Pistols were relatively unknown and only a tiny section of the crowd had come to see the band perform. The second performance saw the Sex Pistols play an incendiary and triumphant gig to a packed crowd of punks and rock fans in a small club in the Yorkshire town of Scarborough. By this point in their career, in the summer of 1977, the band were notorious and forced to perform secret gigs on the SPOTS (Sex Pistols On Tour Secretly) tour.

In my chapter "A Personal History of UK Arena Concerts: Reflections on Gigs over the Past Forty Years" (Smith, 2016a), which was published in *The Arena Concert: Music, Media and Mass Entertainment*, I turned my analysis towards the theme of venues and the role which they play in the concert experience, focusing on the growth of purpose-built concert arenas in the UK.

A further chapter, "An Analysis of the Who in Concert: 1971 to 2014" (Smith, 2016b), which was published in *The Who and Philosophy*, analysed fifteen performances by the Who which I personally attended, focusing on the themes of violence as part of the performance (including Pete Townshend's famous guitar smashing routines) and the way in which the band and their fans survived the tragic loss of the two key members Keith Moon and John Entwistle and discussing how a band is a more complex "being" than simply the sum of its members, based on the principles of Gestalt (Stott & Drury, 2004).

I then turned my focus toward classic punk rock band the Clash and their interaction with their audience in a book chapter entitled "An Analysis of the Clash in Concert: 1977 to 1982" (Smith, 2017), which was published in *The Clash Takes on the World: Transnational Perspectives on The Only Band that Matters*. I focus my analysis on the following interlinked themes: tension and violence in the performance and the audience, the clash between the band's values and the reality of the performance, and "cultural conflict" in all aspects of the performance. I go on to propose the concept of the fifth wall The "fourth wall" is the imaginary "wall" at the front of the stage in a traditional three-walled theatre, through which the audience sees the action (Bell, 2008). At this concert, I experienced a fifth wall that which divided those outside the venue and wishing to gain entrance, from those inside the hall attending the concert. The fifth wall became a focus for conflict, at which punks and non-students fought to gain entry to this all-student concert.

Finally, I expanded my analysis and discussion of the Sex Pistols to form a full text for students of popular music and media studies, entitled *The Sex Pistols: The Pride of Punk* (Smith, 2018).

In this way, I trialled my methodology, taking my first steps into formalising my approach to the analysis of concert performance. These first steps, analysing limited sets of performances by a single band, enabled me to test and refine my approach. This prepared me for the next stage of my analysis. However, as is often the case, my life took an unexpected twist, and my work was halted for a short period.

PHASE 3. THEMATIC ANALYSIS; DERIVING TEN THEMES (2016–2018)

I then suffered a life-changing accident. In April 2016, I fell down the stairs in my own home and broke my neck, damaging my spinal cord and leaving me paralysed from the neck downwards. I spent six months in hospital undergoing physical and emotional therapy, and eventually returned home, able to work online and return to writing using speech technology.

Clifton (2014) who, himself, suffered a spinal cord injury argues that work plays "a prominent part in the narrative of human life" and is "central to persons happiness." He further discusses the relationship between work, hope, and optimism. I soon realised that I needed to return to work, research, and writing to keep my mind active and to remain positive and optimistic about my future and my own well-being.

Towards the end of 2016, I returned to my project, performing a thematic analysis of my narrative accounts, treating them as the "content" (Smith, 2000) for my analysis. My approach was thus: Each day, I read through a small number (usually around three) of my narrative accounts, noting down themes which I deemed relevant and important in terms of my two research questions. Having immersed myself in the accounts, I then stepped back from the material, as recommended by Vallack (2010), waiting for meaning and the final themes to emerge. Vallack (2010) bases her approach within the phenomenology of Husserl (1970). After a period of quiet reflection, I completed my analysis, drawing out final themes which I felt were important in characterising rock performance and answering my research questions. I arrived at ten themes, at which point I felt I had reached saturation (Ando et al., 2014).

The ten themes I arrived at were:

- Icons. Those bands who define rock 'n' roll and rock performance; classic bands like Led Zeppelin, the Rolling Stones, and the Who. Bands that I have followed throughout their careers.
- Persona. The way in which artists take on a new persona in performance such as David Bowie as Ziggy Stardust and Alice Cooper (Vincent Furnier) as Alice.
- Energy. The raw energy that drew me to exciting bands, particularly those of the punk and new wave era such as the Sex Pistols, the Clash, and the Damned.

- Fandom. Those bands who drew and created massive fan bases including pop bands and artists such as Madonna, Prince, and ABBA.
- Venues. The importance of venues in the concert experience: ranging from folk clubs through to arenas and stadiums.
- Communities. The importance of community in rock music. How festivals such as Knebworth and Glastonbury formed their own important communities.
- Politics. Those bands and artists who use music to give political messages including Pete Seeger, Bob Dylan, and Crass. This theme also encapsulates events set up to address political and charitable issues including massive concerts such as Live Aid.
- Art-rock. This theme covers artists who blend art with rock, including performances by David Bowie and Yoko Ono.
- Authenticity. The importance of being "real" and authentic, covering artists such as Bruce Springsteen, Nick Cave, and Patti Smith.
- Maturity. How rock music has reached a stage of maturity where elderly bands such as the Rolling Stones and the Who perform to audiences of all ages.

PHASE 4. CONSULTING THE LITERATURE (2018)

The approach I then took was as follows. I reviewed the literature relating to each theme. This enabled me to set my analysis in the context of the academic literature relating to each theme.

- Icons: I reviewed the literature on those bands whose concerts I had selected to analyse, including Led Zeppelin (Calef, 2011), the Who (Gennaro & Harrison, 2016), and the Rolling Stones (Staubmann, 2013). I also included reference to my own work on iconic bands (Smith, 2013; 2016b). These texts focused on the philosophical constructs underpinning the work of each band or artist. This included, for example, themes such as the occult (Led Zeppelin), violence (the Who), and longevity (the Rolling Stones).
- Persona: I reviewed the literature on the use of persona in rock music including work by Auslander (2009), Lacasse (2005), Marshall (2014), and Cochrane (2010). This informed my analysis in terms of the way in which artists used alternative persona as part of their performance. Auslander (2009) argues that "the visual aspects of musical performance" including physical and gestural dimensions, are important to music.
- Energy: Here I grounded my analysis in my own published work (Smith, 2015; 2017; 2018) and that of others such as Sabin (2002) and Laing (2015). These writings explored the energy of punk rock and new wave

and how this transformed rock performance, making it more accessible to a new generation of rock fans.
- Fandom: I reviewed the literature on fandom in popular music including work by Bickerdike (2015) who discusses fandom in terms of religion and pilgrimage, Fiske (1992) who explores fandom as a cultural economy, Lewis (2002) who writes of an "adoring audience," and Gray, Sandvoss and Harrington (2017) who argue that "most people are fans of something."
- Venues: This theme explores the important role that venues play in the concert experience. I reviewed literature on concerts in pubs (Friedlander, 2018) and clubs (Brocken, 2017) through to the phenomenon of arena concerts (Edgar et al., 2016), from the early days of concerts in ice rinks and cattle sheds to the growth of purpose-built arenas such as the O2 arena in London.
- Communities: Here I reviewed literature which explores the phenomenon of communities as rock music gatherings such as pop festivals (Anderton, 2018). This includes consideration of a historic perspective on the growth of music festivals from the early roots in folk music to major events such as Monterey (Hill, 2017), the Isle of Wight Festival, and Woodstock (Bennett, 2017). I then reviewed literature on festivals which I have personally attended such as the Reading Rock Festival, the Knebworth events (Bannister, 2003), and Glastonbury (Aubrey, Shearlaw & Eavis, 2005).
- Politics: I reviewed recent literature on the interface between politics and music including work by Arvidsson (2016) and Feezell (2017). I also explored literature on the phenomenon of rock as charity events including Live Aid (Grant, 2015), Live 8, and other charitable rock concerts.
- Art-rock: Here I reviewed the literature on performance art (Johnson, 2015; Jones, 2018; Goldberg, 2001) and writings on performances (Auslander, 2016) by artists including Kate Bush (Thomson, 2015), Yoko Ono (Clayson, Jungr & Johnson, 2004), and David Bowie (Waldrep, 2016).
- Authenticity: I discussed the literature on the role of authenticity in live performance (Tetzlaff, 1994; Albrecht, 2008), illustrating this by reviewing Bird's (1994) analysis of the authenticity of Bruce Springsteen.
- Maturity: There is limited literature on the concept of "elderly rock," both in terms of older bands and artists such as the Rolling Stones, the Who, Bob Dylan, the Hollies, and Status Quo, alongside the concept of the elderly rock fan (see, for example, Gibson, 2010). Kotarba (2005) has worked in this area, exploring rock 'n' roll experiences in middle age.

PHASE 5. SELECTING THE PERFORMANCES; TRIANGULATION (2019)

Having identified the themes, I wished to explore these further; as I believed in doing so, I could enrich the arguments and characteristics supporting the themes. In order to do so, I decided to revisit the narrative accounts, selecting ten performances for each theme. I chose the number "ten," as I believed that would give me an appropriate selection of performances to enrich my discussion, based loosely on the principle of saturation as argued by Ando et al. (2014).

I selected the ten performances for each theme based on the following criteria:

- the performances spanned musical genres, in order to draw from a wide range of performance type
- the performances crossed the time dimension, covering the 1970s to the present day and thus allowing me to explore the way in which concert performance has evolved over the years

I then continued to enrich my analysis by watching videos of the artists from the chosen period and read reviews of the artists in performance from music papers of the time using RocksBackPages (https://www.rocksbackpages.com/) as a resource for further reference material. In this way I triangulated my narrative accounts with video evidence and reviews from the period. I updated each narrative account accordingly. Davidson (2001) discusses the use of triangulation to balance subjectivity with objectivity.

The performances which I selected are listed in Table 1.

PHASE 6. FINAL ANALYSIS AND CONCLUSIONS (2019)

In the final phase of my project, I reconsidered each narrative account, addressing my two research questions:

- What constitutes a "good" live performance?
- What are the crucial elements of a live performance?

This enabled me to construct a richer and more detailed answer to the above questions. This also drew out the final themes, as below.

- Personal context. The narrative accounts revealed how important my own personal context was to the concert experience; who I went with, how old I

Table 1.1. Selected Performances by Theme

Theme	Artist	Genre	Year
Icons	Rolling Stones	Classic Rock	1970s
	Led Zeppelin	Classic Rock	1970s
	The Who	Classic Rock	2000s
	U2	Classic Rock	1980s
	Deep Purple	Heavy Rock	1970s
	Status Quo	Classic Rock	1980s
	Elton John	Singer/Songwriter	2000s
	Rod Stewart and the Faces	Classic Rock	1970s
	Bob Dylan	Singer/Songwriter	1970s
	Queen	Classic Rock	1970s
Persona	David Bowie	Art-Rock	1970s
	Captain Beefheart	Alternative	1970s
	Alice Cooper	Heavy Rock	1970s
	Kraftwerk	Electronica	1970s
	Kiss	Heavy Rock	1980s
	Culture Club	Pop	1980s
	Lady Gaga	Pop	2010s
	Twisted Sister	Heavy Rock	1980s
	Screaming Lord Sutch	Rock and Roll	1980s
	The Damned	Punk Rock	1970s
Energy	Sex Pistols	Punk Rock	1970s
	The Stranglers	Punk Rock	1970s
	The Ramones	Punk	1970s
	The Clash	Punk Rock	1970s
	The Prodigy	Dance	2010s
	Dr Feelgood	Rhythm & Blues	1970s
	Elvis Costello	New Wave	1970s
	Siouxsie and the Banshees	Punk	1970s
	The Libertines	Indie Rock	2010s
	Penetration	Punk	1970s
Fandom	ABBA	Pop	1970s
	Wham!	Pop	1980s
	Madonna	Pop	2000s
	Prince	Pop	2000s
	Michael Jackson	Pop	1980s
	Paul McCartney	Pop	1990s
	Bay City Rollers	Pop	1970s
	Slade	Classic Rock	1970s
	Spice Girls	Pop	1990s
	Cher	Pop	1990s
Venues	The Who	Classic Rock	1970s
	Barbra Streisand	Middle of road	2000s
	The Vibrators	Punk	1970s
	Simon and Garfunkel	Singer/Songwriter	1980s
	John Martyn	Folk Rock	1970s
	Yes	Progressive	1970s
	Ringo Starr	Pop	2000s
	Roy Harper	Folk Rock	1970s
	Rainbow	Heavy Rock	1980s
	Bob Dylan	Singer/Songwriter	1970s

Theme	Artist	Genre	Year
Communities	Lincoln Festival	Classic Rock	1970s
	Knebworth Festival—Allman Brothers	Classic Rock	1970s
	Buxton Festival	Classic Rock	1970s
	Glastonbury	Alternative	2010s
	Maryport Blues Festival	Blues	2000s
	Rocking the Castle	Heavy Rock	1980s
	Reading Festival	Progressive	1970s
	6 Music Festival	Alternative	2010s
	Futurama Festival	Punk Rock	1980s
	Hyde Park	Classic Rock	2010s
Politics	Live Aid	Multi-genre	1980s
	Live 8	Multi-genre	2000s
	Red Wedge—The Smiths	Alternative	1980s
	Bob Dylan	Singer/Songwriter	1990s
	Joan Baez	Folk Rock	2000s
	Pete Seeger	Folk	1970s
	Peggy Seeger	Folk	2010s
	Crass	Alternative	1980s
	Edgar Broughton	Alternative	1970s
	Hawkwind	Progressive	1970s
Art-rock	Yoko Ono	Art-rock	2000s
	Bjork	Art-rock	2010s
	David Bowie Tribute	Art-rock	2020s
	War of the Worlds	Rock Theatre	2000s
	Kate Bush	Art-rock	1980s
	Massive Attack	Dance	2010s
	Roxy Music	Art-rock	1970s
	Brian Eno	Art-rock	2010s
	Talking Heads	Art-rock	1980s
	Genesis	Progressive	1970s
Authenticity	Nick Cave and the Bad Seeds	Alternative	2010s
	U2	Classic Rock	1980s
	Arctic Monkeys	Alternative	2000s
	Oasis	Alternative	2000s
	Bob Marley	Reggae	1970s
	Neil Young	Southern Rock	1970s
	Lynyrd Skynyrd	Southern Rock	1970s
	Bruce Springsteen	Singer/Songwriter	1970s
	Ravi Shankar	World Music	2010s
	Patti Smith	New Wave	2010s
Maturity	The Rolling Stones	Classic Rock	2010s
	The Who	Classic Rock	2010s
	Bob Dylan	Singer/Songwriter	2010s
	The Hollies	Pop	2010s
	Status Quo	Classic Rock	2010s
	60s Gold Tour	Pop	2010s
	Led Zeppelin Reunion	Classic Rock	2000s
	Black Sabbath	Heavy Rock	2010s
	The Kinks	Classic Rock	2010s
	The Grateful Dead	Classic Rock	2010s

was at the time, how I travelled to and from the concert, and the social and political context in which the performance was set. Baxter-Moore (2016) has explored similar phenomena in the blogs and forums of fans attending Springsteen concerts.
- Rock concert as "church." Several authors (Cohen, 2016; Harmon, 2014; Pattie, 2007) have written about rock concerts having the status of religious experiences, with the masses travelling to worship their "gods."
- Epiphany. Several writers have written about how they experienced a personal "epiphany" at a rock concert. Morrisey felt that nothing was ever the same once he had seen the Sex Pistols at Manchester Lesser Free Trade Hall (Morrissey, 2013). Others have written of rock concerts as life-changing experiences; Peter Hook also wrote of how his life changed when he first attended the same Sex Pistols concert (Albiez, 2006). In my own case, the closest I got to such an experience was experiencing Bruce Springsteen in concert for the first time in London in 1976 and seeing the Sex Pistols in Whitby in the same year.

This concluded my analysis and has added to the literature and analysis of live rock concert performances.

LIMITATIONS

I recognize the autobiographical nature of this account, and the limitations of my approach. The approach taken is, to some extent, subjective; however, I make no excuses for this as I believe there is strength in the subjective nature of my methodological approach. Ratner (2002) explores the role of subjectivity, and its relationship to objectivity in qualitative research. The late Melanie Jasper (2011) taught me the importance of reflection as an approach to qualitative research. Medhurst (1999) writes of the danger of the "I was there" approach and how emotion, and personal connections to events and memories, can dampen critical analysis. However, Turrini (2013) argues that alternative approaches such as the narrative and oral history (as used by Robb, 2006) are suited to the analysis of popular music.

SUMMARY

This chapter has presented the methodological approach taken throughout this text. The approach is in six phases and took place over a nine-year period. The approach taken is a blended methodology which draws from several approaches including those of Auslander (2008), Vallack (2010), reflection (Gibbs, 1988), and autoethnography (Ellis et al., 2011). The approach taken is subjective by nature; however, I have strived as much as I could to add objectivity to my analysis.

Chapter Two

Icons

This chapter discusses icons; those bands and artists who have reached iconic status and taken on a meaning and an importance which transcends their music. These are artists who have become part of our day-to-day language and culture, icons that many, young and old, look up to and idolise. Artists who sell out stadiums and arenas all over the world and whose lyrics and music mean so much to so many people. Shumway (2014) discusses the making of musical icons, setting them in the context of other cultural icons such as film stars (Judy Garland, Elizabeth Taylor, Cary Grant) and those who transcend genres (Barbra Streisand, Elvis Presley). Shumway discusses how these artists have made their way into the heart of our culture and the hearts and minds of followers all over the world; their legends even transcending their own lifespan.

In this chapter I discuss concerts by ten iconic artists that I have personally attended, including Led Zeppelin, the Rolling Stones, Elton John, and the Who. Each of these bands and artists carry their own legends and, in many cases, links to philosophical concepts including Led Zeppelin and their links to the occult (Calef, 2011), the Who and violence (Smith, 2016b), and the Rolling Stones and their longevity (Baker et al., 2013).

Table 2.1 lists the artists covered within the chapter.

THE ROLLING STONES, KNEBWORTH, 21 AUGUST 1976

By 1976 the Rolling Stones were arguably at the peak of their success. They had just released their thirteenth studio album *Black and Blue*, which gained mixed reviews, but which Scoppa (1976) felt was their best album since *Exile*

Table 2.1. Icons Analysed in This Chapter

Artist	Genre	Date of Performance
Rolling Stones	Classic Rock	1970s
Led Zeppelin	Classic Rock	1970s
The Who	Classic Rock	2000s
U2	Classic Rock	1980s
Deep Purple	Heavy Rock	1970s
Status Quo	Classic Rock	1980s
Elton John	Singer/Songwriter	2000s
Rod Stewart and the Faces	Classic Rock	1970s
Bob Dylan	Singer/Songwriter	1970s
Queen	Classic Rock	1970s

on Main Street, often cited as the Stones' greatest achievement. The Knebworth festival of that year was a massive event of celebration. The band had sold out a big UK tour, and this show was added to satisfy the huge demand for tickets. The Stones had been disappointed with some of the reviews of their recent London Earl's Court concerts. The sound had been poor; with many fans leaving disappointed. Kent (1976) wrote in *New Musical Express* of the "*sheer oppressive enormity of the place*" and how "*one scrutinising peer around the hall will tell you that there's going to be trouble with the acoustics.*"

However, overall, the shows had been a success, certainly in terms of attendance. The Stones played six nights at the cavernous venue, compared to the run of five nights played by Led Zeppelin in 1975. I'd seen their Glasgow Apollo show a few weeks earlier but couldn't resist going to see them again at this big festival show. "*My main reason for doing Knebworth is for people who were disappointed with the sound at Earl's Court. Now they can hear it as it should be in a different setting. Although we played best at Earl's Court, I can understand a lot of the complaints,*" said new guitarist Ronnie Wood (Charone, 1976).

The year 1976 was a long, hot summer in the UK; one of the hottest for many years. Punk rock was beginning to emerge, and Marie and I would see the Sex Pistols for the first time in less than a month (Smith, 2018), but for many of us the old rock guard still represented our main musical interest.

It seemed everyone I talked to was going to make the trip South for this gig. I drove down with Marie and my friend John arriving the day before the concert. Marie wasn't a particularly big fan of the Stones, but she sensed that this was going to be a special event, one to be at and one to be seen at. Everywhere we walked we saw someone we knew, many smoking joints or tripping on LSD. The bad boys of the town congregated outside, trying to suss out a way of getting into the festival without paying. This was as much about bravado and the principle of music being free as it was about the actual cost of a ticket, which at £4.25 was relatively cheap particularly by today's standards, and the price the Stones charge to see them perform today. I'd been to the 1974 (Allman Brothers) and 1975 (Pink Floyd) Knebworth concerts, but the crowd for the Stones was much larger; with a capacity crowd of 100,000 attending the festival, some estimates of the size of the crowd were 250,000.

The supporting bill was pretty strong: Todd Rundgren put in a good set ("I Saw the Light" was one of my favourite tunes at the time), and Lynyrd Skynyrd almost stole the show with a mega version of "Freebird," complete with some superb guitar duelling. The stage was a giant tongue, based on the Stones logo, and two large screens projected the stage action to the back of the crowd. The Stones had planned the event around a large circus, and groups of jugglers and other circus acts mingled with the crowds. There was a long, long, tedious wait for the Stones who came on very late. Many stories circulate about the reasons for the band's late arrival onstage. Some state that it was due to trying to get the sound right; others claim Keith was waiting for delivery of cocaine before he would take to the stage.

It was clear that the Stones had intended this to be a marathon and memorable concert. This was probably one of the longest sets they ever played throughout their career, delving deep into their back catalogue and the many songs that had featured in their set since the 1960s. This started with "Satisfaction" and continued with a mixture of songs from the new album, rock 'n' roll classics, and well-known Stones' favourites such as "Get Off of My Cloud," "Let's Spend the Night Together," "Honky Tonk Women," "Brown Sugar," "Jumping Jack Flash," and "You Can't Always Get What You Want." Keith did his usual solo piece in "Happy," and Mick whipped the stage with his belt during "Midnight Rambler." The Stones finally left the stage at 2 a.m. Marie and I wandered around the back of the site, warming ourselves by the many fires which people had lit. We made our way back to our tent to the final strains of "Street Fighting Man," which was the encore. Although by no means the Stones' greatest performance, their Knebworth appearance remains a landmark in terms of the Stones' career and of rock performances. It was almost certainly their most historic performance since their free Hyde Park concert in 1969, which had been a tremendous success and a remarkable return after the death of Brian Jones. Cannon (1969) wrote in *New Society* of their performance "*If anyone doubts that the Stones are world No. 1 band, they weren't at Hyde Park.*" Although the Knebworth concert was not as excellent a performance as the Hyde Park show, it was certainly as memorable in its own right.

LED ZEPPELIN, EARL'S COURT, LONDON, 24 MAY 1975

Led Zeppelin were initially booked to play for three nights on 23, 24, and 25 May at the massive Earl's Court Arena in London, which has a capacity of 17,000. The venue had been used for concerts before, notably one by David Bowie, at which the sound was reportedly atrocious. Due to what Mel Bush described as *"unprecedented demand in the history of rock music,"* two further dates were added on 17 and 18 May. The total attendance for the five sold-out shows was 85,000. Bush negotiated with British Rail to advertise the ease with which Inter City trains could bring fans in. "The Zeppelin Express Physical Rocket" was how it was dubbed, and the posters for the event featured a picture of Zeppelin riding the express. There was no support act for the shows, and Zeppelin played a long set, around three hours, each night.

This was the first chance to see Led Zeppelin after an almost three-year gap since I'd last seen them at Newcastle City Hall in 1972. I went with my friend John and a couple more mates, and we travelled to London by train, and straight back after the show on the midnight train. It was the day of the Scotland England match at Wembley and the train home was completely packed, full of very drunk (and disappointed) Scots fans (England won 5-1), travelling home after the match. We couldn't get a seat and spent most of the night trying to sleep on the (cold metal) floor of the guard's van, which was pretty uncomfortable!

Tickets went on sale for personal applicants only at various points across the country. John and I queued all night at Virgin Records in Newcastle for our tickets. We arrived late, just before the pubs closed, and the queue grew massively overnight. I took my car and parked it beside the queue, hoping to catch some sleep. Some of the guys in the queue took a dislike to this idea and threatened to turn my car over, so I quickly moved it, on the advice of Bob Smeaton who was next to us in the queue (Bob Smeaton is a double Grammy award winner, and three time Emmy nominated director of music and arts documentaries. Prior to working in film and television, Bob was lead vocalist with the rock band White Heat who I saw many times). I parked the car a few streets away and re-joined the queue. When the box office opened, we were quite disappointed to find that all they had on sale were tickets with pretty poor views of the stage, up the back of the arena. This was often the case in those days, with the best seats being sold at the venue itself, in London.

When we arrived at Earl's Court, we found that our seats had an obstructed view. We were sitting behind a wide pillar and could not see anything. However, we were able to sit on the stairs between the rows of seats for the whole show, which gave us a great view. This was one of the first shows to use videotron screens at either side of the stage, which was very cool for the time, and the first time we had seen colour video screens. All the other screens I had seen before that, usually at outdoor festivals, were black and white, and used a projector. Looking back, the screens were pretty low tech compared to those in use today, but at the time they were streets ahead of anything seen before at a rock concert. The sound wasn't great but was acceptable and used a massive PA system hanging from the ceiling.

The compere for Saturday evening was Nicky Horne who opened the proceedings with something like "Welcome to Earl's Court. For the next three hours . . . your mother wouldn't like it." The Saturday night that we attended is often rated as the best night of the five shows, despite a couple of minor glitches such as Page's guitar cutting out during "In My Time of Dying." "Kashmir" was a particular highlight, and Plant joked. "If you go along the A449, past Droitwich, take the third turn on the right, Kashmir is just up there—it's got a white fence around it." "Tangerine" was dedicated to "families and friends who have been close to us through a lot. It's a song of love in its most innocent stages." "Trampled Underfoot" was simply breathtaking and included Robert unaccompanied leading into "Rip It Up" by Little Richard for a few bars.

A DVD of the show exists. John has a copy and watched it through to remind us of some of the details of the night, particularly Plant's stage banter. Page wore the Dragon Suit, Jonesy his Matador Jacket, Bonham a black T-shirt with a silver sequinned front, and Plant an open "short blue kimono." After "Rock and Roll" / "Sick Again," Plant welcomed us with "Good Evening (audience response). . . . Good Evening (louder response). Last time I was suffering from a touch of cholera, it seems to have worn off, must be all these eastern influences. Our intention is to play between three and three and half hours, and when we say play, we don't mean groove along (sings first line of "Living Lovin Maid" in a goofy voice). We intend to take you on a little journey, some of the experiences we have had which had made the music so different in (emphasis) . . . six and a half years!!" More banter, then "This is the beginning of that journey"—and then they play "Over the Hills and Far Away."

I'll leave the final comment on the gig to John: "I thought the entire set was great with "In My Time of Dying," "Trampled Underfoot," the acoustic set and "Stairway" being the highlights. "Sick Again" was a surprising choice. As you know I am not a big drum solo fan and by then I think "Whole Lotta Love" was sounding a bit 'overplayed,' but minor quibbles on a fantastic experience. I assume the posters must have been sold out by the time we got there, or I would have bought one. All I can say is this was the greatest gig I have ever seen. A great venue, great visuals and sound, and a great time to see the greatest rock and roll band of all time. Like a lot of things, at the time it felt a bit special, but I now realise it was a historic event. Sometimes the sun, moon, and stars are aligned, I feel very fortunate to have been present."

Pete Makowski, writing in *Sounds* (1975), gave the concert a great review:

> After about three and a half hours of music the audience left shattered and satisfied. Those who weren't obviously expected miracles. Zeppelin took away the cold informality of Earls Court and replaced it with a warm magical atmosphere that very few bands can create. The show had the dynamics, excitement and sheer professionalism that some people say represents the ultimate in rock. Somehow I find it difficult to argue with that.

THE WHO, THE ROYAL ALBERT HALL, LONDON, 29 MARCH 2004

This was the first major UK performance by the "Who 2," and the first since Pete Townshend's arrest and subsequent caution (Oswell, 2006). It was preceded by three warm-up gigs at the London Forum. The lineup was Roger Daltrey and Pete Townshend accompanied by Rabbit Bundrick on keyboards, Pino Palladino on bass, Zak Starkey (Ringo's son) on drums, and Simon Townshend (Pete's younger brother) on guitars and backing vocals.

The concert, which was part of a run of shows in support of the Teenage Cancer Trust for which Roger was Chair at the time, was originally announced as a performance of *Tommy*, but for some reason that never came to be, and what was actually performed was a set of Who classics. I went to the concert with my son, David. This was the first time we'd been to the Albert Hall, and we stayed in a hotel close to the venue.

We had quite good seats, near to the stage, on Pete's (right hand) side. Roger had a terrible cold and as a result he was singing in a raspy voice. You could see that it was hurting him when he sang. Pete wore black wrap-around visor sunglasses for the first couple of songs, which made him look cool and moody. Price (2004) says, "But all eyes, tonight more than ever, are on Pete Townshend, who plays with all the pent-up sexual energy, violence and abandon of a juvenile. There's a massive cheer the first time he executes a right-arm windmill." They premiered two new songs "Real Good-Looking Boy" and "Old Red Wine." It was great to see the Who in full flight again. At the end of the show, I could see that Pete was very emotional, with tears in his eyes; something I hadn't seen before. In his autobiography Townshend writes of Daltrey's support and how he felt that he needed to tour to thank everyone else who had supported him. Roger hugged him. "'A longstanding friendship that has turned into a bonded love, founded on a deeper understanding of each other's limitations': Townshend. 'I love him,' shrugs Daltrey. 'We're like brothers, I suppose.'"

It is unfair to attempt to draw comparisons between the current Who 2 and the 1970s Who. The soul of the band does continue to shine through the Who, through Daltrey and Townshend and through the audiences who continue to be part of the spectacle. But it is a different band, and it is impossible to re-create past performances. However, the essence is there, the values remain, and I remain grateful that I can still go to a Who concert, see Roger and Pete play those classic songs, and become part of that experience (Smith, 2016b).

The setlist was a mixture of old and new Who classics. They started with "Who Are You," followed quickly by my personal favourite Who opening songs "I Can't Explain" and "Substitute." There was a short section from *Quadrophenia*, which included "5:15," "Sea and Sand," and "Love Reign O'er Me." Other highlights were "The Kids Are All Right," "My Generation," and closing song "Won't Get Fooled Again." New songs included "Old Red Wine." The encore was "Pinball Wizard" followed by "Amazing Journey/Sparks/See Me Feel Me."

U2, NEWCASTLE MAYFAIR, 9 OCTOBER 1981

It is always a thrill to see iconic bands early in their career, especially in club settings. It was obvious, even in those early days, that U2, and Bono in particular, were very special. Their performances dripped passion and were filled with energy and commitment. And some of those early songs such as "Gloria" were truly excellent.

This gig came a couple of months after we had seen U2 deliver an incendiary performance at the Rock on the Tyne festival at Gateshead Stadium, where Bono clambered up the lighting towers, played the part of the rock star, and generally got everyone onside. The Mayfair was packed to the rafters. Everyone wanted to see this new band. U2 had just released their second album *October* and the excellent single "Gloria." There was something very different about U2; something that it was difficult to get a handle on or describe in the same terms as any other band of the period. To put it in some sort of context, U2 were coming up alongside the Teardrop Explodes and the Bunnymen, both excellent bands. But there was something almost intangible about U2 that seemed to set them apart. Their music came through new wave, but its roots lay deeply and squarely in the 1960s, beat, the Beatles, Stones, soul, religion, spirituality, and, of course, Van Morrison. Jim Green, writing in *Trouser Press*, in March 1982: "People haven't asked U2 if they're the future of rock. They've told them."

What I remember of this gig was a joyous, crazy night with Bono singing his heart out for us, and those great, powerful early songs: "Gloria," "I Will Follow," "Fire," and "11 O'Clock Tick Tock." The U2 who played those club gigs was a raw, hungry, stunning act who were a million miles away from the stadium rock band that they would very soon become. A different time, a different band, a different place. It seems so far away now. But on that night, in the heat and sweat and volume and crush of the Mayfair, U2 were shiny, young, new, and intense. And Bono ran around that stage and sang and sang for all of us. I have probably written this before about other bands, but on that night, in the Mayfair, as we all watched U2, they were simply the best band on the planet.

DEEP PURPLE, NEWCASTLE CITY HALL, 27 FEBRUARY 1973

Deep Purple were the classic heavy rock band of the late 1960s and early 1970s. Characterised by Jon Lord's swirling Hammond organ, Roger Glover's thundering bass, Blackmore's magical guitar playing, and Gillan's soaring, screaming vocals, with Ian Paice providing the thundering back beat. Blackmore was simply a revelation in those days, all in black, wearing his trademark pointed black hat with a silver buckle. His guitar would be up in the air, back and forth against his martial stack creating deafening feedback, and his fingers would weave their way up and down the fretboard like no other guitarist of his era. I recall sitting directly in front of him at one gig, and I could not take my eyes off him; I sat entranced and mesmerised. This was the last time that I saw the classic Deep Purple Mark II lineup in the 1970s. By this point tensions in the band were growing and relations between Gillan and Blackmore were not good. Altham (1973) viewed the band as "five maniacal egotists trying to blow each other off the stage." Both Gillan and Glover were to leave the band before the year was out. This tour came just as the *Who Do We Think We Are* album was released. This is not their strongest album, but it does feature the great hit single: "Woman from Tokyo."

Published setlists from the time show the set as being: Purple exploded onto the stage with a fiery version of "Highway Star." Other songs played included classics "Smoke on the Water," "Strange Kind of Woman," and "Lazy." They closed with "Black Night." My main recollection from the gig was how different Gillan looked. He had grown a beard and was wearing smart jacket and slacks; a very different image to that of previous tours. Reports of shows from that period suggest that you could sense the tensions within the band and the growing distance between the members, but I can't say I noticed anything amiss. I was sitting upstairs with a group of friends, and enjoyed the gig, although not quite as much as previous tours.

A few months later the unthinkable had happened and Gillan and Glover had both departed. I thought that was the end of Deep Purple, which was far from what transpired. In fact, the iconic band continued in many different guises with many different lineups until their recent farewell tour.

MONSTERS OF ROCK, DONINGTON, 21 AUGUST 1982

Lineup: Status Quo, Gillan, Saxon, Hawkwind, Uriah Heep, and Anvil

Are Status Quo an iconic band? Many would argue not, and they are often considered to be a joke, as opposed to a serious band. However, beauty is in the eye of the beholder, and to my mind Status Quo do deserve the term "icon." Consider the statistics. Status Quo have had over 60 chart hits in the UK, more than any other rock band starting from "Pictures of Matchstick Men" in 1968 through to "In the Army Now" in 2010. Twenty-two of these songs reached the top 10 in the UK singles chart. In 1985, Status Quo received a great accolade by being chosen to open the Live Aid event at Wembley Stadium.

This was the third Monsters of Rock festival, and the second time I went to the event. I drove down with my mate Dave, and we had a great time. It was a strong lineup of hard rock bands with Status Quo topping the bill, and a clutch of great support acts in Gillan, Saxon, Hawkwind, Uriah Heep, and Anvil. Tommy Vance was DJ and compere for the day. But the day rightly belonged to Quo, who were worthy headliners. We pushed our way right down the front for their set.

This show is often rated as not one of Quo's best, but I enjoyed seeing them headlining a festival again, and thought they were pretty good. There were some problems with the sound, with some parts of the crowd reporting that they couldn't hear Quo very well, but I think this depended on where you were placed in the field. This was the first time I saw the band with Pete Kircher who replaced John Coughlan on drums. Quo were celebrating their twentieth anniversary as a band. The remainder of the lineup was the classic Status Quo frontline of Francis Rossi, the late Rick Parfitt, and Alan Lancaster. The set was a collection of Status Quo favourites starting with the usual opener "Caroline" followed by a stream of hits including "Roll Over Lay Down," "Whatever You Want," "Rocking All over the World," "Down Down," and their excellent cover of the Doors' "Roadhouse Blues." As always, the closing song was Chuck Berry's "Bye Bye Jonny." Sinfield (2017) felt that "it was Status Quo, 'as laid-back and easy as ever' which gripped the crowd and ensured many remembered Monsters of Rock 1982 as one of the greatest."

ELTON JOHN, RABY CASTLE, 29 JULY 2000

From the Raby Castle website (2019): "Raby Castle was built by the mighty Nevills in the 14th century and is one of the finest and best-preserved medieval castles in North East England. Since 1626 it has been home to the Vane family and is currently the seat of the 12th Lord Barnard."

This was a solo concert with Elton and piano in the grounds of Raby Castle, Durham, as part of a tour of stately homes. Sir Elton said (Northern Echo, 2000): "This really will be an amazing show, as a major concert has never been staged at Raby before. I'm delighted to be part of history by being the first artist to play there."

The concert was heralded as "an intimate evening with Sir Elton," and the flamboyant fifty-two-year-old, who will not have a support act, will be playing the concert without a break (Northern Echo).

This was one of the first concerts I ever attended in the grounds of a stately home. Such concerts are much more common now, but at the time this seemed something quite different and new. It somehow matched Elton John's movement upwards to becoming a "national treasure." It had been some ten years since I last saw Elton in concert. I went with Marie, and we really enjoyed the experience of seeing Elton John perform in such a historic and serene setting. We had seats close to the front, which gave us a wonderful view of the stage and Elton himself. The weather wasn't too good with a little rain as I recall. The tickets were expensive at £50 each, which seemed a lot at the time.

But then we were seeing an icon performing in an iconic venue. It was exciting and a privilege to see such an icon at close quarters. Concerts such as this were the start of many such events to follow, which showcased artists in stately homes around the country and allowed concertgoers to take hampers of food and wine and buy glasses of Pimms and Prosecco at usually inflated prices.

Elton's set that evening covered a range of his greatest hits, all played solo seated at a grand piano. He started with "Your Song" and continued with a stream of well-known songs including "Someone Saved My Life Tonight," "Daniel," "Rocket Man," "Tiny Dancer," and "Crocodile Rock." For encores he treated us to "Don't Let the Sun Go Down on Me," "The Circle of Life" from *The Lion King*, followed by "Bennie and the Jets" and finally "Candle in the Wind," which itself had become iconic as a result of Elton performing his new version of the song at Princess Diana's funeral.

THE FACES, SUNDERLAND TOP RANK AND SUNDERLAND LOCARNO, 1972 AND 1973

The Faces were great fun live; often drunk, always a bit ramshackle to the extent that you wondered if they would fall apart altogether (which, of course, they never did), Rod often very drunk (as indeed were the rest of the band), and a great collection of songs drawn from their first few albums and Rod's solo albums and their growing number of hit singles. I saw them several times in the early 1970s; at the Reading Festival in 1972 and 1973 and at the Lincoln Festival in 1972, they seemed to be playing everywhere in those days. Two memorable gigs took place at Sunderland Top Rank on 5 March 1972 and at Sunderland Locarno on 13 April 1973.

I remember the Top Rank gig very well. This was a big gig for everyone at my school. I took time off school to go to queue for tickets; demand was huge as Rod Stewart and the Faces had recently scored some massive hits with "Maggie May," "Stay With Me," and other great singles. This was one gig that I queued up early for on the night, going straight from school. I was one of the first in the queue with some of my mates and we ended up right at the front, crushed against the stage, where we stayed all night. I can think of nothing worse now; being crushed and unable to move all night, but at the time it seemed great. The gig itself was excellent; Rod and the guys were just amazing. Rod with his now trademark spiky hair, wearing a satin suit, and Ronnie Wood playing his silver fronted Zemaitis guitar. The rest of the band were the late great Ronnie Lane on bass, also recently passed Ian Maclagan on keyboards, and Kenny Jones on drums (who was later to go on and play with the Who, replacing Keith Moon). An iconic band with an iconic singer who was soon to go solo and on to further success, which continues to this day.

Lots of my friends from school were there and we spent days afterwards talking about how great the gig was. My friend John recalls that night:

> I remember the Faces as a good time band, musically rather sloppy and overall a bit ragged. I recall it was the night before one of my mock exams, one of the easier ones I presume; maybe English. My recollections on the setlist are very weak, Internet search suggests "Stay with Me" and "Losing You" which I think I can recall as I always liked those two. The balance of the set was all Faces standard stuff: "Three Button Hand Me Down," "Maybe I'm Amazed," and "Miss Judy's Farm." I think I can remember "Maggie May" and "Every Picture Tells a Story" but I certainly could be wrong.

I'm pretty sure they did play "Maggie May." After the show some of us stood in a big queue to go backstage and meet the band. We waited for a long time but only the first few people in the queue were let in, including some mates from school who reported back that they partied with the band into the next morning.

I remember less about the Locarno gig, probably because I didn't queue up and was at the back of the hall, and the place was packed to the walls. I think the support was a local act, perhaps Beckett, and John Peel was certainly DJ for the night. Peel joined the Faces on stage and is on record as stating several times that this was the best gig he had ever been to, which means that it must have been pretty good! Most of the Sunderland football team were at the Locarno gig and ended up on stage with the band. This was the team that went on to win the FA cup a few weeks later.

John Peel:

And the Faces were my all-time favourite live band. And the best ever gig, I always say this, the best gig that I ever went to in my life, was in Sunderland the night after Sunderland had beaten Arsenal in the semi-final the year, they went on to win the cup, and the Faces were the perfect band to capitalize on that atmosphere. And I saw them many, many times and they were great friends, but there was one song whenever we went to see them–the Pig (my wife) and myself used to follow them around–but whenever they started this one, this is when we sort of got hold of each other. Maybe I'm Amazed.

BOB DYLAN, EARL'S COURT, LONDON, 17 JUNE 1978

This was a big event for me. It had been a long time since Dylan had played in the UK, and I was determined to see him, as I hadn't done so before. It was clear that there was going to be massive demand for tickets for these gigs, which were a string of concerts at the vast Earl's Court Arena in London.

Buying tickets in those days was very different than it is today with the use of the internet. It was announced that tickets would be on sale by personal application only, with a limit of four tickets per person. The tickets were to be sold at various box offices around the country and went on sale on a Sunday morning. Sadly, there was no box office in the North East of England, the nearest being Leeds, Glasgow, or Sheffield. So, I decided to go to Leeds to queue for tickets. I figured that I would need to arrive early, so I drove to Leeds on Saturday morning, one day before tickets were due to go on sale, to buy tickets for Marie and me to see the great man. Tickets were on sale from a music shop (think it was called Barkers?) in the Headrow, which is the main street in Leeds. When I arrived at the shop, there was already a queue, as some fans arrived on Friday night. At some point during the day, the shop decided to give us all numbered tickets to mark our place in the queue, and asked us to move on, to prevent crowding and return later to form the queue when the shop closed. This meant I was more or less guaranteed a ticket! I had a look around Leeds and returned to join the queue around 6 p.m. We then got ourselves in order according to our number on the ticket (looking back it seems amazing that this worked!).

It was a cold, long night queuing outside the shop, but everyone was friendly, and the time passed quite quickly, although I didn't get much sleep. *"I remember queuing in Shaftesbury Ave in London to get 4 tickets, slept out all night under a Transit van!"* (Hunter, 2016). There was evidence of touts, who were staying the night in hotels, and had some young kids queueing for them. By the morning, the queue was massive, and curled round and round the streets. *"I was a 16-year-old American living in London, waited 16 hours overnight on the sidewalk for tickets to see the mighty Bob Dylan in his first UK appearance in 10? years. The wait for tickets with a bunch of other hippies was almost as huge as the great show"* (Palsgraf, 2015).

I bumped into a couple of friends from town and agreed to buy tickets for them as I was only buying two for Marie and me. We were soon in the shop and bought the tickets. There was some disappointment because the tickets which were sent to Leeds were for seats way up the back of the arena, but at least we were in. Also, they had only sent a small number of tickets (around 1,000 or so I think) so only the first couple hundred people in the queue got tickets, leaving hundreds disappointed. I later talked to some friends who went to Sheffield to buy tickets, and the queue was much smaller, and they got better seats! Some others went to Glasgow and there was hardly any queue, with tickets left some days after they went on sale.

Come the night of the show Marie and I took our seats up the back of Earl's Court. The friend who I had bought tickets for kindly bought me a cassette copy of *Street Legal*, Dylan's new album, which was kind. Dylan was wonderful; much better than I had hoped. The sound and the view weren't great from our seats; sound systems weren't so good in those days, and video screens weren't widely used (I don't think there were any for this gig). Dylan was a tiny figure in a waistcoat singing those great songs. His voice was strong, and every time he played his mouth organ there was a great cheer from the crowd. This gig made me a lifelong Dylan fan, and this was the first time of many I was to see the great man in concert.

> I went to one of the Earl's Court concerts too, the week of my 22nd birthday. I bought the tickets from Wilson Peck in Sheffield–started queueing early Saturday evening and it was quite fun. . . . I was so excited, all the months leading up to the concert and then on the night itself. I remember thinking I now understood

why some people scream at concerts! I'd never imagined I'd ever see Dylan, and it exceeded all my expectations . . . (Caroline, 2018)

QUEEN, NEWCASTLE CITY HALL, 3 DECEMBER 1979

This gig came as a pleasant surprise. I didn't think that I would ever see Queen back in the City Hall again. By 1979 they were a massive band and had reached a point in their career where they were becoming much more used to playing arenas and stadiums than in small provincial concert halls. So, I got quite a shock when they announced a UK tour which saw them return to their roots, going back to play some of the smaller venues which they had packed when they were paying their dues in the early days of their career.

The tour included two nights at Newcastle City Hall on 3 and 4 December. Great! I made sure that we got tickets.

As soon as we entered the venue, it was very clear just how big a band Queen now were, and how much of a "show" we were about to witness. A massive extended stage seemed to take up almost half of the stalls (or the "Area" as the tickets always called it in those days). There was a walkway for Freddie to come out into the crowd. A mass of lights surrounded the stage setup, and the drum kit stood majestically on a massive, raised platform. It was very impressive and very different from the early days.

The show itself was ultra-professional, and in parts very staged; at times I felt a little too much so, and my mind reflected back to the early days when Queen were a little more of a raw, unpolished rock band. The Queen I saw in 1979, and from then on, was majestic, pomp-rock, a true spectacle. At each concert, Freddie seemed to have grown a little more in confidence, charisma, and stature; he began to truly command the audience, and his vocal strength also seemed to grow alongside his presence. This would, of course, reach its peak in Wembley Stadium, at Live Aid in 1985, where Freddie and the band stepped up into yet another league. This was the last time I was to see Queen in such an intimate setting. From that night onward, I would watch them from the pitch or stands of a football stadium. It was inevitable that their career would progress that way; their anthems and Freddie's stage presence were made for the rousing sing-alongs of the terraces.

The City Hall show that night saw Queen take us through all their classics in what was quite a long, very impressive set. It was almost as if they were marking their territory as one of the UK's, and the world's, major bands; and they probably were. We left the hall that night, feeling privileged to have seen something truly legendary, unique, and spectacular.

CONCLUSION

These performances all tell a very different story and portray different aspects of what makes an artist "iconic." It is, however, clear that artists become icons when they have assembled a back catalogue of material, a massive following, and a status which transcends the artist, band, and its members. The venue and the audience themselves are part of what defines an icon. In each of these performances, the artist, the venue, and the audience all come together to make the performance itself "iconic."

Reconsidering my two research questions:

- What constitutes a "good" live performance?
- What are the crucial elements of a live performance?

When considering performances by iconic artists, the "performance" begins from the moment the concert is announced and tickets are purchased. Indeed, purchasing tickets can, in itself, be difficult as demand will be high. So, the excitement begins with the act of purchasing tickets. Once the tickets have been secured, the excitement and thrill of looking forward to the performance begins. Sometimes there are many months to wait and a journey to be planned, perhaps with friends. Discussions of the gig, with friends including those accompanying me to the concert, build up the excitement. Travelling to the concert, entering an iconic venue, and witnessing "rock gods" all add to the experience. Sometimes this is an experience that will live with me for the rest of my life. The performance transcends the band, the artist, and takes on a life of its own. Such is the nature of a performance by an iconic band or artist.

Chapter Three

Persona

This chapter will explore the way in which certain artists take on an alternative persona as part of their performance, for example David Bowie as Ziggy Stardust, Kiss, the Damned as Gothic pioneers, Alice Cooper, and Captain Beefheart. I began with a review of the literature on the use of persona in rock music including work by Auslander (2009) who includes persona as one factor in live performance analysis, Lacasse (2005) who discusses the importance of the voice in defining persona, and Cochrane (2010) who links persona to the emotional aspects of music. This helped me to choose ten artists for whom persona seemed a significant element.

Table 3.1 lists the artists covered within the chapter.

Table 3.1. Persona Analysed in This Chapter

Artist	Genre	Date of Performance
David Bowie	Art-rock	1970s
Captain Beefheart	Alternative	1970s
Alice Cooper	Heavy Rock	1970s
Twisted Sister	Heavy Rock	1980s
Lady Gaga	Pop	2010s
Kraftwerk	Electronic	1970s
Culture Club	Pop	1980s
The Damned	Punk Rock	1970s
Kiss	Heavy Rock	1970s
Screaming Lord Sutch	Rock 'n' Roll	1980s

DAVID BOWIE, NEWCASTLE CITY HALL, 2 JUNE 1972, SUNDERLAND TOP RANK SUITE 5, SEPTEMBER 1972, AND NEWCASTLE CITY HALL, 8 JUNE 1973

In 1972 David Bowie took on the persona of Ziggy Stardust, a futuristic rock 'n' roll star. Bowie created the character Ziggy Stardust with the help of his wife Angie Bowie. The name Ziggy Stardust was inspired by a 1960s psychobilly star, the Legendary Stardust Cowboy (Songfacts Newsletter, 2020). However, Ziggy was also inspired by Iggy Pop, Marc Bolan, Gene Vincent, and (according to Bowie himself) English rock star Vince Taylor (Songfacts Newsletter, 2020). The song "Ziggy Stardust" itself also hints at a reference to Jimi Hendrix: "he played it left hand." The image of Ziggy, in terms of makeup, hair, and clothes, was in part derived from Malcolm McDowell's character in the film *A Clockwork Orange* (Songfacts Newsletter, 2020). Although the Ziggy Stardust tour started out as quite a small affair, with poorly attended concerts, it ended with sellout performances around the country and a "farewell" (to Ziggy at London's Hammersmith Odeon).

My first experience of David Bowie in concert was at Newcastle City Hall on 2 June 1972. I'd heard the new single "Starman" on the radio and decided to go along to find out more. So, I wandered along to the City Hall and paid the princely sum of 40p entrance at the door for a seat toward the back of the stalls. The hall was by no means full, as I recall; the support act was the JSD Band. They were "one of the most promising folk–rock bands of the early 1970s" and rated alongside Fairport Convention, Pentangle, and Steeleye Span (Harris, 2020).

I'd heard the *Hunky Dory* LP, and, of course, knew the "Space Oddity" single, but a lot of Bowie's material was still unfamiliar to me. Although this tour is often referred to as the *Ziggy Stardust tour*, the Ziggy LP was not yet released. In fact, it came out a few days after the Newcastle gig on 6 June 1972.

Bowie was great, wearing the full makeup and Ziggy gear, made iconic by his performance on *Top of the Pops* a month later when "Starman" hit the charts. For the time, his surreal, otherworldly persona was unlike anything I'd seen before. Bowie's embodiment of Ziggy Stardust presented crowds with an alternative identity which Blair coined as "counter-hegemonic" (Blair, 2016). Blair argued that such constructions of alternative identities were essential for the time as they "enacted a departure from the everyday," and that the otherworldly quality of Bowie's creation "represented a carnivalesque escape from the increasingly unpalatable social and economic landscape" (Blair, 2016).

During early 1972 the setlist was something like: "Hang on to Yourself," "Ziggy Stardust," "The Supermen," "Queen Bitch," "Song for Bob Dylan,"

"Changes," "Starman," "Five Years," "Amsterdam," "Andy Warhol," "Moonage Daydream," "White Light/White Heat," "Suffragette City," and "Rock 'n' Roll Suicide."

Bowie was back in the North East of England a few months later, at Sunderland Top Rank on 5 September 1972. Although "Starman" had been a hit, he was still by no means a massive star, to the extent that the gig was, as I remember, pretty poorly attended. The thing I remember about this gig was that, surprisingly at the time, David performed the show without any makeup or costume at all. He wore a leather jacket and a pair of jeans. I can also vividly recall a few encores including definitely "White Light White Heat" and "Waiting for the Man." We missed the last bus and walked home after the gig, getting back very early in the morning, which wasn't good as we were at school the next day.

Aladdin Sane was released on 13 April 1973, and by this time the demand for tickets was huge, to the extent that Bowie played a couple of shows on the same night at Newcastle City Hall. The setlist had developed to include songs from *Aladdin Sane*, and the production had also developed since the previous year. Bowie was wearing dresses and having several costume changes and was accompanied by a mime artist. This tour culminated in a show at Hammersmith at which Ziggy announced his retirement. At the time I thought I'd seen David Bowie for the last time. Of course, he was to take on further persona throughout his career.

CAPTAIN BEEFHEART AND THE MAGIC BAND, NEWCASTLE CITY HALL, 5 APRIL 1972

It was very cool to be into Captain Beefheart in the early 70s. I got into him through Frank Zappa, and his vocals on "Willie the Pimp," on the *Hot Rats* album. I then went on to hear Beefheart's *Safe as Milk* and *Trout Mask Replica*. I was fascinated by the very strange sounds that exuded from those albums, so when he came to play at Newcastle City Hall, I bought a ticket straight away.

It was one of the strangest, and best gigs, I have attended. I was sitting pretty close to the front surrounded by some of the most eccentric looking people that I'd ever seen at a gig. A guy sitting a few seats away from me had white hair down to his waist and spent the entire set rocking back and forth in his seat, swinging his long hair about. There was a strong smell of dope in the air, and it was clear that the gig had attracted a lot of local hippies.

Beefheart's show started with a performance from a ballerina and then a belly dancer. Rockette Morton took to the stage and played a manic extended bass solo. Soon he was joined by the rest of the Magic Band, and the Captain who was wearing a massive cloak, and singing in the deepest voice I had ever heard. The band were all dressed outrageously, the music was amazing, experimental, psychedelic, and totally unlike anything I had heard before.

Don Van Vliet was "an only child who showed artistic talent" (Boucher, 2010). He was offered a place to study at art college but "instead hung out at home with his school friend Frank Zappa, listening to old R'n'b records and planning various projects" (Boucher, 2010). It was during this time that he created the Captain Beefheart persona.

The Captain was just unbelievable. His vocal range seemed limitless, and the sounds he made, teamed with the complicated rhythms of the band, gave the performance an avant-garde, artistic feel. The set was pretty unfamiliar to me; it was by no means a greatest hits set. However, that didn't matter. The whole show was just incredible: I was blown away by it all and became a committed Beefheart fan that night.

ALICE COOPER, LIVERPOOL EMPIRE, 14 SEPTEMBER 1975

This was the first time that I saw Alice Cooper. A group of us went to the gig in a couple of cars, all of us excited at the prospect of seeing the king of shock rock. We'd heard the singles, seen him perform "School's Out" on *Top of the Pops* and read about the outlandish stage shows in the *NME* and *Sounds*. "Loud, flashy, articulate hard rock harnessed around superb production"(Kent, 1973), Alice and his band had been on our radar for a while.

Vincent Damian Furnier became interested in performing after he and his friends won a school talent show with a parody of the Beatles (Dunn, Harkema, and McFadyen, 2014). He went on to form several bands after leaving school and in the late 1960s he felt his music needed a "gimmick." He felt that other bands were not experimenting enough with the possibilities of live performance, so he created the Alice Cooper persona and began to play around with stage theatrics based on horror and cabaret traditions (Dunn, Harkema, and McFadyen, 2014).

It was Alice's first concert in the North of England; he had previously only played in London and Glasgow. So, this was our first chance to see Alice in the flesh in his ghoulish horror show. Reviews I'd read promised that the gig would feature snakes, an execution, and babies being sliced up. We couldn't wait!

Support came from Heavy Metal Kids, with Gary Holton on top form, giving his usual super cocky cockney act. We had seats right down at the front and all thought the gig was tremendous. There had been some lukewarm reviews of the *Welcome to My Nightmare* album, largely because Alice had lost all of the original band members, and was now, in effect, a solo artist, rather than Alice Cooper the band. However, we needn't have worried, as this was Alice Cooper at his theatrical best, fronting a stage show that was at times just astounding and, for its time, unbelievable in places.

The show started with the taped voice of Vincent Price booming over the PA system, followed by wonderfully choreographed dancers, who seemed to appear out of nowhere from a giant projection screen, which was the size of the stage. Next Alice suddenly appeared singing the opening lines of the title track. Alice had a giant toy box, and from that jumped devils, bats, and a bunch of skeletons who delivered a nifty dance routine complete with top hats and canes. There was a massive graveyard scene with Alice creeping through the gravestones, dancing demons, giant spiders for "Black Widow" and a cyclops during "Department of Youth. Just wonderful!

Mike Jahn wrote for the *New York Times* that "the group appears to see itself as surrealists, exaggerating several choice American foibles, mainly violence and sexuality" (Jahn, 1971). For the time, stage theatrics on this level were extremely unusual. Alice Cooper himself pushed the boundaries of hard rock, using his persona and overall concept to expand the gig-going experience.

TWISTED SISTER, NEWCASTLE MAYFAIR, 15 APRIL 1983

Twisted Sister were wild, sick, evil, motherf**kas. Going to see Twisted Sister was like going to a military drill, where the sergeant major dressed as a woman, made you swear, and ridiculed you if you didn't join in and go totally crazy. These guys took all the evil, sinister, sleazy, scary bits from Alice Cooper, New York Dolls, Slade, Bowie, and The Stones, dragged them through their worst nightmares of Frankenstein and Dracula, and produced a metal band with an attitude and image like we had never seen before.

Twisted Sister's music was anthems and choruses sung repeatedly over slabs of loud, crashing metal. Oh, and, by the way, they were just great. Perfect for a loud rock night at the Mayfair. Lead singer and 110 percent crazy guy Dee Snider looked like a 6-foot-something biker, dressed in drag, with the tightest, most disgusting bright spandex pants, makeup smeared all over his face like he had been out partying all night, and the wildest mane of bright yellow hair.

It wasn't just the style choices, the visuals, or theatrics of the performance that were unnerving, it was the band's attitude and particularly Snider's brutal interactions with the crowd. I recall him berating us to shout and swear back at him, anyone who was seen to not join in was pointed out and ridiculed. From memory, it went something like this. . . .

"We are Twisted F**in' Sister." "And I am a sick muthaf**ka!" "Are you a sick muthaf**ka?!" "Say it, I am a sick muthaf**ka!" "Hey that f**in' guy up there isn't f**in' saying it! Does he think he is at f**in' Woodstock?! We ain't no f**in' Grateful Dead, maaaan." "Come on man, f**in' shout it. I am a sick muthaf**ka!" "What do we say to f**in' people who don't want to f**in' party seven days a week, 365 f**in' days a year? We are sick muthaf**kas! We are sick muthaf**kas! We are sick muthaf**kas!" . . . There was no escape. In *Record*, David Gans wrote "Snider's speech is slathered, smothered, suffocated in the F-word, the way bad meat is obliterated with barbecue sauce" (Gans, 1984).

Indeed, it felt like the band and Snider, in particular, were using their performance to exorcise an anger or deep-rooted hostility. "I tap into everything negative in my personality. I think about the things I hate, the things I'm angry about. I let it all out—I curse, scream, roll around—and afterwards, I feel good . . ." (Snider in Ganz, 1984).

Indeed, I think that this is what made my first encounter with Twisted Sister a challenging and enjoyable evening. It could so easily have gone wrong and left me and the rest of the audience feeling intimidated or a little freaked out. The performance, however, provided a communal space for the voicing of personal grievances towards the system, the powers that be, or perhaps those just against you having a good time. "What's important is that the performance, graphics, staging and sound be as vile, repellent and loud as possible because the pay-off is not aesthetic satisfaction" (Gans, 1984).

LADY GAGA, NEWCASTLE ARENA, 22 NOVEMBER 2014

Lady Gaga has pushed the boundaries of performance art, brought experimentalism to mainstream fashion, and redefined what it means to be a woman in pop, all whilst churning out catchy pop tune after catchy pop tune (Marshall and Iddon, 2014). Indeed, "in the poster stakes, Gaga has always been a risk taker: she hung herself live on stage for her MTV VMA debut performance, the following year she swept the board whilst dressed in preserved meat and in 2011 she turned up in drag" (Allen, 2014a). I really wanted to see her.

Laura and her friend Christina accompanied me to the ArtPop Ball, when Gaga's ArtRave tour called at Newcastle Arena. We arrived while support, and Gaga friend, Lady Starlight, was finishing her set. She soon left the stage and a series of videos of Gaga were greeted by massive cheers from the crowd.

The stage set consisted of bright white dome-like structures on the main stage which housed the band and formed an entrance to the show. From the stage a series of translucent walkways extended out into the main floor area of the arena. The fans on the floor could walk underneath and between the walkways whilst still being able to see the show through them. There was another smaller stage-cum-walkway at the other end of the floor area. A massive piano, looking something like a futuristic version of the organ from *The Phantom*, was perched on a corner of the setup.

The show itself was a mix of Lady Gaga's hits and tracks from the new album. Lots of loud dance, anthemic sing-alongs, and a few acoustic songs which featured Gaga largely solo on the piano. The latter were, for me, some of the best moments.

Lady Gaga had a number of costume changes into a series of bizarre get-ups including a strange tentacle dress, a golden leotard with wings, some very revealing outfits, and a crazy rave girl complete with big rara skirt and luminous dreadlocks. At one point she was changed by her stylists on stage, dressing down to nothing at all, with her back to the audience. It is clear that Gaga uses her onstage persona and costumes to play around with the concept of gender and what it means to be female. The exaggerated symbols of femininity: the skirts, dresses, big hair, and so on are almost a parody of gender identity, thus bringing focus onto whether such things really are gender signifiers at all. "Just like feminist camp pioneer Mae West, Lady Gaga increasingly performs an outrageous femininity and just like West, Gaga manages to be parodic subject and sexy object at the same time, further unsettling ideas about presumed naturalness of gender and desire" (Horn, 2010). Indeed, Gaga's focus on gender was made more explicit as she addressed the audience and spoke about her support for the LGBTQ community.

Her personal connection to the fans is clear and strong. She talks directly to them, a lot, more so than any other artist I can recall. Her speech is impassioned, urgent, and almost sermon-like at times. The music too has its moments of being pretty powerful stuff. Lyrics about loneliness, loss of identity, and drug reliance take on a particular vulnerability when juxtaposed with the flamboyant visuals.

The images are simplistic and obvious, but I guess that is part of the point, the attraction, the charm, and the power of the concept. Fundamentally, this is a challenging, entertaining, sometimes moving, sometimes a little shocking, show which takes every rock and pop (and art) concept you have ever seen (Bowie, Madonna, Queen, Liza Minnelli, punk, disco, dance, rave, Bette Midler, Black Sabbath, Blondie, Cyndi Lauper, Andy Warhol), mashes them up, twists them, and throws them back out at you in some super bright, often trashy, never boring but always entertaining, postmodern pastiche.

KRAFTWERK, NEWCASTLE MAYFAIR, 5 SEPTEMBER 1975, AND NEWCASTLE CITY HALL, 10 MAY 1981

I saw Kraftwerk twice. The first occasion was in 1975 when they were on tour in the UK in support of their *Radio-Activity* album. I'd heard "Autobahn," which reached No 11 in the UK charts earlier that year but didn't know anything else by the band.

The core lineup for the band that I saw on both occasions was Ralf Hütter on vocals, synthesizer, orchestron, synthanorma-sequenzer, and various strange electronics; Florian Schneider on vocals, vocoder, votrax, and synthesizer; and Karl Bartos on electronic percussion. Hütter and Schneider had originally trained as classical musicians, majoring in piano and flute. However, "bored with the restrictions their studies imposed, they found a new fascination in the electronic music which the West Deutsche Rundfunk radio in Cologne would broadcast late at night" (Gill, 1997). They came to leave behind their traditional instruments and pioneer a technology driven, electronic sound.

I found the gig quite strange. First it took place at Newcastle Mayfair on a Friday night. Now Friday night at the Mayfair in the mid-70s was a heavy metal stronghold, and host to gigs by the likes of Thin Lizzy, UFO, and Judas Priest. So, Kraftwerk were a bit of an off-the-wall proposition for the venue, to say the least. Most of the heavy rock fans stayed away and the ballroom was quite empty for the visit by the German rockers who stood, statue-like at their (then) futurist computer terminals at the front of the stage, making strange robotic moves and playing their electronic rhythms. The stage had boxes of various sizes strewn around and some tall metal cabinets were lined up behind the band. It was quite a bizarre affair, and most of the crowd were having a drink and ignoring the band.

The band themselves stood and sang without any emotion, all dressed in the same strangely sinister dark clothing. This in fact was Kraftwerk's debut performance in the UK and was therefore being reviewed by Geoff Barton of *Sounds*. He stated, "The stage itself can best be described as a supermarket turned on its side. Kraftwerk themselves are an unlikely looking bunch of German chaps. They look like psychopathic versions of Doctor Feelgood" (Barton, 1975). Marie and I found it fascinating, and we didn't realise at the time just how influential this band were going to be.

Fast-forward six years to 1981, and Kraftwerk were back in the UK, touring in support of their *Computer World* album. The tour was entitled the Calculator tour. By now the band were hailed as great innovators, and they were the new darlings of the rock scene. The City Hall concert drew a respectable crowd, but it wasn't by any means a sellout. This time the band brought all of the electronic technology from their studio and took it out on the road. The show also had a substantial visual element, using back-projection of slides and films, synchronised with the music. They had some hand-held miniature instruments, and replica mannequins of themselves. This was much more a show, where sounds and visuals combined to bring a unique sensory experience. I began to understand how special this band was.

CULTURE CLUB, NEWCASTLE CITY HALL, 25 MARCH 1983

Dave and I went to see Culture Club at Newcastle City Hall in March 1983. This is the only time that I have seen the band. At this point in their career, Culture Club had released their first LP *Kissing to be Clever* and had hit the singles chart twice, with the No. 1 single "Do You Really Want to Hurt Me" and a No. 3 hit with "Time (Clock of the Heart)." This was their first major tour, before they became really mega, with the release of the massive *Colour by Numbers* album and the worldwide hit "Karma Chameleon."

I'd been vaguely aware of George O'Dowd's various alter egos. Firstly, as Lieutenant Lush when performing with Bow Wow Wow under Malcolm McLaren's management, then later as Boy George. Boy George was (and still is) a fascinating character, and it was he himself that drew us to the City Hall that night. Indeed, it was definitely Boy George's persona, style, and character that interested me more than the band's output at that stage. "The Boy George persona, which came to international attention with the success of the band Culture Club in the early 1980s, threatened to overshadow completely Boy George the performer" (Gianoulis, 2002).

Support came from the Swinging Laurels, reportedly at the request of George. The concert was pretty good; George looked great in a multi-coloured suit/dress and had impressive dreadlocks. I remember the music as being a mix of pop and reggae, and the sound much quieter than most rock gigs. The gig was sold out and had been for some time in advance.

Despite being drawn to the show based on Boy George's style, flamboyancy, and charisma, I conceded that night that it was wrong to discount his musical talent. His vocals were strong, and his impassioned performance drew you into the music. The songs too had a universality to the lyrics, talking of betrayal and the complexities of youthful experience. Although largely pop-driven in convention, the music was a unique mix of influences, rendering it quite different to other acts of the time. Teamed with Boy George's outlandish presence, Culture Club were extremely original. Retaining his sense of style and eclecticism throughout, "George has proved he is not merely a stage persona, but also a real original" (Gianoulis, 2002). I haven't seen Culture Club since that night, although I did sit in the row next to Boy George on a flight to Munich once.

THE DAMNED, REDCAR COATHAM BOWL, 11 NOVEMBER 1976

The Damned were one of the first punk bands to release a single ("New Rose") (Robb, 2006), and also one of the first to play in the North. Unlike the Pistols, and to some extent the Clash, they played up and down the country a lot, including many gigs in the region.

The Damned's first visit to the North East, and indeed the first time I saw them, was as support to the Flamin' Groovies who had just released their classic album, *Shake Some Action*, which Hull raved about in *Creem* (1976): "the Flamin' Groovies can rock with the best of them (meaning the Stones, the Byrds, the Beatles, the Kinks, etc.)." In the same article Hull argued: "Here, in 1976, there is no Action; hopefully, Shake Some Action will be the grenade which will trigger another rock & roll revolution, the inevitable backlash against disco for the dead." However, as excited as we were to be seeing the Groovies, we were particularly intrigued to catch the Damned, so we arrived early to ensure we saw them.

The audience was a mix of rock fans, not dissimilar to that at any other concert at the time. Cobley (1999) described how the "crowd at such gigs" was "far from the King's Road fashion victims revered in punk literature." Rather there were "denim jackets" and "long hair." This was certainly the audience of which I was a member at this gig. For some reason, even Dave Vanium wasn't wearing his normal gothic outfit or makeup, appearing in a leather jacket. Perhaps the fact that this was a provincial gig made it less important in some ways; it was less likely to be covered by the music press. The Captain was just mad, Brian James was the guitar hero, and Rat was going crazy on the drums. Their set included "New Rose," a manic version of the Beatles' "Help" and some embryonic versions of songs which would be featured on their first album. They were amazing; young, fresh, fast, crazy and blew the crowd away. I couldn't wait to see them again.

Van Ham (2009) compared several of the early punks to "clowns"; the Damned were certainly moving in that direction, building an image which blended gothic horror (Gunn, 1999) with lunacy and vaudeville. Caroline Coon (1982) described Captain Sensible as having "a front as benevolently mad as a village idiot's."

I saw them several times over the years. During a particularly memorable show, the Captain walked on stage naked and took a pee on the audience.

KISS, BIRMINGHAM ODEON, 14 MAY 1976, AND NEWCASTLE CITY HALL, 29 OCTOBER 1983 AND 7 OCTOBER 1984

We'd read all about the weird world of Kiss and their outrageous US stage show in the music papers. The *NME* reported how Kiss were "Bill topping over bands they were supporting but 6 months ago" and how their "style, unashamed derivativeness and a stage persona which is gross in the 'extreme'" were making the band 'so big it hurts!' (Bell, 1976). So, when we saw that they were touring the UK, we just had to go along.

This was their first UK visit and it was a pretty short one too, consisting of four shows in three theatre venues (one night at Manchester Free Trade Hall, one at Birmingham Odeon, and two at Hammersmith Odeon). I drove down with a group of mates to the Birmingham Odeon show.

Support came from my old favourites Stray, with Del Bromham wearing his silver mirror suit. Stray were touring to promote the *Houdini* album. I remember not recognising many of the songs, as most were from their new album, although I think they finished with the old stage favourite "All in Your Mind." Kiss were touring off the back of their *Alive!* double album and their set was built around that. They came over as a hot rock 'n' roll band, complete with the iconic crazy over-the-top makeup. I remember us staring in awe of their massive stacks, although I suspect the show we saw wasn't anywhere near the scale of their massive US stage show, because of the limitations of the venue. They had rocket firing guitars; Gene Simmons spitting blood and breathing fire; Ace Frehley's guitar bursting into flames; Peter Criss's elevating drum riser; Paul Stanley's heavy posing; and various other pyrotechnics throughout the show. We were all very impressed, although we also thought that they didn't quite live up to the hype we had read.

The programme declares: "The KISS experience. KISS is total sensuality. Thundering rock, intense vibration, and soaring freedom. Penetrating energy and exploding emotion stimulate every nerve to unequalled heights" (Programme, 1976). Pretty impressive stuff; however, I couldn't help but feel the band's reputation was as hyperbolic as their show was spectacular.

The volume hadn't been quite LOUD enough and the sound mix wasn't perfect, but it was great to see this seminal live act at such an important point in their career. We ran into an old friend who was studying at Nottingham at the time and gave him a lift home on our way back, which meant that we finally got home in the early hours of the morning, as dawn was breaking. The things you do for rock 'n' roll.

The next time I saw Kiss they had abandoned their trademark makeup and had plucked up the courage to appear before us all unmasked (shock horror). What would these guys look like without the scary face paint? Well actually, they looked OK, and in some ways not too different from their onstage personas. Their new look was displayed to the world on the cover of the *Lick It Up* album, which was released in 1983. Their 1983 UK tour brought them to Newcastle City Hall, and I went along with my mate Dave. Although the guys had gone (semi) straight in terms of their facial appearance, the show was almost as outrageous as ever. The tour programme depicted a tank on the front cover and that tank actually appeared on stage with Kiss on the tour. From the KissFans site: "The stage was still a tank, and the 'turret' moved . . . but there were hardly any pyrotechnics at all! KISS played in some very small venues and the gun had to be shortened for some shows . . . otherwise it would cut the stage in two!! Not every effect had been kicked out of the show however! The band would still end up on the 'gun turret' and the turret would still turn from side to side, puffing smoke" (Kiss Fan Shop).

Support for the 1983 concert were Heavy Pettin', a metal band from Glasgow. Kiss were soon back at the City Hall, playing two nights at the venue in 1984. This time the support was exciting in that it was Bon Jovi, who were up and coming and were touring in support of their debut album. This time we had seats right down the front and came away almost deaf! Kiss were a shit hot rock band in the early 80s, with or without the makeup and the pyrotechnics. For this show, the UK dates had a scaled down version of the US stage show. Two ramps allowed the band to walk from the top of the amplifiers to the stage. The drum riser was covered with black "fur," while the ramps were painted like zebra fur. I remember feeling like the poor cousins because we never seemed to get the full US Kiss experience, I guess because of the logistics of taking their massive show around the world, and also because of the relatively small size of the venues which Kiss were playing in this country, and in the rest of Europe. But, hey, it was still a great show and lots of fun.

SCREAMING LORD SUTCH, SUNDERLAND POLYTECHNIC WEARMOUTH HALL, PROBABLY 1973, AND THE BARBARY COAST SUNDERLAND, 9 FEBRUARY 1984

Picture the scene. It was sometime in the early 1970s, probably 1973. I was in my mid-teens and had started to take gig-going pretty seriously. It was a Saturday night student dance in Wearmouth Hall, which was the student union building of Sunderland Polytechnic. The great thing about those dances at that time was you never knew who you were going to see. There was no internet to check gig listings in those days and I would turn up on a Saturday night with a couple of mates, and the name of the act for the night would be written in chalk on a blackboard at the door. On this particular night, the board read "Screaming Lord Sutch," a name unfamiliar to us all.

David Edward Sutch took on the Screaming Lord persona aged twenty. Johnny Black described it as being "founded on the voodoo antics of American Star Screamin' Jay Hawkins, but distinctively anglicised by his fascinations for Punch and Judy, Max Miller and Jack the Ripper" (Black, 1999). Unbeknownst to us, Sutch was "enormously popular on the club circuit" due to his theatrical antics and his "entertainingly ghoulish" concept (Black, 1999). We paid our entrance fee, which was probably 30p or so, and got ourselves a spot at the front of the stage. We had no idea of what to expect and, in fact, nothing could have prepared us for what we were about to experience.

After some time, a band came on stage playing some basic rock'n'roll. Soon a few guys carried a coffin on stage and set it down right in front of us. We could hear a voice singing, and soon realised that it was coming from inside the coffin. The lid suddenly flung open revealing a guy with long green hair, a face covered with makeup, wearing a cape and a top hat. This was my introduction to the wild world of Screaming Lord Sutch.

Sutch started to prowl the front of the stage. He picked up a large axe and pretended to try to chop our heads off. Girls down the front were screaming. The traditional rock 'n' roll music continued to be pretty basic and formulaic, but the stage show was anything but. During a song called "Jack the Ripper," Sutch paced around the stage threatening to kill any female students that were close by. He was looking for "Mary." At one point he pulled Mary's bloodied head out of his doctor's bag . . . to much screaming from the crowd. It was pure music hall, tacky, yet powerful and great fun. One of the best shows I had ever seen at the time.

I saw Screaming Lord Sutch once more, in 1984. This time the gig was billed as a Wild Rock & Roll Night, and was held at the Barbary Coast Club, Sunderland. In 1984 it had a reputation for fights and earned the nickname "The Barbaric." However, there was no trouble the night of the gig.

The place was full of teds, and we had a long wait before Sutch took to the stage. Much like the first time I saw him, the music was punchy rock 'n' roll; and although the band were tight, it was Sutch's performance we were all there to see. Eldridge described in *Melody Maker* how Sutch "built a reputation through showmanship and an in-built ability for stunts" (Eldridge, 1970). Indeed, the show was very similar to the gig I had attended ten years earlier. Macabre stunts, maniacal laughter, and props that could have been straight from a low-budget horror film. Good fun, perhaps not as powerful the second time.

CONCLUSION

The concept of persona is well documented by Auslander (2004) and other authors. To some extent, it can be argued that all artists take on some form of persona the minute that they step on to the stage. However, the concept of persona takes an entirely different form in terms of the artists discussed in this chapter. These artists actually become a different person on stage, using costumes and makeup to transform into their new persona. And, indeed, we would attend the show expecting to see the new person that the artist had become. I recall going to see David Bowie at Sunderland Top Rank Suite during the Ziggy Stardust tour; he came on stage without any makeup and wearing a leather jacket and a pair of jeans. I was both disappointed and intrigued. I felt cheated because I was not witnessing a true Ziggy show; at the same time, I felt privileged to see Bowie performing "naked." Similarly, I never quite appreciated the Kiss "unmasked" concept. It just wasn't proper Kiss! So, the persona blended into the performer and vice versa. We went to witness the persona and not the artist. The persona became an intertwined part of our expectations, and the performance. Some artists, such as David Bowie, transformed from one persona to another, and Ziggy became the Thin White Duke almost seamlessly; likewise, we accepted and indeed welcomed the transformation. Alice, on the other hand, was always Alice; the crazy scary guy who would put his head into a guillotine, wear a top hat and cane, and sing "Schools Out" at the end of the set. We could predict the persona, the props, the act, and the songs; but that didn't matter, it all added to the performance.

These performances had an additional dimension. I knew that I was going to see a "show"; a performance, rather than a simple concert. To some extent, parallels can be drawn with the pantomime and with the traditional musical hall acts. I went along expecting to be entertained, taken into a different world, a new dimension, and for an all too short few hours transported away from my day-to-day life. I worshipped the persona that the artist had taken on. Ziggy, Alice, Kiss—these performances offered me the ultimate in escapism. I watched, in awe of the cartoon character before me. I wanted the merchandise; the programme, the T-shirt, and the album. It was all part of the story that unfolded before my eyes. These performances were thus unique and stay with me even today. The Ziggy Stardust tour is legendary, and Alice continues to be Alice. I saw part of myself in these characters; I even wanted to be them. Many concertgoers attempted to be Ziggy or Alice. They would wear the makeup and the costume to the show; and in doing so they became part of the performance themselves, which was, of course, their intention. They wanted to enter the world of Ziggy, become Ziggy, and escape from their own lives.

Such is the wonderful world that these artists transported us into; and many still do so to this day.

Chapter Four

Energy

This chapter focuses upon the growth of punk rock, from its infancy in pub rock to its metamorphosis into new wave. Concerts by Dr Feelgood, the Clash, the Sex Pistols, Elvis Costello, Blondie, the Ramones, and Siouxsie and the Banshees are discussed and analysed, drawing from previous published work of the author (Smith, 2015; 2017; 2018) and others such as Sabin (2002) and Laing (2015).

Table 4.1 lists the artists covered within the chapter.

Table 4.1. Artists Analysed in This Chapter

Artist	Genre	Date of Performance
Dr Feelgood	Rhythm and Blues	1970s
The Sex Pistols	Punk Rock	1970s
The Clash	Punk Rock	1970s
The Stranglers	Punk Rock	1970s
Siouxsie and the Banshees	Punk	1970s
The Ramones	Punk	1970s
Penetration	Punk	1970s
Elvis Costello	New-Wave	1970s
The Prodigy	Dance	2010s
The Libertines	Indie Rock	2010s

DR FEELGOOD, NEWCASTLE CITY HALL, 25 OCTOBER 1975 AND 17 SEPTEMBER 1976

In their early days, Dr Feelgood were loud, raw, wild, intense, and just plain amazing. They grew out of pub rock, preceded punk, and were pretty untouchable as a live act. They took the familiar three-minute song formula of pub rock and injected it with a raucous energy which, for the time, felt incredibly unique. In the mid-1970s, glam rock was dominating the charts and the main alternative to this was Prog-rock (Marcus, 2009). Dr Feelgood seemed completely at odds with this musical landscape and, as such, you couldn't help but feel they were something special. "A fierce, gritty riposte to early-70s excess, Dr Feelgood weren't just trailblazers for punk but fleetingly the biggest band in England" (Hasted, 2009).

I first saw them as support for Hawkwind on their 1974 tour and was blown away by the intensity of their performance. I couldn't take my eyes off the two front men, Lee Brilleaux and Wilko Johnson. Wilko strutted backwards and forwards across the stage, playing his Fender Telecaster in his characteristic choppy style, while Lee stared menacingly at us all, dressed in a sharp white suit, wringing the mike and pumping his fist. Sparko and the Big Figure silently and relentlessly provided the rhythm. "Back in the Night," "Roxette," "She does it right" . . . these tunes were intense, three-minute explosions that left you feeling stunned.

The Feelgoods visited the City Hall every year from 1976 to 1979, and I went each year. They were always a great live act, and I never saw them put on anything other than a fantastic performance. The Pistol's Glen Matlock told *Uncut*, "the Feelgoods were really edgy. At the height of prog-rock they went back to three-minute songs played like they meant it. Lee Brilleaux had a brooding manliness about him, he looked like he ran a caravan site on Canvey Island and looked like he'd be after you if you hadn't paid your bill properly. That was the right spirit for a young lad and Wilko had this mad speed-freak thing going on. There was nobody like the Feelgoods. I never saw them do a bad show and I must have seen them about 20 times" (Hasted, 2009).

Dr Feelgood in many ways encapsulated the raw energy which laid the foundations for punk. Julian Temple, director of *Oil City Confident*, a documentary on the band, acknowledged the explosive impact they made upon the 1970s music scene. "In the midst of all that hippy stuff," Temple told *Uncut*, "it was like Reservoir Dogs!" (Hasted, 2009).

SEX PISTOLS, THE WHITE HORSE INN, WHITBY, 11 SEPTEMBER 1976, AND SCARBOROUGH PENTHOUSE, 24 AUGUST 1977

I'd read about the Sex Pistols in an article by John Ingham, which appeared in *Sounds* in April 1976, reviewing an early performance at the El Paradise

Club, Soho. When I later read in *Sounds* that the Pistols were playing in Whitby, I had to see them and took a 60-mile drive to experience them for myself.

Whitby is a seaside town and port in North Yorkshire, famous for its association with Dracula and home to an annual Goth festival. We arrived at the Royal Hotel, which is where the gig was advertised as taking place, walked into the bar, and asked where the Sex Pistols were playing. The staff gave us strange looks; they didn't know anything about the gig and suggested it might be in the pub at the rear of the hotel. We drove around and saw a poster advertising "Saturday Disco Night featuring the Sex Pistols," which led us into the White Horse Inn.

Entrance was 50p, and the venue was empty when we arrived. The Sex Pistols were sitting at a table in the corner. Johnny Rotten was wearing a tam, bondage trousers, and a teddy boy jacket. The place soon started to fill with young people, smartly dressed for the Saturday disco; no one was in punk getup. The DJ, in a corner and surrounded by lights, started to play '70s chart music. After a little time, he introduced "tonight's group: The Sex Pistols."

The Pistols started with a deafening "Anarchy in the UK" which totally threw the disco audience. They just didn't know what was happening; the Pistols performance was well outside their normal frame of reference. After a few songs, the audience were getting restless. John was hanging off the mike stand, staring and snarling at the audience. The DJ sensed that this wasn't going down well with his Saturday disco crowd; between songs he quickly turned off the sound:

> "Thank you for tonight's band the Sex Pistols, now it's back to the disco." And that was it. Glen Matlock remembers the event slightly differently: We were playing in Whitby and they kept telling us to turn it down. . . . The bloke comes up and says "It's no good lads. Look we'll pay you what you're due, but you can't hear the bingo in the other room." We'd played for about 15 minutes. (Savage 2012)

Joe Noble (Smith, 2013): "I was there in 76 great night I was only 15 got in through a bouncer that was my brother's best friend, a teacher at my school told us about them, it was a life-changing experience they were raw loud and exciting, it was the best time to be a teenager ever, I saw them lots of times since."

A month later the Pistols appeared on the Bill Grundy show and achieved notoriety. But for me, and a small number of other people who attended the Whitby concert, it was this first exposure to the Pistols that marked a turning point. I was annoyed that the Pistols' performance had been cut short; however, the drama added to the significance of the event. The Pistols might as well have come from another planet. Garnett (1999) argues that they were "singing from somewhere else, someplace that hadn't existed before and that only existed for a brief moment in time." Those fifteen minutes were enough for me to know that I'd witnessed something special. "My life changed the moment that I saw the Sex Pistols," says Howard Devoto. . . . "Suddenly there was a direction" (Savage, 2012).

By 1977, the Sex Pistols were banned from playing almost everywhere. McLaren decided that they should go out on a secret tour, now referred to as the SPOTS tour (Sex Pistols On Tour Secretly). The nearest gig to me was Middlesbrough Rock Garden, a venue which I often visited for punk gigs, but I had tickets for the Reading Festival that weekend, so I went to see the Pistols in Scarborough.

The Pistols had already played the Penthouse in 1976. Penthouse DJ Matt Watkinson recalls that night "as a wet Thursday and maybe 40 people were in. Word hadn't got round, so not everyone knew what to expect. Some of the older customers shouted "Rubbish!" or "Learn to play!" but they were very good. . . . It was infectious, raucous stuff. . . . It was a great gig, one of the best ever." Local musician John Daniels recalls "a solid band that deliberately tried to provoke an audience reaction, but in a tongue-in-cheek way" (*Scarborough Evening News*, 2006). John Lydon (2014) remembers the gig quite differently: "The hatred! In the front of the stage stood this solid firm of 300 full-on beer monster yobs, who were obviously thinking, 'You softies from down south.'"

We stood for six hours until the Penthouse opened, by which time the queue stretched "down St Nicholas Street and up Westborough" (*Scarborough Evening News*, 2006). It was a small venue, in an upstairs room, and held a few hundred people at most. The place was rammed, the atmosphere electric, and the Pistols were simply incredible. The set was quite short; less than one hour. They played most of the *Bollocks* album. Patrick Argent: "The famous Penthouse rock club in St Nicholas Street had not witnessed anything remotely like it. This time, they delivered a highly charged and simply unmatchable display of the fury, power and frenzy of the punk genre" (*Scarborough Evening News*, 2006).

THE CLASH, WHITE RIOT TOUR
NEWCASTLE UNIVERSITY, 20 MAY 1977

This was the night that punk truly arrived in Newcastle, and the first time I saw the Clash. As the first really big punk gig in Newcastle, it sold out well in advance. Sadly, most of the tickets had gone to students, and not to the working-class kids who the Clash's music was aimed at. You had to be a student to buy tickets, which was the source of some agro on the night of the gig. I was a student at Sunderland Polytechnic at the time and I used my union card to buy tickets.

When we arrived at the Union building on the night of the gig, the entrance was surrounded by a group of local punks trying to get in. There were scuffles between the doormen and the punks, who were angry because they couldn't see "their band" who (in their eyes) were playing for a group of middle-class students. This went on throughout the night. Mensi, soon to form the Angelic Upstarts, was present that night (Robb, 2006), and would write the song "Student Power" about the chasm between the students and the punks.

A similar situation occurred when the Clash played Sussex University. Paul Cecil, who was studying American Studies at Sussex at the time, attended the gig: "A lot of students bought tickets. On the day of the gig itself, large numbers of London punks turned up without tickets and began piling in. . . . Students took one look at them and started to sell their tickets to them. They thought it was scary. It wasn't. Inside the gig it was a really friendly atmosphere. There was lots of pogo-ing and jumping around, getting very bruised bashing into people. It was mayhem but controlled mayhem for about 35 minutes. The Clash played an outstandingly good set—very short, very loud, very fast" (Sussex University website).

In 1977, Newcastle University ballroom was in a small room up a flight of stairs, with the main bar being down on a lower level. The students' union building was a maze of bars, lounges, and a pool room. You could wander around and dip in and out of the gig in the main ballroom.

There was a great sense of anticipation and an air of edginess and craziness that night, as seen at venues up and down the country (Green and Barker, 1999). We had missed out on the Sex Pistols Anarchy tour, which was booked for Newcastle City Hall, and cancelled because of the controversy around the band. So, this was our first chance to see a "big" punk band. The place was packed, largely with students. Some local punks had somehow managed to buy tickets and were crammed around the stage.

Punk was starting to make its mark, but it remained early days. We were at the concert because of the image, rebellion, and to be part of a new youth culture, as much as for the Clash's music (Sabin, 2002). Many were there out of curiosity and because of reports that they had read in *NME* and *Sounds*. I'd read that the Clash was *the* new punk rock band to out-punk (and out-rock) the Pistols, so I had to see them. Support came from the Prefects, Subway Sect, and the Slits. The sound wasn't great for any of the support acts, who all seemed a bit amateur and ramshackle. There was a lot, and I mean *a lot*, of spitting at the band; one of the first times I'd witnessed this.

The Clash were streets ahead of the support acts. There was lots of pogoing and relentless spitting. Poor Joe Strummer was covered in gob. They looked great; just like their pictures on the cover of the first album. Looking back, it's easy to forget just how new, exciting, and radical punk was. The clothes, the image, the attitude were light years removed from the bands I'd been into a few months before (Smith, 2017).

A report in the *Newcastle Journal* (2017) reminisces of the "harum-scarum days of punk rock" recalling the Clash gig at Newcastle Polytechnic in 1978, quoting from an old report of the time which tells of "hundreds of drunken youngsters," "fierce scuffles," "specially trained security guards with dogs and walkie-talkies," and a member of all-girl band the Slits urging the crowd to "wreck the place," and declaring punk "a panto of violent posturing and petty vandalism" and that "shock-horror headlines were the order of the day." It was one of many concerts with violent outbursts outside and within the venue. Cobley (1999) draws connections between masculinity and physically aggressive behaviour and the violence at gigs in the provinces, pointing out the domination of a manual male labour force and that violence may be more probable than in concerts in London, drawing from the Segal's work on masculinity (1990).

Merv Simkins: "I was at this gig, aged 19 with long hair. It was a revelation, these (the bands, all of them) were people who seemed to be living the whole thing intensely. . . . It was like they were from another world. I remember the fighting at the door. . . . I spoke to Mick Jones as he sat on the edge of the stage (you couldn't have done that with Yes or Camel). Don't remember the Prefects but all the other bands did make a vivid impression—a raw, inner-city edge and intensity that seemed to be part of them, not just some stage act—I'd never seen that in any rock band. It was if they'd gone beyond caring about the tedious day-to-day crap the rest of us clung on to, most of all they didn't seem to give a shit if what they did 'worked' as music or art, they just did it, and because of that it was brilliant. It wasn't like a gig—though many other punk/new wave events I saw were—it was like being at an event with stuff going on all around you. I had friends at the time who formed bands, moved to London and/or went for the whole new-wave thing big time pretty much as a result of having been at this one gig" (Smith, 2013).

THE STRANGLERS, NEWCASTLE CITY HALL, 15 JUNE 1977

I first saw the Stranglers at Newcastle Polytechnic Students Union in February 1977. The gig was in a small upstairs bar, rather than the usual main ballroom, and completely packed. The audience was a mix of students and locals, with a smattering of people starting to wear punk gear. A group of fashion students who were in attendance were clearly into punk and would dress in Vivienne Westwood clothing which they must have bought from Seditionaries in London. The Stranglers played a blistering performance featuring early songs, many of which would appear on their first album, *Rattus Norvegicus*. Their only release at the time was the single "Grip"/"London Lady."

Only four months after playing to an audience of around 100 people in a student's union bar, the Stranglers were back in Newcastle, this time headlining the 2,000-capacity City Hall. I remember my surprise as to how they could contemplate playing such a large venue. However, "Peaches" had reached number eight in the singles charts, and their performance of the double A-side "Go Buddy Go" on *Top of the Pops* had undoubtedly boosted the band's exposure.

Although many punk acts had initially dismissed BBC-TV's *Top of the Pops* for its crass commercialism, many of them—the Clash excepted—willingly accepted invitations to appear when their records entered the charts. Partly as a result of this national exposure, the Adverts, X-Ray Spex, the Stranglers, and the Jam enjoyed early success (Salewicz, 1983).

Unlike the smattering of gigs that had taken place in over-eighteen clubs and exclusive student union bars, the City Hall gig also denoted one of the first completely accessible punk gigs in the North East of England. So, despite my scepticism, by June of 1977 punk was making news everywhere (Colegrave and Sullivan, 2001), and the gig sold out.

The Stranglers played an amazing, challenging set: Hugh Cornwell was very non-PC, growling lots of sexist and racist innuendo, no doubt designed to shock (Laing, 2015); Jean-Jacques Burnel looked moody, dark, and dangerous, driving the band with his thundering bass; Dave Greenfield provided swirling Doors-like Hammond organ; and Jet Black was the grumpy looking man at the back on drums. They were one of the hardest working, and most consistent, live acts, and made it through a set of great songs, and hard graft, playing up and down the country throughout 1976 and 1977. Caroline Coon said (1982): "The Stranglers slogged through over four hundred gigs in two years building up an ever-increasing following. They did not jump on the punk bandwagon, but they were astute enough to know which way the rock wind was blowing." It can be argued that the Stranglers were not punk, but more classic rock. Burnel was quoted as saying, "I thought of myself as part of punk at the time because we were inhabiting the same flora and fauna. . . . I would like to think the Stranglers were more punk plus and then some" (interview for Punk77).

The kids at the City Hall didn't care about the "purity of punk" or whether the Stranglers were more of a straight rock band. As far as they were concerned, they were getting their first slice of the action, and were seeing a real live punk rock band. And, of course, they were meant to go totally crazy and spit at the band, and that is exactly what they did. They had read about "punk" and how they were "meant" to behave outrageously in the press, based on reports of concerts in London, and they made sure that they did exactly that. This was a manic gig, and one of the first of many that the City Hall would host in the months to come. It was also the first time I observed a large number of people in punk gear. Cobley (1999) writes of a "bricolage" and "DIY" culture, born out of necessity and that was certainly in evidence at the City Hall with ripped old school blazers, safety pins, and homemade badges the order of the evening. This concert was the first to bring punk to the mainstream in the North East. It was the first major punk concert to be held in a concert hall in Newcastle; many more would soon follow.

SIOUXSIE AND THE BANSHEES, MIDDLESBROUGH TOWN HALL, 13 OCTOBER 1977, DURHAM, 15 APRIL 1978, AND NEWCASTLE, 30 OCTOBER 1978

The Banshees stood out from the rest of the punk bands in their style, their attitude, and the mysterious, somewhat discordant, dark noise that they made. There was an air of danger about them, depth, mysteriousness, and Siouxsie herself was a force of nature, a revelation. In a *Record Collector* retrospective, Kris Needs described them as "fiercely uncompromising, experimental, always progressing but boasting an uncanny pop sensibility" (Needs, 2007). It seemed that the Banshees possessed a strange energy all of their own. They encapsulated the DIY punk ethic but through striking visuals, primeval themes, and sometimes disturbing imagery; they took it to a whole new level.

I first saw the Banshees supporting Johnny Thunders and the Heartbreakers at the Middlesbrough Town Hall on 13 October 1977. Marie and I turned up early specifically to see Siouxsie. The venue was far from full, and this was a raw, ramshackle Banshees; still feeling their way and learning their craft. But you could see that there was something different and special about them. The uniqueness of their music, Siouxsie's style and arrogance, their image, all shone through the amateurishness. Siouxise was full of edge that night, fearless, and obviously out to shock (Liang, 2015). She was dressed in a see-through net top and a leather cap and commanded the stage with crazy dancing and goose stepping. The band were very young at the time and looked it; this was the first and best lineup of the Banshees; with Sioux on vocals, Severin on bass, Kenny Morris on drums, and John McKay on guitar, before they released their first landmark album *The Scream*. I can't be certain what they played that night, but remember being struck by the raw, unapologetic energy that filled the half-empty hall. I am pretty sure they played "Metal

Postcard," "Carcass," T Rex's "20th Century Boy" (Siouxsie announced the song "from one carcass to another" which I remember clearly as I thought it pretty bad taste at the time, as Bolan had died just a few weeks before).

The next time I saw them was at a packed Durham University Dunelm Ballroom on 15 April 1978. By now the Banshees were a proper band, a major force. The venue was packed, the crowd crazy, the Banshees loud and intense, and Siouxsie pure electric magic. As Needs recalled, "The live set was now an amazing beast, mixing the album up with new songs like 'premature burial' while the 'Lord's Prayer' traversed a different irreverent orbit every night. After starting with nothing two years earlier, Siouxsie and the Banshees were now ferociously spectacular" (Needs, 2007).

The intensely dark energy exuding from the band seemed to pervade the audience and there was a scary edginess in the air. As we left the venue, we faced a massive line of skinheads blocking the ramp leading out to the street. "We hate punks!" ... mass brawls ... the police soon arrived. We ran to the car and made a swift, and lucky, escape.

The Banshees first single "Hong Kong Garden" was released in August 1978, they were soon in the charts, and then went out on a full UK tour of major concert halls. I saw them at Newcastle City Hall on 30 October 1978. Support was Spizz Oil (did Spizz really wear a helmet and keep hitting himself on the head, or did I dream that?), and the original Human League. The concert was sold out, and the music and the performance were joyous, swirling, challenging, and totally engaging. From the first crashing, discordant opening bars of "Helter Skelter," through the majestic pop of "Hong Kong Garden," to the closing song, "The Lord's Prayer," Siouxsie had us all totally captivated.

The Banshees, amongst other punk bands of the time, stood for experimentalism, not only within their music but embodied within their whole ethos and presence (Marcus, 2009). They were different, daring, challenging, uncompromising, and produced sounds that came from somewhere dark, adventurous, rhythmic, and yet uplifting.

THE RAMONES, NEWCASTLE CITY HALL, 20 DECEMBER 1977

The Ramones had played the UK a couple of times before they came to Newcastle. They first came across to play two gigs in London in July 1976; one at the Roundhouse as support for the Flamin' Groovies, and a headlining gig at Dingwalls. Their influence on UK punk rock is well documented (Colegrave and Sullivan, 2001; Osgerby, 1999), and these gigs are widely recognised as seminal. The Ramones also toured the UK in May 1977, missing the North

East; the closest they came was Leeds University. Way "up North" we had to wait until their second UK tour of 1977, which brought the boys to Newcastle City Hall. The gig took place a few days before a triumphant return to London where ten rows of seats were smashed, and they played a monumental set of twenty-eight songs to a packed Rainbow theatre; recorded and released as the *It's Alive* double LP.

On 20 December 1977, we finally got to see the Ramones. We'd heard "Sheena is a Punk Rocker," sung along to "Blitzkrieg Bop," and read so much about them. The City Hall was packed with everyone from the region who was into punk rock, including several who had already formed bands, and others who would no doubt go on to do so. Support came from Scotland's the Rezillos (note spelling error on the ticket) who blended an image lifted from '60s sci-fi B movies with frantic and fast surf rock and featured lively singer Fay Fife.

The Ramones lived up to everything we had read and heard. They must have played at least twenty-five songs and yet were on stage for less than one hour. The pace was fast and furious with "1.2.3.4." and straight into the next song, each one a minor classic of teenage rock 'n' roll angst. Joey held high a sign proclaiming "Gabba Gabba Hey." Johnny frantically, yet effortlessly, buzzed furious rock 'n' roll chords out of his guitar, which was down on his knee. It was like nothing else I have seen before or since. These guys had speed down to a craft; as if they were willing themselves to play each song faster than the one before. Before we knew it . . . phew . . . it was all over far too soon, we were left to reflect on what we had just witnessed, and for many to go back home and try to play as fast as those guys.

PENETRATION, THE BEDROCK FESTIVAL, NEWCASTLE POLYTECHNIC 1 JULY 1977, AND THE ANGELIC UPSTARTS, BOLINGBROKE HALL, SOUTH SHIELDS, 16 DECEMBER 1977

Penetration were the most well-established, and in my view the best, 1970s North East punk band. We went to lots of their gigs from early 1977 onwards. They all blur into one now, but what I do remember clearly are some great songs, and Pauline Murray's performance; which was always stunning. I recall listening to "Duty Free Technology" on the radio for the first time and thinking how great it was that local guys had made it. I got to know all the early tracks well before any were released on vinyl. Pauline and the rest of the original band (Gary Chaplin, Rob Blamire, and Gary Smallman) frequented punk gigs in Newcastle and the Rock Garden. The way in which they caught early Pistols gigs, and how that influenced them to form the band is well-documented (Robb, 2006). Penetration were, in turn, a big influence on the North East music scene. They built up a solid following locally and gigged all over the country, becoming quite a "name" band.

The Bedrock Festival took place over the first weekend of July 1977. It was part of broader Newcastle Festival activities; a weekend devoted to local rock talent. The venue was the University Theatre, which is a small hall sited next to Newcastle University. The Friday lunchtime gig was devoted to punk but was moved at the last minute to the dining hall of Newcastle Polytechnic, because the University Theatre took a policy decision to pull out of any punk rock gigs; such was the paranoia of the time. The venue wasn't full; a small grouping of punks, rock fans, and students gathered to enjoy the music of a couple of local bands. Harry Hack and the Big G were first, followed by Penetration, who were starting to build up their own following. Both bands put on a good show, but my memories are of Penetration who had assembled a set of strong, self-penned songs, which became the tracks on their first album, *Moving Targets*, released the following year. My early favourites were "Silent Community," "Firing Squad" (later a single), and Pauline's great treatment of Patti Smith's "Free Money."

Baxter recalls (Delplanque, 2010) Penetration playing an early Middlesbrough Rock Garden gig: "an agile, powerful band who had the then-unusual distinction of being female-fronted. The night I saw them, lead singer Pauline dedicated a song to a lad who had decked his arm with safety pins through the flesh, their war-cry, 'Don't Dictate,' and I think the irony may have been lost on him."

The importance of local bands, including Penetration, Harry Hack and the Big G, Blitzkrieg Bob, and the Angelic Upstarts, in the development of punk culture in the North East, cannot be overstated. Gigs by these bands formed rallying points for punks across the region to come together and celebrate their new identity and enjoy the new music. They were also often the scene of violent clashes between punks, skinheads, and rock fans, and between fans and security staff. Phil Sutcliffe (1979) reported a "fracas" at a Penetration gig at Newcastle City Hall in which "over-aggressive bouncers drove a section of the crowd on to the stage" causing an otherwise peaceful and highly enjoyable concert to "close amid some chaos" with seats smashed and Penetration being banned from the City.

Peter Howard of Harry Hack and the Big G: "Punk was a bit of a shock to a lot of people in the North. At the . . . pub . . . we were all banned for life because one of us was wearing a skeleton earring . . . another gig . . . after the first song the manager marched up and pulled the plug . . . students who'd been watching invited us to finish the gig . . . at the [students'] union" (Butcher, 2012). In the same article, Howard also raises the DIY nature of North East punk: "We couldn't afford Vivienne Westwood up here and the whole punk thing was far more of a home-made affair than the London scene."

Another local North East band who had been heavily influenced by the explosive punk culture was the Angelic Upstarts. The original lineup was Mensi (vocals), Mond (guitar), Steve Forsten (bass), and Decca Wade (drums). Mensi worked as a miner; punk was his escape route from the pits. In an interview for Redstar73 fanzine (2006), he explains how "his childhood had been a totally working-class type background; being brought up on Labour politics, considering the Tories as an enemy." Mond worked in the shipyard as an electrician. They had been influenced by seeing the Clash at Newcastle University: "It was after the White Riot tour. We were basically all from the same council estate and basically it was me going around, knocking on the doors asking if anybody could play an instrument. They were the first ones I found who could play something, actually strum a note. I couldn't play fuck all, so I said, 'Right, I'm the f**king singer, then' (Mensi being interviewed by PunkyGibbon).

I saw the Upstarts several times in those early days, including this gig at Bolingbroke Hall. Their concerts were legendary, partly because of the hardcore troublemakers who came along, and their controversial stage act. An Upstarts gig had an atmosphere of its own. The audience would be strongly committed fans, mostly skinheads and punks (more skinheads as time went on) who bought into the Upstarts socialist and anti-establishment philosophy. Their manager, cum bouncer and minder, was local hardman and ex-boxing champ Keith Bell, better known as "The Sheriff." He could be found at front of stage at their gigs, always ready to jump into the crowd and sort out any fights. Bell went to prison in 1980 for arson (Fitzsimons, 2013).

There were often fights at Upstarts gigs. I always lurked around the back of the hall, feeling quite exposed as one of the few people in the audience with long hair. Their set at the time consisted of "Student Power" ("What a Shower" according to the lyrics; "F**king Shower" live), "Small Town Small Mind," "Police Oppression," and the song that was always a highlight and became their anthem: "The Murder of Liddle Towers." Liddle Towers was a local amateur boxer who died following a spell in police custody in 1976. An inquest into his death returned a verdict of justifiable homicide. The Upstarts song told the story: "Who killed Liddle? The police killed Liddle." The track is a great slab of raw punk; amazingly powerful live. At early gigs Mensi would introduce it by bringing on stage a whole pig's head which he had purchased at the butchers that day. The pig's head would have a policeman's hat perched on top of it, and Mensi would hold it aloft to great cheers from the crowd. The song would start, and he would throw the head into the mosh pit. The audience would kick the head around the floor, throw it about the place, and generally go crazy. I have an enduring memory of a skinhead at Bolingbroke Hall biting the ears. While this was going on, Mensi was screaming and growling the lyrics of the song, wearing the policeman's hat.

Phil Sutcliffe reviewed an Angelic Upstarts gig in *Sounds* (1978) and wrote of "young music screaming for change with no chance of reaching a mass audience except by leasing itself to multinational capital" and declared the band "dangerous" and their performance "barbaric instinctive theatre teetering on the edge of chaos." He goes on to discuss how the North was in some ways "getting there a year too late." The Upstarts drew from their own local politics, writing and singing about "living local issues" which meant so much to them particularly as they "haven't seen much yet outside a ten-mile radius from the council estate they grew up on" (Sutcliffe, 1978).

ELVIS COSTELLO, THE STIFF TOUR, MIDDLESBROUGH TOWN HALL, 9 OCTOBER 1977, NEWCASTLE POLYTECHNIC, 4 NOVEMBER 1977, NEWCASTLE CITY HALL, 22 MARCH 1978, AND SUNDERLAND EMPIRES, 3 MARCH 2020

The Stiff tours were a highlight of the late 1970s rock calendar. These amazing events featured a selection of artists from Stiff records, travelling up and down the UK dropping into concert halls, university student unions, and local theatres. The first tour was known as the Live Stiffs tour or 5 Live Stiffs, and took place in late 1977. This extravaganza boasted a stellar lineup of the new wave aristocracy: a young Ian Dury and the Blockheads, the crazy, wild and 100 percent authentic Wreckless Eric, the Jesus of Cool Nick Lowe (featuring rocker supremo Dave Edmunds), and the enigmatic Elvis Costello and the Attractions.

I first caught the tour at Middlesbrough Town Hall with a group of friends. At the time punk was really taking off around the UK, and the old town hall was packed. I remember seeing Elvis Costello outside talking to a group of kids; my mate Norm recalls him giving them a penny for the guy. It struck us all what an unlikely looking rock star he was, even mores emphasised by his being named "Elvis." We witnessed some great music with wonderful performances, particularly from Ian Dury that night. However, when Elvis Costello and the Attractions took to the stage, something strange happened. The most unlikely looking rock star actually had something special. As Charles Murray, writing for the *New Musical Express* put it, "Elvis Costello and the Attractions look like the kind of kids at my school who hated rock 'n' roll, got to be prefects before everybody else, served as librarians and were astonishingly officious if you returned a book late or did anything freaky in the library. Keep those kids in their school uniforms till their mid-20s, drag 'em through a hedge backwards and you've got Elvis Costello and the Attractions. Except that wowee, they're the hottest little teen combo that ever got the kids sobbing while they frugged at the end of term dance, and for writing teenaged pop songs about adult situations, and for playing monster guitar and singing like a bitch whilst he's doing it. Elvis Costello can't be beat!" (Murray, 1977).

The tour called at Newcastle Polytechnic a couple of weeks later. I enjoyed the show so much, I went along again, this time with Marie. After the gig, we got chatting to Elvis Costello and Captain Sensible in the union bar. The latter was in a somewhat eccentric mood, and show-off that he is, he ate an entire packet of crisps, including the bag, all in one go in front of us.

Elvis Costello quickly graduated to playing concert halls, and the gig of March 1978 was the first of many times that he played at Newcastle City Hall. His image then was very distinct; a strange nerdy mix of Buddy Holly, Hank Marvin, and yet still very cool. On stage he was sharp, stuttering, passionate, and totally enthralling.

His clutch of early singles was impressive. Within a year he had delivered two challenging albums and released the seminal singles "Less Than Zero," "Alison," "Red Shoes," "I Don't Want to Go to Chelsea," and "Watching the Detectives." However, as an artist he was not just prolific, Costello's output struck a chord with those in search of subtlety, depth, and light and shade, which the punk and new wave scenes had so far, for some, failed to provide.

Forty-two years later and I am sitting in Sunderland Empire, once again awaiting Elvis Costello to take to the stage. I wasn't quite sure what to expect. Over the past four decades Costello's career had taken many turns and I wondered which Elvis we were going to get. The angry rocker, the middle of the road crooner, or perhaps a mix?

Elvis was backed by the Imposters which included some familiar faces (Steve Nieve and Pete Thomas of the Attraction, as well as two excellent female singers). He stands at the front, pointing his Fender Jaguar guitar straight at us and spitting out the lyrics of each song in the way I saw him do all those years ago. His ability to command the audience and connect on a deep level was present every bit as much as it had been in the early days and I remember my sense of wonder that he still managed to maintain the agitated energy that pervaded his performances back then. A review of the gig read "Two weeks after accepting an OBE—which he accepted as a tribute to his forbears, and because his mamma told him to—this was a gig that served as a reminder that Costello is still agitated and not quite ready to join the establishment just yet" (Witfield, 2020).

THE PRODIGY, BRIDLINGTON SPA, 22 JANUARY 2010

Like many others, I became aware of the Prodigy when "Firestarter" exploded into the charts, taking the number one spot in 1996. For me, the music demanded attention and it brought with it a kind of intensity and hysteria that reminded me of the sort of wild energy conveyed through the early punk scene in the mid-1970s. Indeed, the Prodigy's Liam Howlett described "Firestarter" as being "not really a song . . . more of an energy." Thompson argued that the track and indeed the band in general "sucked the energy out of life then threw it back at you" (Thompson, 1998).

Despite my initial interest in the band, by 2010 I had still yet to see them live, even though my children David and Laura had suggested we should. So, when the chance came to see them in a small (ish for them) venue, I decided that we should buy tickets and see what they were like in concert. I'd read a lot about Bridlington Spa being a great venue to see a band, so a trip to the seaside seemed in order.

So it was that we set off to drive over the Yorkshire moors on a cold, wet, and foggy night. Not the best night to make the trip, which took us almost three hours (lots of fog and traffic on the moors), but we got there safely and in plenty of time. We went straight into Bridlington centre and found a nice cafe where we sampled their finest fish and chips, which set us up nicely for the show. At around 8 p.m. we went along to the Spa for the concert.

The Spa was already packed when we got in. I was pleased to find that there was a balcony where we could sit down (me being too old for the mosh pit). Luckily, we managed to get three seats, looking over the side of the stage. After two techno-heavy support acts who had succeeded in getting the crowd going, the Prodigy took to the stage. Then followed 75 minutes of heightened energy, crowd mania, and an immersive experience which made us feel like we had temporarily entered a new world. In his book which explores 90s culture, Thompson described how the Prodigy were "inhabiting their own waking dream world" (Thompson, 1998). Indeed, the music, the crowd's reaction, and the energy of the performance felt less like we were witnessing a gig but moreover like we were being invited to experience a strange new universe. Because of this, they were unlike anything else I had ever seen.

The crowd went totally wild and seemed 100 percent invested in the experience. There was lots of moshing and crowd surfing; sweat dripped off the walls. The very loud, relentless beats brought a hypnotic dimension to the night, and the copious amounts of swearing at the crowd felt like the band were corralling and inviting the crowd to stay with them in this moment of intensity. Keith and Maxim were great front men and I remember questioning where they and the crowd in general got all of their energy from. The band were constantly running back and forth across the stage and working the front row along the barrier. To my shame I only knew one song fully ("Firestarter") and sort of recognised a couple of others. But that didn't matter; you didn't need to know the songs to enjoy a gig like that.

The seventy-five-minute set was just about right; given the high energy nature of the whole show. Despite being seated for the majority of the gig, it was almost an exhausting experience. The thumping beats pounding through your chest and the movement of the crowd made it an intensely physical experience.

Rather than brave the moors I drove back via York which took around two hours. We got home around 1:15 a.m., our ears still ringing and our pulses still racing.

THE LIBERTINES, ALEXANDRA PALACE, LONDON, 27 SEPTEMBER 2014

"North London's the Libertines have a place in pop history. A band that burned incredibly brightly, imploded devastatingly quickly and left a total dominance of influence over British guitar music" (Kinney, 2014). Although I was familiar with a couple of their tracks, I must admit to being more familiar with the legend of the Libertines and the Pete Doherty drug saga. However, the band's reputation teemed with the long-lasting legacy of their music meant that when the Libertines reunited in 2014, I was intrigued to see them live. So, David, Laura, Shauna, and I went to check them out at London's Alexandra Palace.

Not only did the Libertines bring musical punk traditions back in vogue, but they also constructed a philosophy and mythology around their output. Drawing from a broad range of poetic references including Tennyson, Keats, and Wilde, the Libertines created a quintessentially British narrative of what it meant to be alive and disillusioned in the early 2000s. They also laid out the means of escaping this state. Many of their songs reference Arcadia, a fictitious utopian land created by Doherty which, when reached by means of travelling on the good ship *Albion*, provides refuge from the establishment (Thornton, 2013).

The Alexandra Palace is a grand venue, set up on a hill overlooking the city. I could not help but think of the image of Arcadia, as I joined the mass of people, as though in pilgrimage, slowly making their way (on foot rather than by boat) towards the building at the top of the summit.

The atmosphere inside was heavy with anticipation. The crowd were mainly made up of people in their twenties and thirties, and I overheard many of them vocalising the reverence they felt on account of being there. The deafening roar that greeted Pete and Carl as they took to the stage did not relent throughout the set. The band clearly meant a lot to their fans and the on-off brotherhood-like friendship of the two front men was most definitely on again. They were clearly enjoying themselves and, looking at the grainy black and white images of them sharing a mike that were being transmitted to the screens, I remember thinking that it could have been John and Paul up there.

The old friends seemed to represent so many things to the entranced crowd before them. Not only did each song bring about renewed roars of recognition, raucous singalongs, and screams of adoration, but the crowd sang along as though in sermon, lyric perfect, and with an intense passion that let you know that they meant every word. This energy was reflected back by the band, who seemed to be charged by the crowd's response, and it felt as though both the band and the fans were mutually invested in the performance.

In the foreword of Welsh's 2011 memoir of the Libertines, Alan McGee, former manager of the band, said, "in managing the band over the last 12 months, I soon learned it's more than a group, it's a belief system. The fans that follow the Libertines are like no other fans I have ever encountered; they are true fanatics. Like all the truly great bands (the Who, the Pistols or the Clash) the Libertines are a mirror image of their fans with all the floors and genius that make up people who are alive and have a go at trying to get out of their mundane existences" (Welsh, 2011).

The story of the Libertines is as much about two friends, their journey to Arcadia on the good ship *Albion*, and their attempt to re-create a time of friendship, fun, and old Englishness as it is about the catchy songs, punk-like rocky riffs, and the moving crowd singalong ballads. They encapsulate a quintessential Brittishness and embody the energy of a youth culture who hoped and dreamed of better times.

CONCLUSION

The energy of punk rock brought with it many changes. The distinction between the performer and the audience was no longer clear in many ways. Several of the audience members at early punk rock gigs went on to form bands themselves. During the concert, audience members often climbed on to the stage and danced, or tried to sing along with the band. There were often stage invasions, sometimes prompted by the performers themselves.

In my earlier writing on the Clash (Smith, 2017), I write of the fourth and fifth walls. The fourth wall is the imaginary "wall" at the front of the stage in a traditional three-walled theatre, through which the audience sees the action (Bell, 2008, p. 203). At the Clash concert, I experienced a fifth wall, that which divided those outside the venue, and wishing to gain entrance, from those inside the hall attending the concert. The fourth wall (that imaginary wall between the audience and the Clash) and the fifth wall are interesting focal points. The invisible barrier between the band and their fans (the fourth wall) was represented by a continual sea-wall of spit; poor Joe Strummer was covered in gob. There was a lot, and I mean *a lot*, of spitting at the band; one of the first times I'd witnessed this. Spitting at the bands was one of the worst things about early punk gigs. There remains debate and confusion as to how and when the practice actually started. Severin of the Banshees has stated that "it was probably that arsehole Rat Scabies from the Damned" who would spit at the audience, while Johnny Rotten is on record as saying "I think the audiences gobbing on stage came from me. Because of my sinuses, I do gob a lot on stage, but never out toward the crowd."

The clashes of culture found a major focal point at the fifth wall, which separated the people outside; the very people who the Clash sang for and to, from *their* band. There were also clashes of culture within the venue where students and punks mixed awkwardly, with sporadic fights, and at the fourth wall, where a wall of spit signified the bursts of energy coming from the bands on stage and from the manic reaction of the crowd that night. Music and concerts in the North East were never going to be the same after this first visit of the Clash.

Although I enjoyed punk gigs, I was often scared. I had very long hair, and looked out of place at a punk gig. The fact that many of the gigs took place in a students' union building added a level of safety. I could blend in with the students, although I was also the subject of taunts from local punks. It was leaving the venue which was the most frightening aspect of the evening. We had to run the gauntlet of a large group of punks and skinheads who, having been denied access to the gig, were determined to vent their anger and frustrations on students, many worse the wear from alcohol, leaving the hall. Some people were seriously hurt. A heavy police presence minimised the violence and the danger and we survived gigs unscathed. "I was at both [Clash gigs]. There was a big fight—I avoided it thankfully—at the first and a lot of windows were smashed as people weren't students or couldn't get in. There was a lot of 'gobbing' at the first and Strummer eventually got angry and took his revenge at the front in similar fashion" (Poolan, 2014).

These were heady, exciting times. My worldview of rock music and performance was transformed, forever. Things would never be the same. Like many others, my view of rock music and bands changed the instant I witnessed Johnny Rotten and the Sex Pistols live on stage. As alluded to above, many others witnessed an epiphany when they first saw the Sex Pistols.

The energy of punk changed the nature of rock performance in so many ways. The wall between the performer and the audience was broken down and could never be rebuilt. Many people hated punk rock music; others saw it as an answer to their social isolation. It gave many young people a voice; a new focus. These performances in the early years were so different, so exciting and so important to an entire generation of young people who felt socially isolated and were waiting for a new way forward; a new set of heroes who they could truly relate to. No longer were their idols distant, on a stage far away in a field or a massive arena. These new heroes were directly in front of them, speaking their language and encouraging them to step outside of their seemingly boring and "lost" lives.

I cannot emphasise how much rock performance was transformed in such a short period of time.

Chapter Five

Fandom

This chapter explores the role of fandom, particularly in relationship to pop music. The chapter begins with a review of the literature on fandom in popular music including work by Bickerdike (2015), Fiske (1992), Lewis (2002), and Gray, Sandvoss, and Harrington (2017). Bickerdike (2015) discusses fandom in its broadest sense, starting with coverage of fans of the Harry Potter series of books. She compares fandom to religion such as, in the case of Harry Potter, many fans make a pilgrimage to King's Cross station in London where the mystical Platform 9¾ lies. She continues, discussing how fans find meaning in following a particular character, artist, or person, in a similar way that many people follow religion. I have explored similar themes in terms of spirituality and how music can help the healing process (Bist and Smith, 2021) in which I discuss how music has helped me through my own healing experience since my accident, and given me a purpose to go on living, alongside the importance of family, several of whom come along to the concerts with me, as they used to before my accident. My life is very different, but music remains a vital part of my life and of my very being. Fiske (1992) discusses fandom in terms of a cultural economy, in which fans often invest in order to find fulfilment. Sometimes, the fan is seeking something which may be lacking in the rest of their life. Again, there are parallels with spirituality.

Lewis's book *The Adoring Audience* (2002) considers "the relationship between fans, stars, media texts and media industries. From Beatlemania to Elvis worship, from science fiction fans and 'Trekkies' to Hollywood films about fans." This collection of essays "examines the way in which fandom relates to identity, sexuality and textual production. Its contributors argue for fandom as a complex and contradictory arena for critical enquiry, rather than a subject to be trivialized and dismissed." Gray, Sandvoss, and Harrington

(2017) argue that we have all become fans of someone or something in a world that is highly dependent upon popular culture and the media.

In order to explore my own understanding of fans and fandom, I chose ten artists largely from the realm of pop music to study. I will analyse a selection of concerts by artists including ABBA, Wham!, Madonna, Prince, Michael Jackson, and Cher. Table 5.1 lists the artists covered within the chapter.

Table 5.1. Pop Artists Analysed in This Chapter

Artist	Genre	Date of Performance
ABBA	Pop	1970s
Wham!	Pop	1980s
Madonna	Pop	2000s
Prince	Pop	2000s
Michael Jackson	Pop	1980s
Paul McCartney	Pop	1990s
Slade	Pop / Classic Rock	1970s
Spice Girls	Pop	1990s
Cher	Pop	1990s
The Bay City Rollers	Pop	1970s

ABBA, STAFFORD BINGLEY HALL, 11 NOVEMBER 1979

I've always had a broad taste in music, and over the years, I've been to see quite a lot of straight pop acts and artists from many varying genres. Although deemed by many to be a "guilty pleasure," ABBA is a concert that I am particularly proud of attending and feel no guilt at all for having done so. Indeed, to my mind ABBA were not just disposable cheesy pop, a viewpoint which, without further exploration, their Eurovision background could potentially lead one into holding. They produced enduring well-crafted songs which, although undeniably poppy in production, did not steer too far away from the rock traditions which usually caught my interest. "By the time 'Dancing Queen' hit in 1976, even the rock community was starting to embrace the group" (Hilburn, 2009). ABBA had a mass popularity, not just with regular pop fans, and this was illustrated by the large venues they were able to fill in 1979 when I saw them on what was only their second UK tour. "To play six nights at Wembley in those days was no mean feat . . . and in the audience over various nights were plenty of rock stars who recognised that the Swedes were to be taken seriously, members of Led Zep, Deep Purple and the Moody Blues among them. Even hipsters like Joe Strummer and Ian Dury were spotted in the VIP area" (Charlesworth, 2014).

ABBA's first UK tour called at smaller venues such as Glasgow Apollo, and I remember regretting missing them then. So, when they announced some dates at larger venues in 1979, I bought two tickets to see them at Stafford Bingley Hall. And so it was that my friend Davy and I managed to catch the band at the height of their fame.

Stafford Bingley Hall was used for gigs throughout the 1970s; Davy and I also went there to see the Who in the mid-1970s. It was a big, old cattle market and smelt like one! For the ABBA concert they laid plastic seats in rows; we were in Row 18, which wasn't too far away from the front. I don't recall there being any support act for this gig. One thing I do remember is we were both were quite tickled that the actor John Forgeham, who played Jim Baines in *Crossroads* (a popular TV soap at the time), was sitting in the next row.

Like Elvis at Las Vegas, ABBA's concerts during this era "opened with a mighty fanfare, a quasi-classical synthesised that pumps up expectations until the four arrive to tumultuous cheers" (Charlesworth, 2014). The crowd was very different from the standard rock audience I was usually part of. There were a few people with long hair like me, some families and a real mix of ages. "ABBA's fans weren't hairy head-bangers or dopers, just everyday folk who appreciated top quality pop" (Charlesworth, 2014).

The setlist included lots of hits such as "Knowing Me Knowing You," "Chiquitita," "Money Money Money," "Dancing Queen," and "Waterloo." The four members of ABBA were accompanied by a band, and by a large choir of local children for "I Have a Dream." The sound at big gigs wasn't great in those days, and I seem to remember that being the case at this gig; it was quite quiet in comparison to a more traditional rock concert. However, the vocals were faultless and the harmonies excellent. The complex arrangements of many of the songs re-solidified in my mind because ABBA deserves a lot more respect than they often get. Davy and I really enjoyed it, and I still look back on this gig with fond memories and feel quite lucky that I got to see ABBA.

After the gig we then drove straight back up to Newcastle, which is around 200 miles. It started snowing as we got further North, and I dropped Davy off at Newcastle City Hall, where he joined the queue for tickets for Paul McCartney and Wings, which went on sale the next morning. I went home for a few hours' sleep, got up, and went to work for a short time, then went through to Newcastle and met (a very cold and tired) Davy who had managed to get the Wings tickets, but that's a story for another day.

WHAM!, WEMBLEY STADIUM, 28 JUNE 1986

In May 1986 Wham! announced that they were to split and that they would play one final concert at Wembley Stadium. My mate Dave and I decided to go! I remember the journey to London well, as we decided that, instead of using the train as we often did when going to concerts in the capital, this time we would try out the North East's new(ish) Non-stop Clipper bus service. The Non-stop Clipper was a double decker bus, converted for longer journeys with a toilet and somewhere to sell stottie sandwiches but it was basically still a standard double decker bus. We decided to sit right up front on the top deck, to get the most out of our Non-stop Clipper experience. Now, I can tell you, it's quite a strange, disconcerting experience, sitting up there on the top deck, overlooking the motorway, cruising for a few hours. Nonetheless, it got us to London safe and on time and also at a fraction of the price of the train. I think we took a bus very early in the morning, which got us down to London early afternoon. Then we made our way across London to join 72,000 eager Wham! fans.

Support for the show came from now disgraced star Gary Glitter and ex–Haircut 100 front-man Nick Heyward. There was also a screening of the new Wham! film, *Foreign Skies*, which was shot during their tour of China. The show was a big celebration of Wham! and featured a career-spanning set of hits, and special guest appearances from Elton John who sang "Candle in the Wind" with George, and Simon le Bon who joined the duo for the encore. However, this show wasn't just about the guests, or even the celebrating of a pop phenomenon.

The show felt very much like a celebration of the fans as well as the band. Around 80.000 people sang along to each song word perfect. The crowd and the band responded to one another intuitively, feeding off one another's energy. Last year Springsteen played at the stadium, but not even he could match the "empathy which George Michael instantly struck up with his crowd" (Sweeting, 1986). George encouraged the crowd to sing along, teaching the audience chants and a three-part harmony at one point. The crowd also knew when to keep quiet too; George sang a heartfelt "Careless Whisper" to a near silent stadium.

There were big video screens and two giant walkways for George and Andrew to get close to the adoring crowd who screamed and screamed. There were also many tears, particularly during the last songs, as the reality hit home that this was the last time we would all see Wham! Perhaps these tears were as simple as marking the sadness brought about by the ending of an era. Or perhaps for some, the band represented something more personal. According to Shuker's definition, "fandom is a complex phenomenon, relating to the formation of social identities, especially sexuality" (Shuker, 2002). Perhaps the sadness expressed was not just due to the music itself but relating to the loss of a shared, collective identity.

We made our way out of the packed stadium, wandered down Wembley Way with the crowds, and across to Victoria where we boarded our trusty midnight Non-stop Clipper, which took us back up North and home. We arrived back early Sunday morning.

MADONNA, EARL'S COURT, LONDON, 2001, AND MANCHESTER ARENA, 2004

I guess this could be classed as a guilty pleasure. I've seen Madonna twice in concert; in London at Earl's Court for the Drowned World tour in 2001 and at Manchester Arena on the Re-Invention Word tour in 2004. I also saw her perform at Live 8 in Hyde Park in 2005.

Going to see Madonna in concert is an experience in itself. There is an air of excitement and anticipation about her shows like no other; you just know that you are going to witness something different and special. Guilty pleasure or not, you have to hand it to her, this lady really does understand the art of performance, and her shows stand above those of other artists, in terms of their production values, concept, and attention to detail.

The 2001 Drowned World tour was the fifth concert tour by Madonna in support of her seventh and eight studio albums, *Ray of Light* and *Music*. The tour was her first outing for some time and featured a major production with many costume changes, sets, and dancers. The show was divided into five segments: Neo-Punk, Geisha-Anime, Country-Western, Latin-Spanish, and Ghetto/Urban. The setlist consisted mainly of songs from Madonna's most recent studio albums, with only a couple of old hits. Each segment had its own theme, stage set, and costumes.

I went with Marie and we were seriously impressed. The tour was a major success and went on to become the highest-grossing concert tours of 2001 (O'Brien, 2018).

The next time that I saw Madonna was with David at Manchester Arena in 2004. The concert took place on 15 August, one day before Madonna's birthday, and some enterprising fans, from the Madonna "Tribe" and thus known as "Tribers," decided that we should all sing "Happy Birthday" to her. The plan began as an idea on a forum thread and ended up as an elaborate operation to get an arena of thousands to simultaneously sing. Fans managed to inform the management team at Manchester Arena, Madonna's personal manager, and the tour's musical director. As we arrived at the venue, we were handed a leaflet instructing us to sing "Happy Birthday" three times after "Papa Don't Preach." Upon finding our seats, we were once again handed a flyer by one of the fan club. "As Madonna started speaking after 'Papa Don't Preach,' backing singer Siedah Garrett interrupted and in that exact moment the crowd came together as one and sang "Happy Birthday," the band and the dancers joined in. Our Queen of Pop was overtaken by emotion" (Madonna Tribe, 2004). It was a great moment, and made the concert extra special for everyone there.

This time Madonna performed several more of her hits, which, for me, gave this concert an edge over the 2001 show. The central theme of the show was unity versus violence. It was divided into five acts with different themes: French Baroque-Marie Antoinette Revival, Military-Army, Circus-Cabaret, Acoustic, and Scottish-Tribal segments. The show began with "The Beast Within," a recitation from the Book of Revelation. Madonna appeared on-stage on a rising platform, striking yoga poses, and performing "Vogue." The Re-Invention World tour was the sixth concert tour by Madonna, promoting her ninth studio album *American Life*. Re-Invention was named as the highest grossing tour of 2004, earning $125 million from fifty-six shows and 900,000 total audience figures. The tour was recorded, and a live album/DVD set was released in 2006.

PRINCE, LONDON, O2 ARENA, 9 SEPTEMBER 2007

The reviews of Prince's output and gigs have always been overwhelmingly positive, with fans and critics alike proclaiming the Purple One as one of the best performers in the world. He was a "compelling and glamourous performer, who continued to dazzle and bewitch audiences" (Sweeting, 2016). Now I don't pretend to be a big Prince fan, but I did go to see him during his record-breaking unprecedented twenty-one-night run at the O2 Arena in London in 2007, billed as the Earth tour. Tickets were priced at a mere £31.21 a pop in order to "make the concerts more affordable, and also entitled the bearer to a free copy of Prince's CD, *Planet Earth*. As usual, the reviews of the time were extremely positive: "Every night, from the moment he hit the stage, he had the audience eating out of his hand with his consummate showmanship and musical genius—his guitar playing, in particular, was extraordinary. You got the feeling that he was simply pleasing himself, but the fun was mightily contagious" (totalproduction).

I enjoyed the gig much more than I had anticipated; Prince included several of his hits, and some amazing covers. The stage was modelled in the shape of his trademark symbol, and he used it to its full extent, popping up at various different places during the evening. You can see shades of many influences in Prince's music and style, but the artist who he most reminds me of is Sly Stone; now there is someone who I have never seen and would love to (but I doubt I will get the chance to now). The strange thing about my attendance at this Prince concert was the fact that I was not a fan. However, the magnitude of his fan base, and the positive reviews I had read of his live performances drew me to make a pilgrimage to London that night. I wanted to experience the same thing as the Prince fans experienced. I was trying to understand why he was so popular; I was intrigued by his massive popularity and felt that there must be something I was missing out on. Indeed, I did enjoy the performance, and at certain moments I almost became a fan. At the very least I came away understanding a little more about the phenomenon that was Prince, his music, and his fans.

MICHAEL JACKSON, ROUNDHAY PARK, LEEDS, 29 AUGUST 1988

Ashleigh was massively into Michael Jackson around the release of his *Bad* LP. I also wanted to see him, but his tour of the UK sold out straight away, before we decided we should go. So, we agreed to drive to Leeds, on the off chance of picking up tickets outside Roundhay Park. It was actually quite difficult to buy tickets that day. There were touts outside the venue, but they were asking a lot more than face value for the tickets. We eventually managed to buy a couple for a reasonable price, and we excitedly entered the gates of Roundhay Park.

Roundhay is a large park to the North of Leeds city centre and has hosted concerts in the past by massive acts such as the Stones, Genesis, and Springsteen. Laura, David, and I went to see Robbie Williams there a good few years after this Michael Jackson gig.

Support for Jackson came from Kim Wilde, who put in a good performance; but everyone was, of course, waiting for the main man. "More than 60,000 fans turned out for the concert which was hailed at the time by critics as perhaps the most dazzling two hours of showmanship ever witnessed in Britain" (Hutchinson, 2020). It also happened to be Michael's thirtieth birthday on the day of this concert, so it was even more special, and fans were clearly buzzing with anticipation.

"When the opening fanfare reached a climax, he shot out of the stage in a Jack-in-a-box and stood motionless in front of a sea of adoring faces for a full two minutes" (Hutchinson, 2020). Jackson then opened with "Wanna Be Startin' Somethin'" and went on to play a selection of his well-known songs, going right back to the days of the Jackson Five. He was, as you would expect, a great showman and performer, and the crowd loved him, cheering his every dance move. Ashleigh was just amazed.

As well as his exceptional showmanship, the mysterious, otherworldly quality of Jackson himself is perhaps what also helped captivate his fans.

"Perhaps Michael was beginning to draw crowds from distant solar systems, let alone Terence Trent D'arby and Jack Nicholson," wrote a reviewer at Jackson's 1988 Wembley gig. "Certainly, the air of unreality was tangible enough to take home in cans" (Sweeting, 1988). "Part of the Jackson mystique is his capacity for making 72,000 people willing accomplices in his dream-world, however ludicrous or irrational that might be" (Sweeting, 1988).

Jackson returned to Roundhay a few years later as part of the *Dangerous* tour, although we didn't attend that gig. Laura and I had tickets to see him at the London O2 gigs, which, due to Jackson's death, never took place.

Jackson's fan base was, of course, massive, crossing the world, all ethnicities, genders, and religions. Again, one can draw parallels with religion; many fans were totally devoted to Michael Jackson. His music and dexterity as a dancer and performer cannot be faulted. In many ways he was the ultimate pop star and pop performer. Although the allegations of sexual molestation, of course never proven, may have diminished his fan base to some extent; they also polarised the same fan base, making some fans even more devoted to Jackson. What cannot be argued about is a strong musical legacy which lives on. Jackson was, without doubt, a pop star with significant musical ability; unlike many other pop stars whose music is much more "lightweight."

Jackson and his legacy have, like many other artists who have been accused of terrible acts, suffered from what, today, is termed "cancel culture." Cancel culture is defined by the Urban Dictionary (Damaso and Cotter, 2007) as a "modern internet phenomenon where a person is ejected from influence or fame [because of] questionable actions. It is caused by a critical mass of people who are quick to judge and slow to question."

PAUL MCCARTNEY AND WINGS, NEWCASTLE CITY HALL 10 JULY 1973, AND PAUL MCCARTNEY, GLASGOW HAMPDEN PARK, 20 JUNE 2010

My one big concert-going regret is never seeing the Beatles. I was just too young to have seen them in concert, being only nine when they last toured the UK. So, when Paul McCartney started to tour again, with his band Wings, I was determined to see him. However, I also missed the first time Wings played in the North East, which was a "secret" last minute gig at Newcastle University, McCartney and Co. simply turning up in a van and asking to play. I remember a girl at school coming in and telling me that her brother had seen Paul McCartney the night before (he was a student at Newcastle University), and at first not believing her. Anyway, my first real opportunity to see McCartney in concert was on the Wings 1973 concert tour, which called at Newcastle City Hall on 10 July 1973. The tour was to promote the band's new album *Red Rose Speedway* and the single "Live and Let Die" from the James Bond film of the same name.

Wings' lineup at the time was Paul and Linda McCartney, Denny Laine (ex-Moody Blues; guitar and vocal), Henry McCullough (ex-Grease Band; guitar), and Denny Seiwell (drums). The support group for the tour was the excellent Brinsley Schwarz who Paul and Linda asked to accompany them after seeing them perform at the London Hard Rock Cafe a few weeks previously.

I hadn't managed to get tickets for the show, which had, of course, sold out immediately, but I wasn't going to let that stop me. So, I went along to the City Hall on the night to try to score a ticket outside. After wandering around outside the venue for some time without having any luck and still being ticketless, a shifty looking guy came up to me and asked me if I needed a ticket for the show. I explained that I did, and he offered to get me into the venue if I paid him a few pounds. I don't remember exactly how much he charged me, but it wasn't too expensive, not much more than face value. I gave him the money and he walked to the door of the City Hall with me, placing his hand on my shoulder. The doormen obviously had "an arrangement" with this guy and let me pass through. I'd been told that once inside I was on my own, ticketless, but that if I stood at the back of the hall, I would be OK; which, indeed, I was.

The Wings set that night was quite short in comparison to later gigs I saw, and it just seemed to fly over. I stood at the back of the City Hall almost not believing that I was actually seeing Paul McCartney in concert. I remember wondering if the rest of the audience were feeling the same, as the atmosphere was quiet and reserved, almost as if the audience were entranced. "McCartney politely suggested before each number that the audience make some noise" (Gambaccini, 1973). This was very different from the infamous screaming of Beatlemania. Towards the end, however, the nervous tension seemed to lift. A review from the Oxford leg of the tour stated, "Five persons stood up and that broke the Oxford reserve. Within 20 seconds almost everyone was on their feet, half the crowd was rushing forward 2 zealots had leaped on stage" (Gambaccini, 1973).

The set was a mixture of Wings and McCartney songs and a couple of Denny Laine tracks. Standouts for me were "Maybe I'm Amazed," "Live and Let Die," and "Hi Hi Hi." I was surprised that they played the Moody's "Go Now," which was just great to hear. They also played Denny's song "Say You Don't Mind," which had been a hit in 1972 for Colin Blunstone. The closest that we got to a Beatles song was the encore, which was Little Richard's "Long Tall Sally," which Paul used to play with the Fab Four. A great concert, and I was buzzing and on a high for days afterwards.

Thirty-seven years later, Laura and I went to see Paul McCartney at Hampden Park in Glasgow. Support came from Sharleen Spiteri, who put on a good set for the arriving crowds. There had been talk of a half empty stadium, but by the time Paul took the stage the place was packed. It has been around twenty years since he last played in Scotland and the crowd were well up for seeing him and joining in. So, lots of singing along all night.

Unlike my first experience seeing Paul McCartney and Wings, the crowd were a lot more laid back, a mix of people who'd come to McCartney's career at different times and stages. I'd say the atmosphere that night was one of nostalgia and celebration of the huge contribution McCartney has made to rock and pop. The set was a mix of Beatles classics, Wings tunes, and Paul solo material. Highlights for me were "I've Just Seen a Face," "Day in the Life," "Hey Jude," and (surprisingly for me) "Mull of Kintyre," for which Paul and his band were joined onstage by a massive pipe band, and we all joined in with a massive Hampden sing-along. Great stuff. We were out of the carpark around midnight and home around 3 a.m., pretty tired, but worth it.

I remain an avid Beatles fan and regularly play their music, even today. Like many others, the allegiances we form with artists in our youth stay with us throughout our lives. Like some of the other artists I explore here, the Beatles music has much more depth and breadth (and quality) than other pop acts. Indeed, the Beatles transcend rock and pop music; their musical legacy will last for many years to come and possibly indefinitely.

One other interesting anecdote arises from the first time I saw Wings at Newcastle City Hall without a ticket. My friend Colin and I were speaking of the concert recently. Colin reminded me that he was with me that evening and his recollection is that the doorman came up to us and about ten or so others and said, "Paul has told me to let a few people without tickets into the concert," and then let us enter without paying anything. Colin swears down that this is what actually happened. This is one example of how my memory can play tricks and how I cannot rely too much on narrative accounts which have been written a long time after the event. Such reflections are affected by the weaknesses of my memory and elements of nostalgia.

SLADE, SUNDERLAND LOCARNO, 18 NOVEMBER 1971, LINCOLN FESTIVAL, 28 MAY 1972, AND SUNDERLAND EMPIRE, 12 APRIL 1978

Slade were, no question, one of the best live acts out on the road in the early 1970s. With their loud, stomping, and often aggressive profile, the band also garnered a particular kind of fandom which sometimes exhibited some pretty extreme behaviours. "A bunch of Americans witnessing the Slade armies for the first time, went away completely shattered by the scenes they had witnessed" (Charlesworth, 1973). Wilder and more raucous than the band themselves, Slade fans were a force and energy unlike any other.

I saw Slade twice, maybe three times, at Sunderland Locarno in October/November 1971 and January 1972. The first time I saw them was just as they released their No. 1 smash hit "Coz I Luv You." The ballroom was packed for these guys. Support was Steamhammer, who are perhaps best known for their track "Junior's Wailing," which was covered by Status Quo.

We all sat cross-legged on the floor, which was customary practice back in those days. However, when Slade came on stage, Noddy wasn't having any of this sitting on the dance floor. Slade were a loud rock band, and we were commanded to "Come on, up on your feet, everybody." The crowd jumped up and crushed to the front of the stage, suddenly energised.

The opening number was their cover of Ten Years After's "Hear Me Callin'" (it always was in those early days), and it was amazing. It started quietly and slowly with Noddy singing in (for him) quite a low voice, then after a few bars the pace picked up, and Dave Hill's guitar, Jim Lea's bass, and Don Powell's drums came crashing in at an amazingly loud volume, so loud that I thought my ears would go. By then Noddy's voice was his normal raucous scream. And the crowd went crazy—completely bananas.

Slade were just coming out of their skinhead phase; their hair was starting to grow, but you could still see signs of crew cuts. Except for Dave, whose hair was already growing right down his back. Nod was wearing a cap, a checky shirt, braces, and jeans. The set included all of the tracks from *Slade Alive!* and quite a few covers; favourites of mine were "In Like a Shot from My Gun," their excellent cover of John Sebastian's "Darling Be Home Soon," which took the mood and the pace down a notch, the rocking "Get Down and Get With It" during which we all had to follow Nod's instructions and "stamp our feet" (as long as we had our boots on), their new single "Coz I Luv You," with Jim soloing on his violin, their cover of Janis's "Move Over," and they closed with "Born to Be Wild," an ear-piercingly loud cover of Steppenwolf's classic. It was all over too soon, but it was amazing. Slade were a force to be reckoned with. They played wild, fast, and very, very LOUD. The set was short, probably around an hour, but furious and by the end we were all ringing in sweat and totally exhausted.

I saw them again a few months later. By that time, they had released "Look Wot You Done" and were becoming chart heroes. But the live set was perhaps even wilder, more raucous, and louder than before. It was as if the fans had been given permission to tap into the energy produced by the band and, rather than merely observing, embodied what the music stood for.

The next time I saw Slade was at the Lincoln Festival in 1972. The band managed to change a difficult situation into a major success. "They were terrified of that audience . . . completely overawed by it all . . . it was an underground audience and Slade had become a pop band. Their fears were justified" (Charlesworth, 2006). This time, the fans had channelled their energy into making it clear their disapproval of Slade's recent direction. There was booing, people throwing things, and a very menacing atmosphere. However, the band came out confidently and played a rock-heavy set, winning the crowd back round.

"We got booed when we walked on stage . . . the first time that had ever happened to us. . . . We carried on regardless . . . two minutes into our set, the rain went off. Then all the lights came on. Suddenly, the whole audience stood up. They had been sitting down all day. . . . people began going berserk. The place just exploded. . . . The next week, we were on the cover of every music paper in the country. . . . The impact of that gig was amazing" (Holder, 1999).

Six years later and Slade's now infamous fans were set to "wreak havoc" again (*Sunderland Echo*, 1978). The next time I saw Slade was at Sunderland Empire, a gig which ended with serious damage to the first few rows of the seats. Support came from local rockers Geordie. I was quite close to the front, with a group of friends, and we watched the first few rows of seats collapse under the weight of fans pushing, shoving, and generally going crazy. By the end of the concert all that was left of the first five or so rows was a pile of smashed up wood.

"Seats and brass rails were smashed and twisted at the Sunderland Empire last night, as rock group Slade worked a young audience to fever pitch . . . although there was an audience of only 800—less than half the theatre's capacity—they had been very involved in the performance, and at times some became carried away with the highly charged atmosphere" (*Sunderland Echo*, 1978). It seemed that at times, Slade's fans garnered more attention than the band.

THE SPICE GIRLS, MANCHESTER ARENA, 4 DECEMBER 1999, AND THE O2 ARENA, LONDON, 15 DECEMBER 2007

Laura was a big Spice Girls fan, and a proud member of their fan club, so when the Christmas in Spiceworld tour was announced we decided to go to see them in Manchester so that her Christmas would come early that year. The tour was a complete sellout as "girl power" had dominated the UK for the past three years. The tour included eight massive arena shows in Manchester and London in the run-up to Christmas 1999. The tour occurred between the albums *Spiceworld* and *Forever*. It was their first tour as a four-piece girl group as Geri Halliwell (aka "Ginger Spice") had left the band the year before to pursue a solo career. We managed to get great seats through the fan club sale, right down at the front. It was our first visit to the massive Manchester arena and Laura's first proper concert experience.

The stage set was complex and extremely impressive. It consisted of a small platform surrounded by Christmas trees from which ran a very long runway leading to the main stage in the middle of the arena. The band (guitar, drums, bass, brass, and a small string section) were in a pit in the middle of the main stage. The centre of the main stage raised up and rotated and above there were the usual lights and a massive Christmassy ice pillar. The girls entered the arena on the small stage and then made their way over to the main stage. During the concert they moved between these two stages, sometimes moving up and down and revolving round and round, all to the delight of the crowd. The show was in three acts.

Act 1: Forever Spice. They started with "Spice Up Your Life" and the place went crazy. I could hardly hear them for the screaming. Laura loved it; she had taken two of her Spice Girls dolls and was waving them at the girls. The rest of the first act featured the songs "Something Kinda Funny," "Say You'll Be There," "Right Back at Ya," "Step to Me," "Mama" (where they were joined by a choir), "Too Much," and "W.O.M.A.N." The last song of the first act was "2 Become 1."

Act 2: Supergirls. The girls played the parts of superheroes on the revolving stage. The songs in this act were: "Stop," "Holler," "Who Do You Think You Are," "Never Give Up on the Good Times," "Wannabe," and "Goodbye" (with the choir returning).

Act 3: It's Christmas! (the Encore). The girls returned to the peal of church bells and performed "Viva Forever" and a Christmas medley comprising "Merry Xmas Everybody," "I Wish It Could Be Christmas Everyday," and a reprise of "Wannabe." The crowd, of course, gave them a standing ovation. All great fun and a spectacular show.

What struck me as interesting about the Spice Girls was their huge female following. Usually, crowds of young girls would congregate to scream at boy bands, and this was the first time I'd seen droves of young girls interested in screaming at women. Guest (2016) discussed how the Spice Girls, with their messages of girl power and "friendship never ends," brought an accessible, non-political version of feminism into the mass media and made it acceptable for girls to celebrate other females.

Eight years later: The Spice Girls held a press conference in London, announcing that they were to reunite to the delight of millions of fans. They revealed that they were going to embark on a world concert tour as a celebration of the group's legacy and a final farewell to fans. Eleven concerts were announced in North America, Europe, Asia, Oceania, Africa, and South America, and we were informed that we had to pre-register for tickets on the Spice Girls' website. Lucky "winners" were sent a code, allowing them to buy tickets for the concerts. Initially only one night in London was planned, but it sold out in only thirty-eight seconds, and more dates were quickly added. Concerts continued to be added, and they eventually played a massive seventeen nights in London at the O2 Arena, and three nights at Manchester Arena. Laura wanted to see her childhood heroes again, and we were lucky enough to get tickets for the opening night, thanks to a friendly Spice Girls fan from Germany who gave us a code to buy tickets when they first went on sale, having not been successful ourselves in the initial draw.

Our trip to Planet Spice started on the train from Durham station down to Kings Cross, onward to a hotel to dump our bags, and then to the huge O2 Arena to take our seats for a nostalgic trip back to the days of Girl Power!! Laura bought a T-shirt (perhaps I should have got one), and there was a buzz of excitement transmitting around the whole of the arena.

We had pretty decent seats on the arena floor about halfway back and with a great view of the stage. The first bit of excitement came when *Pop Idol* winner Will Young took his seat a few rows in front of us, to massive cheers and screams from the crowd. There was an atmosphere of almost nervous anticipation as the fans waited to witness what many of them had dreamed about for almost a decade.

The show began with a video of five young girls playing inside a house. They find a magic box, open it, fireworks appear, and they all wish that they can become pop stars when they grow up. Cue the music for "Spice Up Your Life" and videos and press cuttings of the Spice Girls. The girls then appeared on five massive high platforms and the whole place erupted. I have never heard such loud screaming go on for so long. The 20,000 strong O2 crowd gave the Spice Girls a reception unlike anything else I have seen. Breathtaking. Girl Power had returned to London. "Two things loomed large in my mind. The peculiar sensation of hearing thousands of women screaming at an all-female band and another broadsheet comment, this one from a forty-six-year-old working class mother after the girls first gig. She had taken her daughter along, wanting her to realise that life is 'all about going out and getting what you want . . . and showing that girls don't just have to sit at home doing the washing up.' It's a simple wish but one all to easily dismissed by the critics" (Rogers, 2008).

"Spice Up Your Life" was followed by "Stop," and their reunion single "Headlines (Friendship Never Ends)" closed the first act. The second act had a jazz theme: "The Lady Is A Vamp" and a showgirl-style performance. The girls performed jazz versions of "Too Much" and "2 Become 1" with the girls dancing around pink and white poles. In the third act each of the girls took a solo spot, each singing one of their hit singles, with the exception of Posh Spice who started the sections with lots of catwalking to a remix of "Like a Virgin." Next came "Mama" with images of the Spice Girls with their mothers and their own children. After a medley they finished with "Goodbye" and the concert ended with the slogan "SPICE—MISSION ACCOMPLISHED." The encore was (of course) their biggest hit and debut single "Wannabe" and "Spice Up Your Life."

CHER, MANCHESTER ARENA, 23 OCTOBER 1999

I'd always wanted to see Cher in concert, ever since hearing her early material like "I Got You Babe," "Bang Bang," and "Gypsies, Tramps & Thieves"; all great songs. I had loved her 1990s come-back hit "Believe" and its crazy Auto-tune when it came out, so when she announced a UK tour, I persuaded Marie to go to the Manchester Arena gig. We bought tickets quite late and ended up with cheap seats right up at the top of the massive arena, which Marie found quite scary. I was little frustrated because, after we had bought the tickets, Cher added a Newcastle date to the tour. However, I put that aside in my mind, and we stuck with going to the Manchester gig.

I remember being firstly struck as to the diversity of the audience. The age range and mixed audience profile was testament to the far-reaching effects of Cher's almost forty-year career. "I'd been wondering who might go to a Cher concert and it turns out the answer is pretty much everybody. Families (three generations' worth), groovy silver surfers, younger pairs smooching as they juggle plastic pints, whooping teens, gangs of glittery twentysomethings on girls' nights out (lots of rhinestone cowboy hats), giggling middle-aged women, a few elegant transvestites and some very young very cute gay men" (Flett, 2004). It was obvious that Cher had acquired a fan base as rich and varied as her career.

The gig itself was impressive; the set was a mix of songs from throughout her career and featured a lot of costume changes. At times, these changes left the audience waiting around a little too long, with Cher offstage for a couple of songs leaving a group of dancers to entertain the crowd. At one point a nostalgic video sequence was shown with lots of clips of Cher, some with Sonny, from the 1960s, again underlining the breadth of her career. Large production numbers, disco balls, costumes, lights, interpretive dancers . . . the show was spectacular.

Cher is an artist who has continually "surprised" and "defied expectations," a theme that was expressed through the gig itself (Bego, 2001). The long pauses whilst waiting for a new Cher to emerge, the video screens showing footage from her various TV, film, and music performances, the wide range of musical styles. For me, the show itself symbolised and, at times, explicitly showed the many rebirths that Cher has undertaken. "Of course, the music was almost beside the point. This was a pilgrimage for the faithful to bow at the spike-heeled feet of the goddess of survival" (Himmelsbach, 1999).

THE BAY CITY ROLLERS, SUNDERLAND LOCARNO, 1974

Ok, I'll admit it. I saw the Bay City Rollers and survived to tell the tale . . . just.

In the history of pop, the Rollers are sadly often seen as a joke. "Despite record sales of 120m, the UK's first boy band has virtually been written out of pop history" (Sullivan, 1999). Actually, I think the Rollers deserve more respect than they ever get. A bunch of kids from the Scottish estates who played music for young people like themselves . . . could it be argued that the Rollers actually embodied the ethos that foundered the punk movement? Why then, despite their record sales and huge fan base, are they so often dismissed and considered to be an embarrassment.

Garratt explored the idea that bands with a predominantly female fan base are often rejected. "Screaming at pop groups is not something many of us talk about because, like a lot of women's experience, it has been trivialised, dismissed and therefore silenced" (Garratt, 1982). In her 1982 essay, Garratt presented the idea that bands which attract a lot of female attention are subsequently considered to be an embarrassment and not worthy of remembering. She quotes a *Birmingham Evening News* reporter as stating, "when their fans are old enough to start looking for 'real' boyfriends, the Rollers will soon be forgotten" (Garratt, 1982).

The Bay City Rollers played in Sunderland at the Locarno, just as they were taking off. It was probably in early 1974, when "Shang-a-Lang" was hitting the charts. They played on a Friday, which was a normal rock night, and a strange choice of billing. The normal faithful rock/hippy crowd, who went every Friday come what may, stayed away in droves, but I decided to go along with a couple of mates just to see what it was like.

The ballroom was full of young girls and a smattering of skinheads. On any other Friday, I would have known almost everyone in there; that night I saw almost no one I recognised, other than a handful of regulars who, like us, had come out of habit and curiosity.

I couldn't actually hear much of the Rollers set over the screaming, and the sound wasn't wonderful. I do remember them singing hits such as "Shang-a-Lang," "Remember," "Saturday Night," and "Summerlove Sensation" (all from their first LP *Rollin'*) alongside a number of covers such as "Be My Baby." Musically they were quite average, no astonishing displays of vocal or instrumental excellence. However, the way the band worked the crowd and communicated their catchy pop-driven tunes was very impressive; Les on his knees at the front singing to the girls and all of the guys hamming it up, drawing on the energy of the fans.

That night was eventful for me for another reason. I was walking around the balcony when a skinhead came up to me and punched me hard in the face for no reason at all. I was dazed, and walked away; not very hurt, but pretty shocked. One of the guy's friends came up to me, asked if I was OK, and explained that his mate was just edgy, and didn't like guys with long hair. Just a case of being in the wrong place at the wrong time, I guess, but it did spoil the rest of the evening for me. I never did go to see the Rollers again, which is something I regret.

CONCLUSION

I found this one of the most difficult conclusions to write. I reflected upon it for some considerable time before finally sitting down to write this. My initial thoughts of fandom were of superficial, transient fans who were devoted to their idols in their youth and teenage years and then moved on as they grew older. I also began to think of pop bands whose music was, again, superficial, and would not withstand the test of time. However, having read these accounts, and the literature around fandom, I realised that the topic is much more complex. Indeed, many of the artists that I have covered in this chapter built up significant catalogues of music which is of high-quality and will remain with us for many years to come. I'm thinking principally of Paul McCartney, his legacy from the Beatles, Michael Jackson, and Prince. Also, my thoughts of fandom as a transient phenomenon are far from the truth. For example, the Spice Girls fan base returns after many years, just as big and strong and perhaps even bigger than before. Although, on one level you could argue that the Spice Girls music is somewhat superficial pop, they also make a statement about "girl power" and, through that, feminism.

So, fandom is not as simple as I first thought. The parallels to religion are strong, with fans building a community who make pilgrimages to see their idols. Many become fans for life and return to see their idols again in middle age. So, fandom runs much deeper and is an important part of many of our lives, including my own. Many of these pop idols start as part of a band, such as Paul McCartney and the Beatles, Michael Jackson and the Jackson Five, and George Michael and Wham!

However, their music and fame continue when they become solo artists and they retain, and in some instances expand, their fan base. Thus, the main themes which I can draw from these narratives are those of pop as a religion, linkages to the media and the use of media to support and promote fan bases, and lifelong allegiances to artists. This is another chapter where linkages to rock as church and spirituality can also be drawn.

Jerry Garcia states about the Grateful Dead and their fan base, the Deadheads, which remains strong to this day, even after the passing of Garcia and the band: "We're like liquorice. Not everybody likes liquorice, but the people who like liquorice really like liquorice." Such are the power and complexities of fan communities. They can polarise music communities; there are those that actually idolise the artist and will stick with them throughout their lives. Others, however, cannot see the attraction at all. Fandom is a strange beast.

Chapter Six

Venues

This chapter discusses the important role that venues play in the concert experience. I discuss concerts in pubs (Friedlander, 2018) and clubs (Brocken, 2017) through to the phenomenon of arena concerts (Edgar et al., 2016), from the early days of concerts in ice rinks and cattle sheds to the growth of purpose-built arenas such as the O2 arena in London. The discussion then proceeds to analyse performances in football stadiums such as Wembley Stadium. Table 6.1 lists the artists and venues covered within the chapter.

Table 6.1. Artists and Venues Analysed in This Chapter

Artist	Genre	Venue	Date of Performance
John Martyn	Folk Rock	Festival / Pub	1970s
Yes	Progressive	Concert Hall	1970s
The Who	Classic Rock	Cattle Market	1970s
The Vibrators	Punk	University	1970s
Bob Dylan	Singer/Songwriter	Aerodrome	1970s
Simon and Garfunkel	Singer/Songwriter	Stadium	1980s
Rainbow	Heavy Rock	Ice Rink	1980s
Roy Harper	Folk Rock	Folk Club	1970s
Ringo Starr	Pop	Arena	2000s
Barbra Streisand	Middle of the Road	Arena	2000s

JOHN MARTYN, LINCOLN FESTIVAL, 28 MAY 1972, READING FESTIVAL, 26 AUGUST 1973, AND LONDONDERRY HOTEL, SUNDERLAND, 1973

I saw the great John Martyn several times in the 1970s. The first time was at festivals: the Lincoln Festival in 1972, and then Reading in 1973. I remember the Reading appearance well; John appeared early on the Sunday afternoon with the great Danny Thompson on bass. At that time John was very much the folk hippy troubadour, and the song that we all knew was "May You Never," which appeared on the *Solid Air* album. I later saw Martyn at a gig at Newcastle City Hall on the Glorious Fool tour. The gig programme summed my thoughts up well, "Who can fill a hall with sound using just a guitar and an echoplex? Who wears natty suits, complete with braces? Who has gained ecstatic reviews for every album he has released in the last ten years? The answer to all these questions is John Martyn" (Gig Programme, 1981). Many years later I also saw him play at the Sage in Gateshead, a purpose-built concert hall famous for its attention to sound and acoustics. However, although enjoying all of these performances, it was in the upstairs room of a pub in my hometown of Sunderland, where I experienced what was, for me, the most memorable time I witnessed John Martyn play.

A beautiful Edwardian building, the Londonderry stood in the middle of Sunderland city centre. During the 1970s, pubs were increasingly being used as music venues, bands favouring more independent, intimate, personal environments and rejecting more corporate, traditional music hall and theatre settings (Savage, 2009). It was precisely the intimacy and intensity offered by the upstairs room of the Londonderry which elevated this particular John Martyn gig to being the best time I ever saw him. It was 1972 or 1973. Around this time John was beginning to experiment with his echoplex, and the wall of sound he built up within the small space was just amazing. The tone of his voice and guitar echoed again and again, filling the room with layers of sound. It was tremendous and not what I was expecting at all. John was exploring the use of his voice as an instrument, intertwining it with his echoing guitar, and creating sounds unlike anything I had ever heard before. There was a rare humanity to the concert, at times I was unable to tell if I was hearing the sound amplified through the PA system, or organically coming from Martyn himself. The intense resonance of the music and the intimate setting gave the gig a very physical quality as Martyn's guitar and voice vibrated through the room. For me, the venue itself brought added authenticity and soul to John's performance. "If British music has a soul, it resides in small venues. In hundreds of pub back rooms, grotty gig venues, DIY spaces and sweat soaked basement clubs where lives are changed and occasionally, history made" (Naylor, 2020).

Indeed, despite the sometimes low-fi setups, pubs for me brought a special quality that other venues simply did not offer. There was a feeling that you were part of the performance itself due perhaps to the close proximity you were able to have with the performer. Sometimes pubs offered the chance to mingle with bands before or after the gig, and there was a sense that there were less boundaries or barriers between the performers and audience. When writing about the Liverpool music scene, Leonard and Strachan stated, "throughout the 1970s, the pubs provided popular venues for Liverpool's rock music scene, staging performances by local and visiting bands and providing spaces in which musicians would hang out and interact" (Leonard and Strachan, 2010).

I saw John once more before he sadly passed away. That was at a concert at the Sage Gateshead in 2007. The Sage is a purpose-built music venue and centre for musical education, which, due to its careful and innovative design, "boasts world class acoustics" (Sage Gateshead, 2020). John was playing the *Solid Air* album, and to be honest, I wasn't sure what to expect. By then his health was poor, and he had lost part of his right leg and was in a wheelchair. But his spirit and voice were still great, and the concert was simply spell binding. However, despite Martyn's magic still being very much present that evening, the perfectly balanced acoustics and grand concert hall of the Sage could not, for me, transport it in quite the same way as in the past. John sadly passed away two years after that gig, and we lost a unique spirit and talent.

YES AND TALES FROM TOPOGRAPHIC OCEANS, NEWCASTLE CITY HALL, 8 DECEMBER 1973

As well as the huge part pubs played within the UK 1970s live music scene, city halls were also extremely important within the gig-going landscape. In recent decades, the need to travel has become a regular requirement if wanting to catch a tour; however, then city halls provided local people with the opportunity to experience the majority of touring artists (Friedlander, 2018). For me, it was the Newcastle City Hall which provided me with the opportunity to see many of the big-name bands.

The Newcastle City Hall opened in 1927, originally a space for civic functions, talks, and events. However, during the 1960s and increasingly in the 1970s, such spaces began to be used as gig venues to meet the demand of larger audiences wanting to access touring bands (Friedlander, 2018). Indeed, had it not been for the City Hall, I as a schoolboy would have found it very difficult to attend gigs if I'd had to travel as is now often customary.

I have seen Yes many times; however, one of the most memorable occasions was during the *Tales from Topographic Oceans* tour when it called at Newcastle in December 1973. Yes played at the City Hall for two sold-out concerts on two consecutive nights. I went to the first night's performance, along with a group of mates. This tour was a bold, possibly foolish, move by the band; they decided to play the whole of their new concept album during the second half of the concert. In many ways, this represented the ultimate in prog-rock pomposity and self-indulgence and was one of several factors that made some young music fans tire of the bands of the time, and which would ultimately result in the emergence of punk rock (Udo, 2017).

The first half of the concert was devoted to a run-through of the band's previous opus *Close to the Edge*, which, for me, is a much more palatable musical piece than *Topographic Oceans*; the title track "Close to the Edge" is lengthy with meandering instrumental parts and several segments, but it does at least have a recurring melody and is actually a "song." *Topographic Oceans* did not make for easy listening that evening. At the time it confused me. For many, the album represents a masterpiece, a groundbreaking piece of popular music which raised the level of the genre and truly synthesised rock composition with classical music. I must admit I found it hard going, and it is still one of my least favourite Yes albums. Of course, the musical dexterity and technical virtuosity of the players was clear and fully on display that evening, but the soul of the music was lost in that very virtuosity.

I now wonder how much the venue itself influenced my discomfort when sitting through the *Topographic Oceans* recital. Sat in rows in a traditional theatre-like setting, the music seemed to take on even more of a pompous style rendering it even less accessible to me. Akin with classical conventions, the performance didn't move me and there seemed to be a great distance between performer and audience, which was not just physical.

The day was saved by an encore of "Roundabout," which reminded me that the sharp, bright innovative Yes who astounded me a few years earlier still did exist, and that they could still fuse rock, jazz, and pop and blend that mix with lyrics which hinted at hippy ideals and values, and yet at the same time confused me and took me through so many twists and turns.

THE WHO, STAFFORD BINGLEY HALL, 4 OCTOBER 1975

During the 1970s audiences got bigger and the demand for larger venues increased. Gigs began to take place in a variety of locations, many of which were not originally designed for music performances. "All performances take place somewhere, inside or outside, in spaces designed for other uses" (Kronenburg, 2012).

The Who had not performed since the summer of 1974, as they had been working hard on the *Tommy* film. They recorded their new album *The Who by Numbers* during the spring of 1975 and toured the UK in October. Although the tour was meant to be promoting *The Who by Numbers*, they actually only played "Squeeze Box" from that album at Stafford. One or two other songs from the LP sometimes featured as part of their set. The show saw them return to playing quite a lot from *Tommy*, with a mini-set featured in the middle of their show, presumably linked to the success of the film.

Bingley Hall is a large 10,000-capacity exhibition hall in Stafford, England, located on the site of the Staffordshire County Showground. The County Showground hosts a variety of events, including antique fairs, dog shows, and motor shows. It is situated in the centre of the UK and close to major motorways, making it an accessible from the North and the South (Bingley Hall, 2020). During the 1970s and 1980s, before the emergence of purpose-built arenas, it was a very popular concert venue. Acts that performed there included the Who, Pink Floyd, Fleetwood Mac, David Bowie, ABBA, the Rolling Stones, Bob Marley, and Queen. This was the first rock concert to be held in Bingley Hall. The Who were out to prove themselves "The Greatest Rock and Roll Band in the World."

"Eight thousand people made their way into the middle of nowhere . . . magnetically pulled towards the new Bingley Hall . . . you could smell the disinfectant in this agricultural barn before the bodies began to sweat" (Charone, 1975). Indeed, before Who fans descended upon it, Bingley Hall had been used as a cattle barn and minimal adaptations had been made in preparation for the show. For me, this added an immense amount of character, and the venue provided a strange, surrealist quality to the night, which enhanced the experience. "The architectural venue can have a highly significant effect on the character, power and relevance of the performance adding layers of meaning and expression for both performance and audience" (Kronenburg, 2012).

I attended the second of two nights, driving down to the concert with a couple of mates, all three of us squeezed into my two-seater MG sports car. This was a set of classic Who. They started with "Substitute," played lots from *Tommy*, and closed with "Won't Get Fooled Again." Like Zeppelin, the show made use of lasers which shone out over the crowd. This was billed as "the first stage act in the world to employ high-powered lasers" (Townsend, 2012). I remember being quite worried that they might hit me in the eye. Lighting operator John Wolff confirmed my fears: "If a beam stands still, it can blind someone" (Neill & Kent, 2007). These were the Who's first performances in 14 months, and the band were simply on fire, with lots of mike swinging by Roger Daltrey and arm twirling by Pete Townshend. The Who played for two hours, with no encore. Pete didn't smash his guitar, although the crowd was willing him to do so. Apparently the Who had used a raised podium for Moon and his drums on the first night, but this didn't work out and was scrapped for the second concert. Charlesworth (1975) described "Townshend adopting his classic legs-apart stance and spiralling his right arm roughly across the strings of his Les Paul."

THE VIBRATORS, NEWCASTLE POLYTECHNIC, 10 JANUARY 1977

Ballrooms, pubs, and city halls were the main providers of musical entertainment in the 1970s; however, another important provider of gig venues of the time were students' unions (Fonarow, 2013). Often responsible for bringing more obscure or alternative music to cities, the downside of the students' union gigs was that in order to gain entry, you had to be a student. The Vibrators was a gig promoted by the Alternative Rock Society in collaboration with Newcastle Polytechnic Students Union and was the first punk rock gig to take place in Newcastle. Mark, the promoter, said, "Jan 77 was originally the Buzzcocks, but they cancelled at very short notice, and the only band we could get to replace them was the Vibrators. There were very few punk bands in existence at the time" (Smith, 2020).

I was particularly excited about seeing the Vibrators again. Marie and I had seen them a month earlier at Middlesbrough Rock Garden and had been quite impressed by them. Their single at the time was "We Vibrate," which had quite a catchy riff to it.

The gig took place in the Green Bar, a small bar upstairs in the Students Union building. Marie and I were right down the front, facing Knox. The music was loud, pounding, and exciting. All around us, the crowd were going crazy. Some were starting to do "the Pogo," the new punk rock dance which involved jumping up and down while standing straight, bolt upright. Soon the crowd would start spitting at the band, although I don't recall any spitting on this occasion. Sometimes the front man would be covered in spit, which was very unpleasant for the band and anyone close to the front (we soon started standing close to the back!). These were incredible times, I felt something new was happening in music, and in the tiny union bar, I had my eyes opened and became a convert to punk rock.

Much like pubs, students' unions were intimate settings with little physical or social barriers between you and the band. They often were responsible for showcasing innovative, experimental, and alternative acts, which often resulted in such venues being "at the forefront of emerging music scenes" (Fonarow, 2013). Indeed, the Green Bar at Newcastle Polytechnic was that night responsible for launching punk music into the North East, something for which I am incredibly grateful.

BOB DYLAN, BLACKBUSHE AERODROME, 15 JULY 1978

Towards the end of the 1970s, gig-going was becoming increasingly popular, and the UK music scene did not have the infrastructure to support the large audiences which big name acts would attract. Indeed, demand for Dylan's run of concerts at Earl's Court in 1978 was so high that a massive open-air show was added. At first, I wasn't sure whether to go to see him again, but in the end, I couldn't resist going along. I travelled down on my own but ran into a group of friends when I arrived at the gig. They had a spot pretty close to the front, so I joined them there.

The attendance at this event was huge: 250,000 people arrived at the gigantic airfield to see Dylan. There were people everywhere! "Maybe it was the site, flat and uncomfortable, especially if you happened to be sitting on the runway, but the great British festival spirit never seemed to permeate the multitude" (Sutcliffe, 1978). Indeed, audiences of that size were extremely unfamiliar to UK music fans of the time and I can imagine that some people may have even felt unsafe due to the magnitude of the crowd and event.

The lineup was very strong indeed. Dylan was supported by Eric Clapton and Band, Joan Armatrading, Graham Parker and the Rumour, and Lake. I don't recall much about the supports, other than Clapton, who went down well with the crowd. It was a hot day, and a great atmosphere. Dylan performed a set which was similar to that he performed at Earl's Court. I remember him wearing a top hat, and that there was a long wait before he took to the stage.

The sound wasn't too great, and if you were at the back of the gig, I suspect you saw very little, particularly as there were no screens. We were quite close to the front, and had a good view, so I really enjoyed the event. I count myself incredibly lucky to have found a spot so near the front. For the hundreds of thousands of people behind me, the gig must have been quite a different experience.

After the gig I spent hours in queues to get the train back across London and start my journey home. I later learned that my friend John had also gone down to the gig on his own, neither of us realising that the other was going.

SIMON AND GARFUNKEL, WEMBLEY STADIUM, 19 JUNE 1982

I never thought I'd get the chance to see Simon and Garfunkel in concert. I'd seen Paul Simon once at a concert in the London Palladium in the 1970s but felt that the chance of a reunion with Art Garfunkel was slim. However, Simon and Garfunkel did reunite for a free concert in New York City's Central Park on 19 September 1981. The Central Park concert was attended by over 500,000 people, a recording of it was released as a live album, and the duo then went on to go on a world tour in 1982–1983, including a performance at London in June 1982.

During the late 1970s and throughout the 1980s, stadiums provided an answer as to how to house large crowds and stage big events (Kronenburg,

2012). However, something felt odd about going to see a folk-based act in a vast stadium, and I wondered if the songs would get lost in such a huge venue.

In many ways, I needn't have worried. The beauty and power of those simple songs transfixed the crowd of 72,000 people. The stage set was similar to the Central Park concert, and as far as I recall, there was no support act. The atmosphere was one of delight, not only for the opportunity to see the duo but also in being reunited with their music.

On one hand, I believe that the stadium setting enhanced the experience. The masses of people, the spellbound silence shared by thousands, and the magnitude of two old friends playing simple songs but able to transfix such a huge crowd. Kronenburg explores the idea of "shared identities," where large-scale events such as stadium gigs allow gig-goers to "feel unity and explore their identity in relation to a larger whole" (Kronenburg, 2012). On the other hand, a part of me wishes I could have experienced Simon and Garfunkel in their early days, when they were able to look you in the eye as they played. "Today's gig crowd might be comfortable, safe, able to see and hear well, but will their experiences be as powerful and as persistent as it was for those in the more basic venues of the past" (Kronenburg, 2012). Who knows which I'd prefer, however, for me, the Wembley show was a surprisingly wonderful experience nonetheless.

RAINBOW, WHITLEY BAY ICE RINK, 8 SEPTEMBER 1983

Before the construction of arenas, often the venues of choice for bigger bands in the 1980s were cold and cavernous ice rinks. For me, this meant a trip to Whitley Bay.

Built in 1954, the ice rink was a great attraction for all your skating needs. However, in the mid-1970s, the rink was repurposed so that it could also host live music events (Steel, 2012). This involved soundproofing the venue and ensuring it met safety standards for the time.

In 1983, I visited the ice rink to see Rainbow play. This was now Rainbow MK VIIII (!) and the lineup was Ritchie Blackmore (guitar); Roger Glover (bass); Joe Lynn Turner (vocals); David Rosenthal (keyboards); Chuck Burgi (drums). Support came from ex-Runaway Lita Ford.

Whitley Bay Ice Rink was a pretty awful venue for a rock concert. It held a lot of people but standing on top of an ice rink covered in wooden boards was not the best setting for a gig, and it was always soooo cold. Rainbow's performance made up for it. Ritchie was on excellent form, controlling his guitar and the band with strange almost magical hand gestures. A bootleg recording exists of the show. It was a long set by Rainbow standards, probably around two hours. Very loud and a storming performance. One of the best times that I saw Rainbow live. I think Ritchie's Strat was smashed into pieces, which he threw into the crowd, if I remember correctly. This was the last time I saw Rainbow. The next time I saw Ritchie, it was back in Purple at their massive comeback show at Knebworth.

ROY HARPER, BUDDLE ARTS CENTRE, WALLSEND, 30 SEPTEMBER 1986

The Buddle Arts Centre in Wallsend was North Tyneside's community arts and creative industries resource and gained a deserved reputation as one of the most distinctive and innovative arts facilities in the North East. When the centre closed in October 2008, it brought to an end the latest phase of a history stretching back more than 130 years. The Buddle Arts Centre was one of the first facilities of its kind in the North East. "The core of the facility was the intimate performance space and exhibitions gallery" (North Tyneside Council, 2019).

I saw Roy Harper at the Buddle Arts Centre in Wallsend on 30 September 1986. The Buddle is a sadly missed local venue that played host to many concerts over the years, although this was the only occasion that I attended a gig there. The Buddle was housed in an old school, and the concert room was a small intimate venue. It was great to see Roy close-up again; just him, his acoustic guitar, his songs, and his great banter with the crowd. I can't recall the exact set, but I do remember that I was pleased that he played a lot of old favourites. I think that included "When an Old Cricketer Leaves the Crease," "Tom Tiddler's Ground," "Me and My Woman," "I Hate the White Man," and "One of Those Days in England."

The venue had a communal feel, and it felt like the audience were put on the same level as the performer. Chatting to audience members and with lots of interactions between Roy and the crowd, it felt like we could have been at a local folk club. As Friedlander states, "intimacy and the expectation of a two-way interaction is pivotal to an engaged experience" (Friedlander, 2018).

RINGO STARR, LIVERPOOL THE MUSICAL; OFFICIAL OPENING OF THE EUROPEAN CAPITAL OF CULTURE, LIVERPOOL ECHO ARENA, 12 JANUARY 2008

In the mid-1980s, arenas began to be built and served as the go-to option for bands who could attract a large audience. I have attended many gigs at many different arenas; however, I have only once experienced the opening of such a new venue.

This concert was the official opening of the European Capital of Culture at the new Echo Arena. "The ceremony launched a yearlong celebration and signified the culmination of a decade of regeneration in the city" (Liverpool Echo, 2008). Tickets had been allocated by a ballot and had gone largely to residents of Liverpool, with some sent overseas and to other parts of the UK. As the lineup for the event became clear, Laura and I decided we would like to go along, so we set about trying to get a couple of tickets. Some tickets were going for silly prices on eBay, but we managed to buy a couple for less than face value from someone in Germany.

The arena is a short walk from the centre of the city, and we got there in plenty of time for the show. We were both quite excited about going to the new Echo Arena to see Ringo at the launch of the Capital of Culture!

The new Echo Arena has a modern design, with some ideas obviously taken from the O2. It's not quite the size of Manchester MEN, but it's much better than most of the other arenas that we've been to. It felt spacious, however not to cavernous, and the seats were comfortable too.

Our seats were at the back of the arena, but with a direct view of the stage. From listening to the people who were sitting around us, it was obvious that most were from around the globe; the block of seats had obviously been allocated for international punters.

The show had been billed as Liverpool—the Musical, a musical based on the history of the city of Liverpool and featured many local stars: The Wombats; the Christians, Shack, Connie Lush, Echo and the Bunnymen, the Liverpool Philharmonic Orchestra, the Farm, and Pete Wylie. The stage was pretty cleverly set up with the orchestra on a multilevel stage playing from behind a net screen, and clever use of video footage of Liverpool and the Beatles. The bands played a mixture of their own material and some Beatles classics; Echo and the Bunnymen and the Wombats doing most to lift the mood of the crowd.

At one point we saw a crowd of children each holding a box of light marching through the local St Georges Square (this had been filmed the previous evening); the children then entered the building and walked through the audience up onto the stage.

As we neared the end of the show, Liverpool-born TV producer Phil Redmond took to the stage and introduced Ringo who joined us to an enormous cheer from the crowd. Ringo was joined by Dave Stewart and a band and began with "Liverpool 8," his new single at the time. He then sung "With a Little Help from my Friends," with the help of the entire arena singing along with him. To close, he led us into "Power to the People" ("this one's for John"), and it sounded like the roof might have lifted off the arena.

Then we took the short walk back to our hotel, through the streets of Liverpool; this was a pretty memorable event and lived up to all the expectations that we had for it.

BARBRA STREISAND, O2 ARENA, LONDON, 18 JULY 2007

This was my first visit to the O2 Arena London, and one of the first concerts to be held in the new arena. The O2 is a massive indoor arena located in the centre of an entertainment complex situated on the Greenwich Peninsula in London. It is, of course, named after its main sponsor, the telecommunications company O2 and has a capacity of 20,000. It is the first American-style, multipurpose arena in London, the second largest arena in Europe (after the Manchester Arena), and the busiest concert arena in the world. "With the completion of the O2, AEG has given London what it has always needed: a world class entertainment destination. Under our already iconic roof in Greenwich lies a state-of-the-art live music club, 11 screen multiplex cinema, exhibition centre, an entire street of bars, restaurants and leisure attractions, and most breathtaking of all—the O2 arena. . . . The O2 is the first purpose-built music venue since the Royal Albert Hall in 1871. The wait has definitely been worth it" (O2 Arena, 2020).

The O2 was an ideal and obvious venue to host a concert by Barbra Streisand. I'd fancied seeing Barbra in concert for some time and regretted missing her previous visit to the UK. I'd read of her reputation as being the consummate live performer, and the greatest and biggest star in the world. "Barbra Streisand is the only artist ever to receive Oscar, Tony, Emmy, Grammy, Directors Guild of America, Golden Globe, National Medal of Arts and Peabody Awards and France's Légion d'honneur as well as the American Film Institute's Lifetime Achievement Award . . . she is the only performer to have number one albums in five consecutive decades . . . her 51 gold albums, 30 platinum and 18 multi-platinum exceed all other female singers" (Barbra Streisand, 2020).

The publicity around this series of four UK dates (three in London, with a date subsequently added in Manchester Arena) was as much about the price of tickets as Streisand, her music, and her performance. Prices ranged from £100 to £650 a seat, with the whole of the floor area of the O2 being priced at £550 and upwards. I stumped up £100 for a ticket for the first night, right up on the upper level.

I arrived early at the O2 to allow time for a good look around the venue and the surrounding complex and must say I was impressed. The arena is a plush venue, sited with a larger complex, with bars and restaurants on every level. I took my seat, right up "in the gods" for the first half of the show, which started with the crowd giving Streisand a standing ovation before she even sang a single note. Soon her powerful, emotion-filled voice rang through the arena and we were treated to classic Streisand: "The Way We Were" and "Evergreen"; those familiar tones bringing tears to the eyes. I much prefer hearing the ballads to the stage hits and wasn't disappointed. I could spot some empty seats downstairs, some of the expensive seats remained unsold, so during the interval I made my way down to the floor level and sat in an empty £500 (ouch!) seat. No one challenged me so I enjoyed the second part of the concert with an excellent view.

The latter half featured more classics: "What Are You Doing the Rest of Your Life?" "You Don't Bring Me Flowers," and "(Have I Stayed) Too Long at the Fair?" along with a question-and-answer session, which got a little lost in the vast arena. For the encores I became a little more daring and moved right down front; I was now sitting about five rows from the front in a seat that would have been priced at £650, with a great view of Barbra as she stormed through "Don't Rain on My Parade" and touched us all with a moving version of Chaplin's "Smile."

CONCLUSION

Reflecting upon the different venues covered within this chapter makes me realise how important the venue is to the performance. Indeed, it is not unreasonable to conclude that the venue is part of the performance itself. Each venue offers a different experience and a different audience community. Folk clubs offer small intimate settings in which a regular clientele meet to discuss and enjoy different acts and artists. There is regular and easy communication between the artist and the audience. It is almost like you are witnessing the artist perform in your front room. You can talk directly to the artist, and many artists enjoy the communication, banter, and heckling between the audience and themselves. Roy Harper is an example of such an artist. He enjoys and encourages banter between the crowd and himself.

However, concert halls offer a much more formal performance experience. The audience are usually seated, that in itself preventing a closeness between the artist and the audience. The stewards at a concert hall will often prevent dancing or even standing up. I have been at performances in concert halls where the artist or band have encouraged the crowd to ignore the stewards and storm the stage. Indeed, my account of attending a Slade concert at Sunderland Empire, in the Fandom chapter, recalls how the crowd started smashing up the seats to get closer to the band.

Arenas offer a very different experience. Crowds of between 10,000 and 20,000 can attend the event. The expectation is of a larger "show," with large screens, perhaps fireworks and other pyrotechnics. Audiences may have travelled long distances to the concert and the performance becomes more of an event. Some modern arenas, such as the O2 Arena in London, are very plush and offer expensive bars and restaurants within the complex. Some shows, such as Barbra Streisand for example, are very expensive to attend and become corporate events where large groups of people pay significant amounts of money to attend preconcert meals, with guaranteed seats in the first few rows. The performance has become an event, a "big night out," for which people spend a lot of money, perhaps several hundreds or even thousands of pounds to attend.

Stadiums are, again, a very different sort of performance experience. Up to 100,000 people may attend the concert, perhaps with patchy sound or a poor view of the stage. However, there is a great sense of community and a feeling that the audience are attending an important and substantial "event." Of course, the only artists who can command appearing at a large stadium concert are those with massive followings such as the Rolling Stones, the Who, and, using the example in this chapter, Simon and Garfunkel.

Venues often play an important role in the development of a particular music scene; for example, the importance of public houses in London, and further afield, in the development of the pub rock scene of the mid-1970s. Also, venues played an important role in the development of punk subsequently. The importance of local venues as rallying points and for providing the opportunity to experience punk rock became obvious in my own experience. For example, Middlesbrough Rock Garden was an important venue, hosting all of the major punk bands and providing a "home" for the local scene.

Middlesbrough is a large town situated on the South bank of the River Tees. The local economy is dominated by the nearby chemical industry. The Rock Garden in Newport Road, Middlesbrough, was the venue for punk rock in the North East. Everyone (the Sex Pistols, the Clash, the Damned, Adam and the Ants, 999) played there. It was an old Bier Keller, which was basically a room with a stage, a bar, a few tables and benches, and a small kitchen, where they served the best burgers I have ever tasted. As the years went on, the gigs started to attract more and more local punks and skins, and were often marred by violence. Alex Baxter recalls (Delplanque, 2010): "In my teenage years, I was a regular at the Rock Garden, a small, rather dingy venue on Newport Road which catered for the rock music crowd, and was next door to the more sophisticated Marimba, a club aimed at the 'supper set' with its light, easy listening style entertainment. There was nothing 'easy' about the listening at the Rock Garden, however." It was actually a very dangerous place to visit. Every time I went, I felt in fear of violence, and there were fights at almost every gig I attended there.

So, the venue is an intricate and important part of the performance experience, and the two cannot be separated.

Chapter Seven

Communities

Here I first reviewed literature which explores the phenomenon of communities as rock music gatherings such as pop festivals (Anderton, 2018). This includes consideration of a historic perspective on the growth of music festivals from the early roots in folk music to major events such as Monterey (Hill, 2017), the Isle of Wight Festival, and Woodstock (Bennett, 2017). I then reviewed literature on festivals which I have personally attended such as the Reading Rock Festival, the Knebworth events (Bannister, 2003), and Glastonbury (Aubrey, Shearlaw & Eavis, 2005). I then selected ten festivals I had attended and reviewed and analysed my narrative accounts, drawing conclusions as to the importance of communities in rock performance. Table 7.1 lists the festivals covered within the chapter.

Table 7.1. Festivals Analysed in This Chapter

Festival	Genre	Date of Festival
Lincoln Festival	Classic Rock	1970s
Knebworth Festival	Classic Rock	1970s
Buxton Festival	Classic Rock	1970s
Glastonbury	Alternative	2010s
Maryport Blues Festival	Blues	2000s
Rocking the Castle	Heavy Rock	1980s
Reading Festival	Progressive	1970s
6 Music Festival	Alternative	2010s
Futurama Festival	Punk Rock	1980s
Hyde Park	Classic Rock	2010s

LINCOLN, MAY BANK HOLIDAY WEEKEND, GREAT WESTERN EXPRESS FESTIVAL, 1972

I was fifteen years old and so excited about going to my first real pop festival. My dad drove me and a couple of mates down on the Friday night, after we'd been to the local Mecca ballroom. We arrived in the early hours of Saturday morning, having missed the Friday night bands, and slept in a big crash tent for a few hours.

We soon ran into a group of other lads who had also come down from Sunderland. This was a frequent occurrence, and the more such music events I attended, the more I became aware of the comradery and community evoked by festival going. "A distinct sense of togetherness and shared identity began to emerge, with music festivals as the epicentre of this" (Simonelli, 2012). I would see the same group of lads at local music gigs and in pubs around the town and they would all attend the same music festivals. This group was known as the "boys," a 1970s phenomenon referring to groups of young men who hung out together, listened to the same music, and, on some level, possessed a shared group identity and mentality. Bowie's "London Boys" and "Boys Keep Swinging," as well as Thin Lizzy's "Boys are Back in Town" for me epitomise the spirit and ethos of the "boys" culture. "Groups of young men, referred to as 'boys,' would travel to music events and particularly festivals adopting gang-like attitudes of belonging and shared ideals, most notably in relation to the music they listened to" (Simonelli, 2012).

Between us, the boys and I built a cabin out of bales of hay and planks of wood which were lying around in the fields. There must have been around twenty of us sleeping in there. We were quite close to the stage, and I pretty much stayed in that cabin all weekend. We could also stand on the roof and watch the bands from there. There was a massive (and very empty) press enclosure which divided the crowd from the stage, so no one could get very close to the bands, which was bad planning. The weather was wet, the rain not letting up most of the weekend. But I didn't care; this was my first pop festival, and I was determined to enjoy every minute.

The festival itself created the strange illusion that you had stepped outside of the conventions and expectations of ordinary life. A large black and white screen above the stage showed movies on it throughout the night and I was able to watch Marlon Brando in *The Wild One*, which was banned in the UK (!) at the time. People were openly selling dope with price lists on their tents. Hari Krishnas were giving out free food to anyone who wanted some. Many people were walking around the site completely naked. Indeed, the microsociety created by the festival did not operate under the same traditions and systems of our everyday experience. Once we passed through the gates, those inside were all unified under this new set of rules and freedoms. "Festivals represented the communal creation of alternative realities, often based around hippy values and utopian ideologies which directly opposed the runnings of everyday society" (Robinson, 2015). I'd never experienced anything like it, even before the music began. The lineup for the remaining three days of the event was really strong.

Saturday. Nazareth opened the day around noon. I remember them playing "Morning Dew" and thinking that they were OK. They were followed by Locomotive GT, Roxy Music, who were playing their first major gig, and Heads, Hands & Feet, featuring the great Albert Lee, who I remember playing "Warming Up the Band." The first band I have strong memories of was Wishbone Ash. They had just released *Argus*, and their set consisted of all the classic Ash songs: "Time Was," "Blowin' Free," "Jailbait," "The King Will Come," "Phoenix," and so on. They were just wonderful at that time. Helen Reddy did not perform, and was replaced by Rory Gallagher, who had stayed on from the Friday to play again, as I understand his Friday set was cut short because of the weather. The Strawbs featured the classic Cousins/Hudson/Ford lineup at the time. This was before any of the hits. Stone the Crows were next up. This was their first performance after Les Harvey's death, and Steve Howe from Yes stood in on guitar. Maggie Bell's performance was highly emotional, and the crowd gave her the strongest reception of the day, sensing how real the blues was to her that night, coming only a few weeks after she had lost her boyfriend. Rod Stewart and the Faces closed Saturday night. I remember Rod wearing a silver lame jacket and that they were pretty ramshackle, but good.

Sunday. The Natural Acoustic Band started the day, followed by Focus who warmed the crowd up with "Sylvia," and Brewers Droop who were a raunchy boogie band who popped up at a few festivals in those days. Spencer Davis played with his new band, which was heavy on steel guitar and country oriented, followed by the Incredible String Band. Lindisfarne were the first band to get the crowd going and were a big hit of the weekend. We were all on the roof of our cabin, singing along to the North East anthem "Fog on the Tyne." Average White Band were followed by the Persuasions who were an a cappella soul band and were impressive. The next big hit of the day was Slade, who just tore the place apart. They started this performance with a lot to prove to a "hippy" crowd, who viewed Slade as a pop act. By the end of the performance, everyone was singing along and converted. They were just great. Monty Python's Flying Circus, with the entire cast, did all their great sketches: Dead Parrot, Lumberjack Song, Argument; great fun. The Beach Boys closed the evening and were wonderful singing all the hits. Great end to a great day. The morning featured some folk acts, who had been moved to the main stage because the folk tent had been damaged by the weather. I remember Jonathan Kelly performing and singing "Ballad of Cursed Anna," which is a favourite of mine to this day. Jackson Heights, featuring Lee Jackson from the Nice, started the main part of the day off, followed by Atomic Rooster, Vincent Crane collapsing (as he normally did) during "Gershatzer." Vinegar Joe with Elkie Brooks and Robert Palmer were next up, followed by the Sutherland Brothers. The next two bands were both up and coming at the time: Genesis and Status Quo. They were both festival favourites, Peter Gabriel with his shaved forehead, telling those great stories to introduce beautiful songs such as "Musical Box," and Quo were still trying to establish themselves as a proper rock band and shake off the pop image, which they were doing very well with tracks such as "Someone's Learning" and "Is It Really Me?" Don McLean sang "American Pie," and the rain stopped for him. Humble Pie were something else. Steve Marriott was at the top of his game. Sha Na Na, still featuring in all our minds from the Woodstock movie, had us all singing along. Joe Cocker closed the festival. He came on very late as I recall. There was a long wait, and he took to the stage in the early hours of the morning. I remember him singing "The Letter" and "Cry Me a River." He was good, but I was tired and cold by then and all of my mates had gone to sleep.

I felt extremely grateful to have experienced my first festival that weekend in Lincoln, particularly as "it was amazing that the festival even happened in the first place as there was a lot of opposition from officials and locals who wanted to ban it" (Whitelam, 2018). Indeed, the festival had been met with so much opposition that it was marketed as "the festival they couldn't stop" (Whitelam, 2018). I caught the train back on Tuesday and arrived home tired, unwashed, and determined to go to as many festivals as I could.

KNEBWORTH PARK, THE BUCOLIC FROLIC, 1974

This was the first of the great 1970s one-day festivals to be held at Knebworth Park. I went along with my mates John and Gillie, catching a bus to Stevenage and then making our way to the site on the Saturday morning.

We arrived just in time for Tim Buckley, who came on early in the day just as the crowds were entering the site. I remember his deep booming voice echoing around the field, but little else about his set. Next up was the Sensational Alex Harvey Band, who were already a favourite of ours, and a great festival crowd pleaser.

We made our way to the front to get a good view of Alex, Zal, and the others who started with "Faith Healer," which was still quite a new song at the time. Alex was an amazing front man, had no fear at all and was also a bit of a philosopher: "Don't pish in the water. Don't buy any bullets, don't make any bullets and don't shoot any bullets." You couldn't get more of a contrast than Alex Harvey followed by John McLaughlin and his Mahavishnu Orchestra, but such a rich mix of music was quite commonplace at 1970s events.

> The diversity of the music at festivals in the 1970s exposed us to a greater range of musical influences and helped to broaden and blur the boundaries of musical identities. Hippies were exposed to rock, rock fans to jazz, jazz fans to folk etc, resulting in a sense of extended community and acceptance. This role of festivals as an audible and visual celebration of public and counter-cultural community, enabled music fans to come together as a whole, rather than sticking to their self-identified musical tendencies. (Anderton, 2018)

This is to say, rather than festivals showcasing just one particular type of genre, these mixed genre events resulted in audiences being exposed to music and, indeed, people they would otherwise not have encountered.

And so it was that John McLaughlin took to the stage. John was dressed entirely in white, and he and his band took us through a wonderful blend of jazz, rock, and classical music, which swept through the field. The Mahavishnu Orchestra was a big band, featuring Jean Luc Ponty, who had recently made his name playing with Frank Zappa. Van Morrison was just amazing, and at his peak, in the early 1970s, and his set at Knebworth was great. His band on the day was a three piece, which was very small for Van, and a contrast to the Caledonia Soul Orchestra who I saw him with a few weeks later.

I was never a big fan of the Doobie Brothers, they were a bit too funky for me; however, my friend John recalls them as the highlight of the day. They went down OK with the crowd, but by then everyone was waiting for the headliners. "Jessica" and "Ramblin' Man" were real favourites that summer, played at all the festivals, and the Allman Brothers Band had a reputation for being THE Jamming band, renowned for playing long sets and mega versions of their songs, particularly "Whipping Post." They didn't let the crowd down. Gillie, John, and I spent some time wandering around the site that day, and Jessica was constantly playing in the background. The Allmans came on late and played until well after midnight. Gregg Allman said at some point during the set, "We are going to play every damn song we know" after continued shouts for "Whipping Post."

We slept the night on the site and got the bus back home the next morning, running into some of John's school friends on the bus. John comments that "this was overall a very exciting day, with a diverse, even eclectic, lineup which happened a lot at the time and gave everyone a chance to appreciate lots of different styles of music" (Smith, 2014).

THE BUXTON FESTIVAL, 1974

My friend John and I attended the 1974 Buxton Festival. I'm not sure if it is a pleasant memory or not; and those of you who attended any of the outdoor Buxton events will know why I say this. Terry Battersby puts it well on the UK Festivals site: "I managed Buxton in 72/73/74.They should have been campaign medals issued" (Battersby, 2018). I myself managed to attend in 1973 and 1974 and know what he means; I hold my medal with pride; the Buxton festivals were a real endurance test.

Buxton is a town high up in the peak district and the festival was sited up on a moor. You couldn't imagine a worse place to hold a pop festival. All of the three outdoor festivals (there were some indoor events which preceded them) suffered from poor weather, lots of wind and rain, and after 1974 the organisers abandoned the idea of holding any further festivals.

I drove down to Buxton with my friend Gilly, who also came to the 1973 event with me. We arrived on Friday afternoon, finding the place cold and windswept. Not being the most prepared festivalgoers at the time, we didn't have a tent and planned on sleeping in the car (not easy in a tiny MG Midget), or in sleeping bags on the ground. When we arrived on the moor, we saw lots of people building makeshift huts from planks of wood. I asked them where they found the wood, and they pointed me to a storehouse in the next field.

So off I went to retrieve some wood for us to build our own shelter. I was leaving the store with some planks under my arm with a few other guys, when we were stopped by a policeman, who asked us where we were taking the wood. He quickly bundled us all into the back of a police jeep and took us off to a temporary police cabin which they had set up for the weekend. Once in there they searched us, took statements, and made us wait a few hours, telling us that we would probably be charged with theft for taking the wood. When they eventually did let us go, we had to walk back to the site, where I found my mate Gilly lying asleep by the car. The bands had started by that point, and we went into the arena and caught as much of the show as we could.

I remember seeing Man and Mott the Hoople that night. Mott started with "Golden Age of Rock 'n' Roll" and were just great. I slept in the car and Gilly slept in a sleeping bag underneath the car. We were both frozen; it was truly awful. Highlights of the next day were Humble Pie (Stevie Marriott was awesome in those days and a big festival favourite), and Roger Chapman and the Streetwalkers. Anyone who was there will remember the magic moment in that dull rainy day when the sun came out during "My Friend the Sun," as Roger sang "He's there in the distance" to a great cheer from the crowd. The Faces were OK, but it wasn't the best time I saw them; by this point they had added a horn section to the band. I remember keeping warm in the Release tent and chatting to Caroline Coon. My friend John was also there with a group of mates, although I don't recall us running into each other. He recalls: "My own recollections were that the weather was terrible, wet and cold, the facilities non-existent and I slept in my dad's car with three other mates. The Friday bands were good Mott, Man and Lindisfarne. On Saturday there was the famous "My Friend the Sun moment" which I do recall, and Humble Pie were great. The Faces came on late and I remember the stage being pelted with bottles—reports on the Web said this is because they refused to play an encore . . . those were the days!!!" (Smith, 2014).

Indeed, the somewhat trying experiences endured by those who attended Buxton festival brought a new dimension to the sense of community there. In Anderton (2018), it is thought that adverse weather conditions, uncomfortable sleeping arrangements as well as other adverse experiences can act as a bond between those who shared these experiences. "Even if one did not directly interact with said persons at the festival itself, just knowing that they were in attendance, and therefor privy to the experience as a whole, acts as an unspoken understanding of the adversities faced, however trivial" (Anderton, 2018).

Postscript: Several weeks after the festival I received a letter summoning me to attend my local police station where I was issued with a formal caution for "stealing" the wood; and that was the last I heard of it. I did run into a couple of the lads who were in the jeep with me at Reading and Knebworth over the years and we always said hello. I wonder where they are now.

GLASTONBURY FESTIVAL, PILTON FARM, 25–27 JUNE 2010

It had been thirty years since I'd last been to a three-day festival and stayed for all three days (Reading in 1980). So, when my children David and Laura expressed an interest in attending Glastonbury, I was keen to check out a modern festival. So, they, my wife Marie, and I secured tickets and eagerly anticipated our first Glastonbury experience.

We travelled down in a campervan we'd hired specially for the occasion. We arrived on the Wednesday, although the main acts were not scheduled until Friday. Thursday was spent exploring the massive site; and although dedicating a day to this, the four of us still left the festival feeling as though we'd only experienced a fraction of it.

There were many aspects of Glastonbury that reminded me of my old festival experiences. Lots of displays of hippy values with areas dedicated to charities, environmental activism, and promoting messages of green living. Certain parts of the site were themed around mystical and New Age traditions with "the Stone Circle," "Arcadia," and "Shangri-La." However, amongst all of this were definite indicators of the effects of modern consumerism and commercialism. "While promoted as an ethical festival that celebrates its anti-commercial countercultural cool, Glastonbury reflects a modern cathedral of consumption. Vast areas of food vans all selling gourmet meals" (Flinn and Frew, 2014). Fields filled with clothing, trinkets, and even antiques for sale. The healing field where you could purchase a massage or any number of pricey complementary therapies . . . it felt you could easily fill the four-day festival experience sampling the shopping opportunities the site offered.

Whilst not denying that Glastonbury's roots of an original 1970s festival were evident and, on the whole, it still did a lot to reject a completely corporate feel, the signs of postmodern ideals were ever-present. "Festivals have gradually evolved to mirror the cultural demand for consumerism and extended youth, and the pressures of the market have impacted upon Glastonbury, transforming it into a hedonistic landscape of endless partying, eating, drinking and spending" (Anderton, 2011).

Although partly impressed by the vast site and the varied opportunities it offered, the highlights for us were watching Gorillaz, Muse, Ray Davies, and Stevie Wonder who turned out all the hits for us. We all had a great weekend; the festival is so big we gave up on the idea of trying to see all of the bands that we had planned and just enjoying what we managed to catch.

So, despite the large screens showing adverts and sponsorship messages between bands, and the blatant differences between 2010 Glastonbury and festivals of the past, the family and I still vowed to visit the festival as often as we could. We managed a further three visits.

MARYPORT BLUES FESTIVAL, 27 JULY 2003 AND 24, 25 JULY 2010

Maryport Blues Festival was a festival held in the small Cumbrian town of Maryport, celebrating all things blues. "The festival sees musicians perform in a marquee, pubs, an outdoor stage and on the street" (BBC News, 2018).

My first visit to the festival was in 2003, when I witnessed something very special. The Groundhogs had reunited for the first time in thirty years, reforming their classic lineup of Tony McPhee, Pete Cruikshank, and Ken Pustelnik. The Groundhogs are a very important band for me and I must have seen them around fifty times over the years. This particular occasion brought me to Maryport on a hot Sunday afternoon in July.

David came along with me and took some photos whilst the Groundhogs played a short but energetic set of some of their classic tracks. The bands played in a large marquee down by the harbour. In later years, the festival moved its home to near the rugby club. It was great to see the original lineup again and to experience the delights that the small town of Maryport had to offer.

I visited the festival on three other occasions over the years. My fourth and final time was in 2010 with Marie. This year we decided to attend the Saturday and the Sunday. We drove across on Saturday afternoon and checked in at the Ship, in Allonby, which is about five miles up the coast from Maryport. Allonby is a lovely town with wonderful views of the sea and a great coastline, and the Ship is a nice pub offering rooms for bed and breakfast. On the Saturday evening we ventured into Maryport centre for the blues trail. The place was jam-packed with people, and there were queues to get into all of the pubs, so we retreated to the rugby club where the main marquee for the festival was situated. The attendance was pretty good, although there were rumours that ticket sales were slow and that this may have been the last festival due to funding problems. In fact, the festival managed another eight years before being sadly cancelled (BBC News, 2018).

The Saturday night was headlined by Mica Paris and Booker T. Booker T was excellent. He still used his famous Hammond organ and Lesley cabinet, and he treated us to favourites such as "Green Onions," "Time Is Tight," and great renditions of "Dock of the Bay," "Ain't no Sunshine," and "Hold on I'm Coming." It was a rare chance to see a true legend (his only UK date in his European tour of the time), and he didn't disappoint.

We were up early on Sunday morning and had a walk along the beach, which blew away the cobwebs and got us ready for the day. We drove into Cockermouth and had a look around Wordsworth's birthplace before going into the festival later in the day. Headliners were Canned Heat and Robert Cray. It was Canned Heat who I had really come to see. The band consisted of the original drummer who has been there throughout since the 60s and the recently returned-to-the-fold Larrie Thompson on bass and Harvey Mandel on guitar. They were billed as the Woodstock lineup as those three guys all played at that famous festival. They opened with "On the Road Again," which set the pace for a host of blues and boogie tunes, including the other hits "Going up the Country" and "Let's Stick Together." They still sounded great. We returned to the Ship on Sunday night and drove home Monday morning. Another great blues festival.

ROCKING THE CASTLE FESTIVAL, 17 AUGUST 1985

"Conceived by Jones and Loasby as a way of signalling the end of Rainbow's down to earth tour, this wasn't actually meant to be the birth of a dynasty, just a one off day out, but it was so well received that Monsters of Rock became a tradition that dominated the 1980s" (Dome, 2015). A single-day festival held in Donington in the East Midlands, I attended the Monsters of Rock several times throughout the 1980s. Donington 1985 signified the festival receiving a name change, presumably due to the lineup being a little more mixed than the usual heavy metal fare.

The lineup for this, which was the sixth Donington Festival event, was ZZ Top, Marillion, Bon Jovi, Metallica, Ratt, and Magnum. It was a beautifully hot day and one of the best Donington festivals I can remember in terms of the weather. Marillion were a massive hit with the crowd, "Misplaced Childhood" having just been a chart hit. Bon Jovi were energetic and delivered a polished performance: You could tell they were on the cusp of massive things. However, everyone was there for the headliners and the air of anticipation grew in the buildup to ZZ Top's set.

At some point during the afternoon, the ZZ Top car flew over the audience, suspended from a helicopter. This prompted huge cheers from the crowd and a deluge of bottles and cans being thrown up into the air. Thankfully, none of these hit the flying limo! When the band eventually took to the stage, the crowd were so excited to see the boogie kings that the atmosphere became electric. Their classic tracks, tongue-in-cheek humour, and unique style resulted in them delivering a memorable set that both delighted and united the audience.

The Donington crowd brought together a set of individuals, who, through style, attitude, and, of course, music, were able to come together as one for a day. "The 70,000 odd fans were, undeniably an awesomely collective phenomenon. Herd-like, ugly, faceless: A sense of single-mindedness prevailed wherever one looked" (Hoskyns, 1981). Indeed, the single genre festival gave space for, as Lopez and Leenders would term it, a "self-expansion opportunity" (Lopez and Leenders, 2019). That is to say, for the duration of the festival, audience members were enabled to express a part of their identity, which, for the most, would be supressed or rejected in everyday life. The Rocking the Castle event was a space of acceptance, somewhere to fit in rather than stand out. "These kids are here to participate in a group fantasy, a fantasy in which divergences in style are tolerated and ultimately ignored" (Hoskyns, 1981).

THE READING FESTIVAL, 11–13 AUGUST 1972

I first went to the Reading Festival in 1972 and continued to go every year until 1980. I'd already been to the Lincoln Festival in May 1972, so I felt, as a fifteen-year-old, I was already a hardened festivalgoer. I didn't know anyone who wanted to go to Reading, so decided to go along myself. My parents weren't keen on my idea of hitching, so I agreed to go by train.

The festival took place over the weekend of 11–13 August 1972 starting on Friday afternoon. For some reason I decided to get the train down to London early on the Thursday night, arriving around midnight. Having nowhere to spend the night I took a tube to Piccadilly Circus and found an all-night cinema. It was showing Elvis films that night, I paid my money and sat close to the front. The cinema was quite empty; the audience was a few couples, some Elvis fans, and several people alone like me, and just looking for somewhere to spend the night. I emerged, very tired, from the cinema in the early hours of the morning and went across London to get the train to Reading.

I didn't have a ticket for the festival, so when I arrived, I joined the queue and bought a weekend ticket. In those days it was all about seeing the bands, so I stayed in the queue to get a good spot in front of the stage. All I had taken was a sleeping bag; no tent, no change of clothes (I told you that I thought myself a hardened festivalgoer).

The Friday lineup was: Good Habit, Nazareth, Cottonwood, Steamhammer, Jackson Heights, Genesis, Mungo Jerry, Curved Air. The music started at 4 p.m., and there were two stages set alongside each other to make for quick changeovers. I positioned myself close to the front somewhere between the two stages, so I had a good view of both. There was a press enclosure right down the front, and an area where the Hells Angels would encamp, so you couldn't get that close to the stage. I got talking to a guy next to me; he was also alone, still at school and a similar age. We stuck together throughout the weekend, keeping each other's place in the crowd, and sleeping there on in our sleeping bags. This seems crazy now, but, hey, I was young and just so excited about seeing the bands. You could sleep in the main enclosure in those days; you had to leave in the early morning so that they could clear up and get ready for the next day. Some clearing happened during the night; this didn't make for a good night's sleep as there was a danger that someone stood on you (this happened to me several times). The organisers stopped letting people sleep in the main enclosure a few years later; a punter was run over by a vehicle that was driving around collecting litter.

The casual familiarity that often existed at festivals was liberating. You felt you could chat to people freely and the normal social restrictions that applied to life outside of festivals did not exist within the gated community. "Often friendships and connections, although only lasting for the duration of the festival, would be more intense and expansive than those casually made outside of the festival environment" (Laing and Mair, 2015).

The Saturday lineup was Jonathan Kelly, Solid Gold Cadillac, Man, Linda Lewis, Focus, Edgar Broughton, Jericho, If, Johnny Otis Show, Electric Light

Orchestra, the Faces. I watched all of the bands, and also took some time to have a look around the stalls in the arena. I didn't see any need to venture into town (that would come in later years) and spent the entire weekend within the confines of the festival. The weather was quite warm, sunny with a little drizzle now and then but nothing major, and certainly nothing compared to the rain I had experienced at the Lincoln festival earlier in the year.

The Sunday lineup was Sutherland Brothers, Gillian McPherson, String Driven Thing, Matching Mole, Stackridge, Vinegar Joe, Status Quo, Stray, Roy Wood's Wizzard, Mahatma Kane Jeeves, Ten Years After, Quintessence. John Peel and Jerry Floyd were comperes for the weekend. Jerry was the regular DJ at the Marquee Club, who organised the festival at the time. I spent most of the weekend chatting about music to the guy that I met on the first day and we struck up quite a friendship. I made a few friends at festivals in those days and would sometimes see some people every year, but I never ran into this guy again. "The relationships, connections and acquaintances fostered at festivals, often coloured the festivals themselves with memories being shaped around the people we met" (Laing and Mair, 2015).

I left as Quintessence took to the stage as did many others to catch the last train to London. The tubes had stopped, so I walked across London. I'd missed the midnight train, so I spent the night in Kings Cross station. By Monday morning, I was stiff, tired, and scruffy. I got the first train home and went straight to bed.

BBC 6 MUSIC FESTIVAL, SAGE GATESHEAD, 21 FEBRUARY 2015

The BBC 6 Music festival is a weekend festival, which, every year, takes place across a number of venues within a chosen UK city (BBC 6 Music Site, 2020). In 2015, the BBC 6 Music Festival decamped to the North East with events in the Newcastle O2 Academy on Friday, the Sage Gateshead on Saturday and Sunday, and a range of venues across Newcastle throughout the weekend. David and Shauna came up from London for the weekend, and we all (Marie, me, David, Shauna, Laura, Dale) trooped across to the Sage for the Saturday evening festivities.

The Sage had been transformed into a festival cum nightclub, with all of the halls open, simultaneously featuring music. All of the seats had been removed from the floor level of Hall 1, and the atmosphere was one of excitement.

The first act that Marie and I caught was Kate Tempest, who was introduced by Don Letts. Now there's a face from the past. The last time I remember seeing him was 1977 in Newcastle Students Union and he was holding a big camera, filming the Clash. He was managing the Slits at the time and went on to be a member of Big Audio Dynamite. Kate Tempest got the crowd going with her spoken word hip hop music. We wandered into Hall 3 and found Stuart Maconie playing soul sounds, and then out onto the concourse to watch Jungle. For me, the highlight was Royal Blood, who made a loud intense blues noise and played to a packed Hall 1. It's hard to believe that two guys (guitar, vocals, drums) could produce such a wall of classic rock music, in the tradition of Hendrix, Zeppelin, and Cream. Great stuff. The others all reckoned Hot Chip as the highlight of the night. Laura and Dale went off to the Boiler House after the Sage closed at 11 p.m., for further 6 Music fun.

It felt very special that a national event chose to come to the North East. Not only was it convenient to experience a festival on our doorstep, it also showcased the city, transforming it into a creative space. "Urban festivals not only promote tourism to cities but also imprint it as a cultural hub where creative things are happening" (Van Alst and Van Melik, 2012). Indeed, I heard from my daughter, Laura, that friends from all around the country were travelling to Newcastle for the event, and my son, David, and his wife made the trip from London. For the duration of the weekend, Newcastle was re-imagined as a musical and artistic landscape and took on new cultural significance.

FUTURAMA 2 FESTIVAL, QUEENS HALL, LEEDS 14, SEPTEMBER 1980

This was the second Futurama festival, and it took place at Queens Hall, which was in the centre of Leeds. The Saturday lineup featured U2 (low down on the bill), Echo & the Bunnymen, Soft Cell, and Siouxsie & the Banshees (who headlined). I attended the Sunday with my mate Dave, and it featured the Psychedelic Furs, Gary Glitter, the Durutti Colum, Classix Nouveaux, Young Marble Giants, Hazel O'Connor, the Soft Boys, Flowers, Naked Lunch, Blurt, Artery, Notsensibles, Vice Versa, Desperate Bicycles, Frantic Elevators, Athletico Spizz 80, Brian Brain, Tribesmen, Boots for Dancing, and Household Name.

We arrived during the afternoon and missed some of the bands. Queens Hall was a cavernous building in Leeds, which was originally a tram and bus depot. It was used as a concert venue during the 1980s. It has since been demolished and is now a car park. When we arrived, it looked like a war zone. Punk fans from all over the North, and further afield, had decamped there for the weekend, and had been in the venue all night, sleeping on the floors; there was trash everywhere.

We saw faces that we recognised from Middlesbrough Rock Garden, which had closed for the weekend as everyone was going to the festival. We chatted to a few people; everyone was talking about how great Siouxsie (who had headlined the Saturday night) had been. There were stalls around the place and pop-up art performances in dark corners of the hall. I recall one performance which involved a guy having a crap in a bucket; we moved on. The bands were playing on a stage at the end of the massive hall.

"Futurama gathered the provincial post-punk micro scenes that were congealing in many cities in the north and beyond, building upon a vaguely coherent strand of moving beyond punk by adding a strand of industrial angst and futuristic ambiguity" (Trowell, 2017). The Festival felt very different from anything I'd experienced before, and the crowd seemed on board for whatever the weekend had to offer. "Futurama went against the grain, large festivals emerging from the hippy and rock scenes had settled on events such as Glastonbury and Reading, which excluded punk, post-punk and the north from this culture." Indeed, the festival seemed to want to showcase bands which other festivals, so far had not touched (Trowell, 2017).

This was an opportunity to see bands who went on to stardom: The Frantic Elevators became Simply Red, and Vice Versa became ABC. There was a great mix of bands at the event, and the atmosphere was wonderful, really friendly. Although on the surface this festival appeared messy and shambolic, it is actually one of the best I have every attended for the musical range and the attitude of the crowd. "Leaving aside the organisational inadequacies and general filth of the occasion, the line-up of bands looked quite tasty" (Gill and Penman, 1979).

Highlights of the day were Hazel O'Connor, who was in the charts with "Eighth Day" and became the robot from "Breaking Glass," Durutti Column featuring Vini Reilly's meandering guitar, and 4" Be 2" who were a proto-Oi! band featuring Jimmy Lydon (John Lydon's brother) and also at one point featured Youth of Killing Joke. But the highlight was an incredible performance by Notsensibles, a punk band from Burnley who had some success with their single "I'm in Love with Margaret Thatcher." Their set included a lot of tongue-in-cheek songs, all performed in their strong Northern accent. They'd brought a large contingent of fans, who all sang along with every daft song. Notsensibles motto was "all we want to do is make silly records and play silly gigs."

The festival ran very late into the night (inevitable given the incredible number of bands who were performing), and we left around midnight during the Psychedelic Furs set to drive back up North and home, thus missing the headliner who was (also incredibly) the now shamed star Gary Glitter. The Futurama festival had a history of choosing off-the-wall headliners; on another occasion the closing act was a reformed Bay City Rollers (now that must have been something to experience). A crazy, mad, fun event with some great bands. Happy, happy days.

QUEEN, HYDE PARK, 18 SEPTEMBER 1976

During the 1970s, free festivals were a relatively common phenomenon. The biggest of these was held at Hyde Park in London, where "one could listen to free music for hours from some of the best bands in Britain . . . nowadays this is so rare that it is big news if it happens but, in those days, free concerts were a regular event" (UK Rock Festivals Site, 2012).

The last open air festival event I went to in the long hot summer of 1976 was Queen in Hyde Park. A group of us went down to London by train on a day return ticket, returning straight after the concert on the mail train which pulled out of Kings Cross at midnight. This was a free concert, which drew a crowd of over 150,000, and was organised by Richard Branson. The lineup consisted of Supercharge, Steve Hillage, and Kiki Dee. Kiki Dee had just been No. 1 in the charts with Elton John and their massive hit "Don't Go Breaking My Heart." There were lots of rumours that Elton would join her onstage for the song, but he didn't; instead, she was accompanied by a life-size cardboard Elton figure, and we all had to sing the Elton parts with her. Steve Hillage was quite popular at the time, and was great on the day, lots of glissando guitar, and amazing psychedelic trippy versions of the Beatles' "All Too Much," and Donovan's "Hurdy Gurdy Man." There was a big fight in the crowd during his set. But the day belonged to Queen.

It was quite a brave move headlining such a major event at what was still a relatively early point in their career, but they pulled it off and were as majestic as ever. Their set was relatively short, around an hour, because of curfew and time restrictions. Apparently, Queen were prevented from returning for their usual long encore by the police. This was just before they released the *Day at The Races* album. Freddy was amazing, although from where we were standing, he was a tiny white figure shining across the massive sea of people (no big screens to watch in those days).

CONCLUSION

This chapter has presented a number of narrative accounts of festivals which I have been lucky enough to experience, starting in the early 1970s. I remember those early festivals vividly, perhaps more so than more recent events. I was so excited, at fifteen years old, to be attending a real pop festival. Those early events had a sense of freedom about them. When I entered the confines of the festival grounds, I felt I was in a different world; one where anything was possible. Drugs were openly on sale, and the bands played well into the night. There didn't seem to be any curfews at the time. I met others of a similar age from all over the country, some I would meet at various events, year by year. There was little security and little evidence of police presence. Once I was in the festival site, I felt free and able to do anything I wanted. In the early days, I was interested only in witnessing as many bands as I could. The lineups were excellent: Genesis, Rory Gallagher, Rod Stewart and the Faces, Status Quo, the Edgar Broughton band, and others. Bands I followed for many years to come. Later came the temptation of the local pubs, particularly at the Reading festivals. The early Knebworth festivals featuring the Allman Brothers, Pink Floyd, and the Rolling Stones were all very special events.

Soon, I would meet many other "boys" from Sunderland. Some of these I already knew from the town; others I met for the first time and they became lifelong friends. The boys were a mad crowd, with lots of shenanigans, diving in the river and having confrontations with groups of lads from other parts of the country. However, the boys were not limited to men alone; the group also included several female members, some were partners and wives of the male boys; others were not. The Hells Angels were always in attendance; down the front sometimes with their motorbikes. At the Buxton Festival, the Angels drove through the crowd on motorbikes, and eventually took control of the festival. John Peel, also, always seemed to be the DJ. And, of course, I must not forget the "Wally" chant which went on into the early hours of the morning, and the stories about who the legendary Wally actually was! Jesus Jessop would appear, dancing naked at the front of the stage, much to the delight and cheers of the audience.

There was a real sense of community about these early events. My regret is that I was too young to attend even earlier Reading festivals, when they took place at Plumpton and the legendary Isle of Wight festivals in the late 1960s. In later years, we would regularly attend Glastonbury as a family. Again, there was a sense of community, a joint "friendship" where everyone would support and help each other.

Festivals appeared in other venues, such as the Futurama festival, which was a strange event in the cavernous Queens Hall of Leeds, which was later to become a car park (and which was little more than a car park when the festival took place!). All of these events, of course, gave me the opportunity to see many bands over a short period for a relatively low cost.

I miss attending festivals. It just isn't practical in my current, disabled situation. They were, and remain, important events in the rock music calendar and collections of performances which themselves become legendary. I'm so pleased that I got to see the Rolling Stones at Knebworth, Glastonbury, and their return to Hyde Park; and that I also saw Queen perform at their legendary free concert in Hyde Park. Heady days!

Chapter Eight

Politics

This chapter discusses the role of rock in discussing and supporting social causes, politics, and charity. The chapter draws from recent literature including Arvidsson (2016) who discusses the intersection of rock music and politics, and Feezell (2017) who explores the influence of rock music on politics. I discuss the phenomenon of rock as charity events including Live Aid (Grant, 2015), Live 8, and other charitable rock concerts. I go on to discuss and analyse performances by artists who use rock music to pursue political issues including Bob Dylan, Joan Baez, Pete Seeger, and modern anarchic acts such as Crass. I selected ten performances relating to politics and analysed these. Table 8.1 lists the artists and events covered within the chapter.

Table 8.1. Artists and Events Analysed in This Chapter

Artist / Event	Genre	Date of Performance
Live Aid	Multi-genre	1980s
Live 8	Multi-genre	2000s
Red Wedge—The Smiths	Alternative	1980s
Bob Dylan	Singer/Songwriter	1990s
Joan Baez	Folk Rock	2000s
Pete Seeger	Folk	1970s
Peggy Seeger	Folk	2010s
Crass	Alternative	1980s
Edgar Broughton	Alternative	1970s
Hawkwind	Progressive	1970s

LIVE AID, WEMBLEY STADIUM, 13 JULY 1985

The 1985 Live Aid concert was brought about by Bob Geldof and Midge Ure after the success of the charity single "Do They Know It's Christmas." Both the song and the live event were organised in response to the 1984 Ethiopian famine. Geldof and Ure planned two events, one in the UK and one in America. They wanted the concerts to be huge in order to raise as much money for the cause as possible. "The show should be as big as is humanly possible. There's no point in just 5000 fans turning up at Wembley, we need to have Wembley linked with Madison Square Gardens and the whole show to be televised worldwide . . . in that way, lots of acts could be featured and the television rights, tickets and so on could raise a phenomenal amount of money" (Geldof, 1985).

I was lucky enough to go with a couple of friends to the Wembley event. We missed out on tickets when they went on sale and the only way we could get there was to buy tickets for a coach trip from Middlesbrough. So, we had to get up at 4 a.m., drive to Middlesbrough, and join a coach which left at 5 a.m. for London. We arrived well before noon, had a couple of drinks, and entered the stadium, which was, of course, completely packed so we found a spot in the stands right at the back.

A few minutes later Status Quo took to the stage with "Rockin' All Over the World" and the day started. This was Quo reunited one year after the split, with Alan flying over from Oz to join Francis and Rick. Their short set also featured "Caroline" and "Don't Waste My Time." A fitting start to a day which not only held great political and historical significance, but also showcased some of the greatest live performances in rock history.

Queen's performance is, of course, often rated as the greatest live performance by any band. Freddie certainly commanded the crowd that day and it propelled them to superstardom. Their well-planned set was a medley with short sections of their anthems: "Bohemian Rhapsody," "Radio Ga Ga," "Hammer to Fall," "Crazy Little Thing Called Love," "We Will Rock You," and "We Are the Champions." They had apparently been rehearsing their short set for days, to ensure perfection, and it showed. U2 weren't far behind them in terms of performance, with Bono showing how great a front man he was. They played two songs: "Sunday Bloody Sunday" and a lengthy version of "Bad" during which Bono dragged a girl from the rush down front to dance with him on stage, and which also included snippets from Lou Reed's "Satellite of Love" and "Walk on the Wild Side," and the Stones' "Ruby Tuesday" and "Sympathy for the Devil."

For me, however, the highlights were the Who and David Bowie, as I was, and remain, a big fan of both acts. Bowie started with "TVC15" (a strange and poor choice I felt, and remember being disappointed on the day), "Rebel Rebel," which was excellent, "Modern Love," and then "Heroes" (we all sang along and it was pure magic). I still feel that with a better choice of songs, though, Bowie could have eclipsed Queen and U2.

The Who performed "My Generation," "Pinball Wizard," "Love Reign O'er Me," and a blistering "Won't Get Fooled Again" with much mike swinging by Daltrey and lots of arm twirling by Townshend.

Other stand-out memories of the day were: Elton and Kiki singing "Don't Go Breaking my Heart." Paul McCartney suffering from sound problems and being very difficult to hear for much of "Let It Be" although I gather it was fine on TV. Geldof drawing massive cheers every time he set foot on stage. Seeing the cameras pick out Charles and Diana over in their enclosure. The amazingly camp Bowie and Jagger "Dancing in the Street" video. The awful, sad, and moving video of starving children played to the Cars' "Drive." Phil Collins playing Wembley and JFK courtesy of Concorde.

But the truly unforgettable moment came for me at the end, and will stay in my mind for ever. That was the finale, with the entire stadium singing along to "Do They Know It's Christmas?" with Bob Geldof leading us, and everyone else on stage. I've never seen, felt, or heard anything like it before or since.

Not only did the event bring important political issues into the public arena, Live Aid demonstrated the power of music and collective action. Indeed, the concerts showed how music is capable of being "more than a mere soundtrack to politics, but as the substance of politics" (Street, 2013). Starting with "Do They Know It's Christmas" and culminating in the two Live Aid shows, music itself was able to motivate, unite, and educate members of the public in a very special way.

We walked out of the stadium to the coach park, all of us still singing "Feed the World." Then it was a long coach ride back to Middlesbrough. We arrived back around 5 or 6 a.m., then drove home. Twenty-four hours with hardly any sleep, just an hour or so caught on the bus, but a day I will remember forever.

LIVE 8, HYDE PARK, LONDON, 2 JULY 2005

Twenty years after the original Live Aid shows, Geldof and Ure once again announced that they were going to stage a series of benefit concerts. This time the events were in response to the Make Poverty History campaign ahead of the G8 summit. This time, ten concerts were to be held around the world in order to show solidarity for and raise money for global action against poverty (Tilden, 2005).

Chapter Eight

I was so excited about this event for three reasons: firstly, because I'd been in Wembley Stadium for Live Aid; secondly, to see the Who; and thirdly, and most of all, to see Pink Floyd again as they had announced they would be reuniting for the show. We (me, Marie, David, and Laura) all went, staying the weekend in London. I'd managed to get tickets for the Gold Circle, which took us right down the front, next to the stage, so we had an excellent view of the entire day's events.

Bob Geldof opened the proceedings, followed by Paul McCartney with U2 performing "Sgt. Pepper's Lonely Hearts Club Band" (It was twenty years ago today! Wonderful!). Then U2 performed "Beautiful Day" (with a verse of the Beatles' "Blackbird"), "Vertigo," and "One" (including a segment from "Unchained Melody"). Coldplay were next up and played "In My Place," "Bitter Sweet Symphony" (joined by Richard Ashcroft), and "Fix You." David Walliams and Matt Lucas then came on stage in the role of their Little Britain characters Lou and Andy and introduced Elton John who played "The Bitch Is Back," "Saturday Night's Alright for Fighting," and "Children of the Revolution" (with guest Pete Doherty). Bill Gates was then next up on stage to introduce Dido who sang "White Flag" and "Thank You" and "7 Seconds" with Youssou N'Dour.

Stereophonics were followed by R.E.M. who were introduced by Ricky Gervais. R.E.M. performed "Imitation of Life," "Everybody Hurts," and "Man on the Moon." Then Kofi Annan introduced Ms. Dynamite who was followed by Keane and Travis. Bob Geldof joined Travis to sing "I Don't Like Mondays." Brad Pitt was next on stage to introduce Annie Lennox, then came UB40, Snoop Dogg, and Razorlight.

Bob Geldof then introduced twenty-four-year-old Birhan Woldu, the starving Ethiopian child whose image was so powerful in the video shown at Live Aid. Madonna took to the stage, embraced Birhan, and held hands with her as she sang "Like a Prayer."

Madonna was followed by Snow Patrol, the Killers, Joss Stone, Scissor Sisters, and Velvet Revolver. Then Lenny Henry presented Sting who sang the same songs as he performed at Live Aid: "Message in a Bottle," "Driven to Tears," and "Every Breath You Take." Next Dawn French introduced Mariah Carey, and David Beckham presented "his friend" Robbie Williams who got the crowd really going with "We Will Rock You," "Let Me Entertain You," "Feel," and "Angels."

Now we were moving to the legends; the bands that I had really come to see. The Who played "Who Are You" and "Won't Get Fooled Again." They were followed by an event which I never thought I would see, the reunion of Pink Floyd.

David Gilmour had announced the reunion less than a month before the gig, on 12 June 2005: "Like most people I want to do everything I can to persuade the G8 leaders to make huge commitments to the relief of poverty and increased aid to the third world. It's crazy that America gives such a paltry percentage of its GNP to the starving nations. Any squabbles Roger and the band have had in the past are so petty in this context, and if re-forming for this concert will help focus attention, then it's got to be worthwhile" (pinkfloydz.com, 2005). They opened with "Speak to Me," "Breathe," and "Money." Waters then said, "It's actually quite emotional standing up here with these three guys after all these years. Standing to be counted with the rest of you. Anyway, we're doing this for everyone who's not here, but particularly, of course, for Syd" (scratchpad.fandom.com, 2005). The screens showed video footage from their past shows, and a film of the pig from the Animals flying over Battersea Power Station whilst the band played "Wish You Were Here." They then closed with "Comfortably Numb." For me it was a very emotional experience. I found "Wish You Were Here" particularly powerful; you felt they were singing the song for Syd, which, of course, they were. Syd sadly passed away the following year. With Wright's subsequent passing in 2008, this was to be the final concert to feature all four playing together.

It was left to Paul McCartney to close the show with "Get Back," "Drive My Car" (with George Michael), "Helter Skelter," and "The Long and Winding Road." He finished with "Hey Jude" to which everyone sang along, and which seemed to go on for ever. We left Hyde Park as the crowd continued to sing "Na Na Na Na Na Na . . ." The show was originally scheduled to close at 9:30 p.m., but seriously overran and went on until just after midnight.

RED WEDGE TOUR (FEATURING THE SMITHS), NEWCASTLE CITY HALL, 31 JANUARY 1986

Red Wedge was a collective of musicians, who set out to engage young people with politics, and the policies of the Labour Party in particular, during the period leading up to the 1987 general election, in the hope of ousting the Conservative government of Margaret Thatcher (Rachel, 2016). Fronted by Billy Bragg, the collective also included Paul Weller and the Communards lead singer Jimmy Somerville. Red Wedge organised a number of major tours and concerts. The first and most memorable, took place in January and February 1986, and featured Billy Bragg, Paul Weller's band the Style Council, the Communards, Junior Giscombe, and Lorna Gee. The core touring acts were joined by other guest bands throughout the tour.

The City Hall concert featured Billy Bragg, Junior Giscombe, the Style Council, the Communards, with guests Prefab Sprout, and, as a big and very welcome surprise, the Smiths. It was the Smiths who stole the show, and their performance that night sticks in my memory as one of the best I have ever seen, by any band.

All of the bands performed short sets. The Communards were impressive, Jimmy Somerville's soaring vocals were amazing, and the Style Council were also good. I seem to recall Dee C Lee guested with them and sang "See the Day." Local heroes Prefab Sprout also went down well, but it was the Smiths who stole the show.

There had been whispers around the hall that something special was going to happen. Without any real warning, the Smiths were announced and stormed straight into "Shakespeare's Sister," followed by "I Want the One I Can't Have," "Boy with the Thorn in His Side," and "Big Mouth Strikes Again" ("our new single"). There is something about a short set; it allows a band to focus and to maintain a high level of energy and passion throughout. The Smiths were simply phenomenal that night; there was a buzz about them at the time, and everyone was delighted to see them perform. But it was more than that. It was as if they had decided to put everything into those four songs; the power, the intensity, and Morrissey's and Marr's performance were a step above anything I had seen them deliver before (or since) that night. It was as if they knew that they were simply the best band on the planet at the time, and they came out with the confidence and ability to deliver a world-class, stunning performance. We sat there, feeling that we were witnessing something special. It was that good. It was the best time I saw the Smiths, and a performance that will stay with me forever. Perfect rock 'n' roll in four songs and twenty or so short minutes.

Johnny Marr said afterwards: "The Red Wedge gig at Newcastle City Hall was one of the best things we ever did. Andy and I had done a couple of gigs already with Billy Bragg in Manchester and Birmingham the week before. . . . I was telling Morrissey about it and he was fairly up for just doing an impromptu show. So, we drove up to Newcastle, without telling anyone. I walked into the sound-check . . . the other bands were a little bit perplexed as to what we were doing there. We had no instruments, so we borrowed the Style Council's equipment and just tore the roof off the place. In the middle of the set, we just walked on to this announcement and the place went bananas" (Marr, 2014). In a 1986 *NME* interview, Morrissey said, "When we took to the stage the audience reeled back in horror. They took their Walkman's off and threw down their cardigans. Suddenly the place was alight, aflame with passion!" (Morrissey, 1986).

This gig was an example of music's ability to tap into the energy of youth culture in order to inspire and unify. The electrifying performances I witnessed on the Red Wedge tour were symbolic of the political unrest within left-leaning communities, and the gig itself embodied the passion displayed by the movement as a whole.

BOB DYLAN, NEWCASTLE, TELEWEST ARENA, 19 SEPTEMBER 2000

I took David to this gig, for his first taste of Dylan in concert. This was one of the better times that I have seen Dylan, and David was impressed enough to come and see him with me on several more occasions in the years that followed. We had bought tickets quite late and, as a result, we ended up with seats which were quite far back. Still our view of the stage was OK.

The arena was full this time, after a far from sold-out gig at the same venue in 1998. Dylan and his band were in great form and the set featured a lot of his better-known songs. There was a mix of electric and acoustic versions, and the encore contained a surprising seven songs. He finished with a lovely acoustic version of "Blowin' in the Wind."

Seeing Dylan in this setting could seem far removed from the protest singer he originally was considered to be in the 1960s. "Journalists and historians often treat Dylan's songs as emblematic of the era and Dylan himself as the quintessential 'protest singer,' an image frozen in time" (Dreier, 2011). Indeed, his off-and-on engagement with politics, coupled with his status as a musical legend, means that one could easily attend a Dylan concert without appreciating his political significance. However, his "peace and justice songs" have a timeless resonance and, when performed, their message is unavoidable. "'Blowin' in the Wind' and 'The Times They are A-Changin' in particular will forever be linked to the progressive movements of the 1960s and used to rally people to protest for a better world" (Dreier, 2011).

JOAN BAEZ, SAGE GATESHEAD, 28 FEBRUARY 2007

I've only ever seen Joan Baez once in concert. This was at the Sage in 2007. The place was sold out, and full of fifty- and sixty-something ageing folkies and rockers who had all come to see the legendary protest singer.

Joan was on stage very early, shortly after the published time of 7:30 p.m., and sang for over an hour. The performance finished around 9 p.m. Her voice was clear and beautiful, and she performed a set of classics such as "The Night They Drove Old Dixie Down" and "Diamonds and Rust." Joan seemed to enjoy the evening and commented upon the beauty of the Sage as a concert venue. Between the songs she told little humorous anecdotes of her experiences and the many great people she has worked with over the years, both musically and politically.

A friend of Martin Luther King Jr., Baez was an activist during the civil rights movement, and all through her career has dedicated herself to supporting social justice. One of the original protest singers, Baez is considered by many to have been instrumental in the 1960s progressive movement (Street, 2003). Simon Frith examines the ways Baez uses her voice and music as a "text" to support and "evoke ideals" (Street, 2003). Indeed, her songs remain as powerful as her voice, and she received a rapturous response from the North East crowd.

PETE SEEGER, NEWCASTLE CITY HALL, 8 MARCH 1978

I only ever saw the legendary Pete Seeger once, at the Newcastle City Hall in 1978. It was one of the simplest, yet most powerful performances I have had the pleasure of attending. I went along with a friend, neither of us massive folk fans, but the legend of the man transcended musical boundaries and drew us to the City Hall that night.

Seeger performed alone; seated centre stage on a simple wooden chair for much of the performance, accompanied only by his banjo, and sang all those great songs. He told us stories, sang his own tunes, and covered traditional and contemporary folk songs. There was a purity, authenticity, and truth about his performance; Seeger was completely in tune with the audience, and we all sang all with him to classics such as "Where Have All the Flowers Gone?" "If I Had a Hammer," "Turn! Turn! Turn!," "Little Boxes," and "We Shall Overcome."

"One of Pete Seeger's greatest achievements was incorporating political activism into music and realising that liberation struggles need a sound-track" (Lynskey, 2014). Indeed, Seeger showcased how simple music can hold great power. Seeger himself stated, "My job is to show folks there's a lot of good music in this world and if used right it could help to save the planet" (Whitehead, 2014). The title "legend" is often applied to many different artists and musicians, but few actually deserve it; Pete Seeger is one who undoubtedly and absolutely does.

PEGGY SEEGER, THE SAGE, 22 OCTOBER 2018

Although I was much more familiar with the music of her brother Pete, I was very much looking forward to seeing Peggy Seeger in concert. I knew of the track "I'm Gonna Be an Engineer" and, of course, knew of her marriage to Ewan MacColl, who wrote "The First Time Ever I Saw Your Face" for Peggy herself. I was intrigued to hear more of her output, so when she announced a concert at the Sage, I was keen to go. So, Jacky and I met up with Laura and Dale ready for an evening to see Peggy Seeger.

As a political activist, who has spent most of her life campaigning, Peggy Seeger's music speaks of working-class struggles, feminism, environmentalism, and social injustice. Her two-part set included tracks which focused heavily on such themes and reflected her political beliefs. Particularly striking was "Reclaim the Night," a dark folk song examining sexual violence and consent, which Peggy performed a cappella. However, although the set had many sombre moments when such tracks were performed, Peggy managed to deliver these serious messages whilst still keeping the evening warm and full of charismatic banter.

Seeger created a friendly, light-hearted, and good-humoured relationship with the crowd. She joked between tracks and encouraged the audience to speak up and sing along with the songs, unifying the crowd and giving the evening a traditional folk feel at times. Indeed, the Belfast review stated, "Seeger's greatest asset is her uncanny ability to dissolve the gap between artist and audience" (*Belfast Review*, 2017).

At the age of eighty-three, Seeger treated us to stories about her fascinating life, mentioning her late husband, Ewan MacColl, and her brothers Mike and Peter. There was the sense that we were seeing a living legend perform.

Seeger "saw folk music as inherently political" referring to it as "the expressions and artistry of people who are not in power" (Freedman, 2017). It was evident from this concert that Seeger's performance was not just a musical expression but moreover an externalising of a set of beliefs.

CRASS GIGS IN MIDDLESBROUGH, EARLY 1980s: DO THEY OWE US A LIVING? COURSE THEY F***ING DO!

Crass were an Essex-based art collective and punk band who advocated for animal rights, environmentalism, and feminist ideology and promoted anarchism. "They formed in 1977, a compelling mix of anarcho-punk, avant-garde art and, despite singer Steve Ignorant's protestations that he hated hippies–vegetarian free thinkers who worked and lived out of a commune" (Swash, 2010). I was lucky enough to see Crass live twice in the early '80s. I went to both gigs with my friend Dave, the first was in Middlesbrough Rock Garden, and the second a year or two later in Middlesbrough Town Hall Crypt.

I have very vivid memories of the Rock Garden gig. The Rock Garden was an amazing venue, an old beer kellar, with sticky floors and full of punks and some of the edgiest looking skins you have ever seen. Dave and I went to many gigs there; it was always exciting, and we often felt in fear of our lives, particularly as we both had long hair, and didn't come from Middlesbrough.

For Crass the place was packed, so packed that you couldn't move. We were the only people in there with long hair; everyone else was a punk or a skin. There were black and white TVs all over the place, at first showing static and flashing screens and then images of war crimes, the Holocaust, Hiroshima, and so forth.

Crass were just great. Dave and I loved "Owe Us a Living," "Banned from the Roxy," and "Shaved Women" and its "Screaming Babies, Screaming Babies" chorus; the whole place went wild and sang along. Imagine being in a room full of punks, so full that you can't move, the sound is loud, deafening, and the place is going wild, beer is being thrown everywhere, and you are getting pushed all over. Well, that's what it was like. Dave and I drove home singing "Screaming Babies."

We were back to see Crass again a year or so later at the Crypt. In comparison that gig was quite tame, as I recall. Not as full (the crypt is a bigger venue) and nowhere near as wild or scary. There was no other band like them, nor has there been since. I picked up this comment from YouTube: "CRASS! are the most influential punk band ever, not to mention, the PUNKEST band ever. they were not about the bull shit, and never sold out. they were a true punk band and spoke what they knew was right, not caring who opposed" (Smith, 2013).

For me, Crass didn't just communicate their ideologies through their lyrics, the band itself seemed to embody all that they stood for. In a time when punk was dominated by men and masculinity, the fact that Crass had two women members and explored gender issues felt refreshing and very different for the time. Their output did not just garner a set of music fans as followers, moreover they "inspired a loyal, motivated and open-minded fanbase, many of whom wore the Crass logo as a badge or tattoo and went on to campaign for animal rights, anarcho-feminism and anti-road groups" (Richards, 2019).

THE EDGAR BROUGHTON BAND IN CONCERT, 1971–2005: OUT DEMONS OUT!!!! REBEL ROCK AT ITS BEST

Edgar Broughton is one of my all-time heroes. During the early 1970s he was uncompromising, fearless, and a composer and singer of some great rock music. My early memories of Edgar were gigs at Sunderland Locarno and at festivals such as Reading 1972 and Buxton 1972. Edgar was usually sporting a snazzy karate suit, and singing tracks from the early EBB LPs such as "Freedom," "Evil," "American Soldier," "Apache Drop Out," and, of course, "Out Demons Out."

Edgar always had a lot to say and wasn't frightened of speaking out against the police, the government, and anything he didn't feel was right. He was (and still is) a big man with a deep booming voice, often compared to Beefheart. But there was much more to Edgar. His guitar work was pretty tasty, and his songs crossed genres and defied categorisation.

Onstage I often felt as if Broughton was speaking directly to me. The simplistic politics that his music was centred around felt very identifiable, and audiences were clearly inspired by all that the band stood for. Indeed, after seeing the band at the 1969 Buxton Festival, John Peel wrote, "Many of the bands we've been listening to for the past year or so have forgotten all of the things they said about money when they didn't have any. Perhaps they could do something for the thousands who've trekked round the country to hear them. They'll probably kill me for mentioning this but the Broughton band really do this when they can and they're broke but honest as a result. That's another reason for loving them" (Peel, 2019). Indeed, the EBB represented working-class people and unified its audiences, making them feel like they had a voice.

I saw Edgar Broughton in the Locarno a few days before the now (in)famous Redcar gig (which I regret not attending) where Edgar and the band turned up and played from the back of a lorry after being banned from playing on the seafront. He encouraged us all to come along to Redcar, to bring our friends and our cars and to mess up the town and the local police force. Edgar ended up spending the night in a Redcar jail, and wrote the song "(Judge) Called Me a Liar" about the experience. One night I recall him telling us not to buy the "Out Demons Out" single, as that would only give money to the record company. Instead, he encouraged us to buy a spray can and spray "Out Demons Out" on walls around the town.

As we moved into the mid-1970s, Edgar and the guys had graduated to playing the City Hall circuit. Although the music was still strong, I felt they lost some of the immediacy and passion that I had experienced in a club and festival setting. The EBB had some great songs. Favourites of mine were "The Poppy," "Green Lights," and "Hotel Room." As we came to the end of the 1970s, the EBB had all but disappeared from the scene. The last time I saw them they were called the Broughtons, and were supporting (Ian) Gillan at the City Hall.

It was many years before I saw them again; however, in 2006 they were back, and my friend Will and I caught their gig at Sheffield Boardwalk. I went backstage before the show, said hello to Edgar (Rob) and the guys, and got them to sign my gig flyer. The set that night included all of the well-known tracks, starting with "Evening Over Rooftops" and continuing with "Speak Down the Wires," the strange story of "The Moth," "Why Can't Somebody Love Me," the great boogie of "Momma's Reward," "American Boy Soldier" with lyrics updated to comment upon modern war, the proto punk metal of "Love in the Rain," "Hotel Room," and "Out Demons Out" as an encore. In introducing the latter song, Edgar told the crowd that the demons are still out there and explained that we needed to chant; just as we did in the old days!

HAWKWIND, SPACE RITUAL TOUR, SUNDERLAND LOCARNO, 23 DECEMBER 1972

The Space Ritual tour called at Sunderland Locarno in 1972, and was as epic as the legends suggest. "Silver Machine" and "Master of the Universe" were great favourites at the Mecca (the Locarno) at the time; the dance floor always filled up when they came over the PA. So, when it was announced that the band were coming to play as part of their Space Ritual tour, there was a lot of excitement and huge anticipation for the gig. This was the classic Hawkwind lineup with Robert Calvert on vocals; Dave Brock on guitar and vocals; Nik Turner on sax, flute, and vocals; Lemmy on bass guitar and vocals; Dik Mik and Del Dettmar on synthesizers; and Simon King on drums. The gig was everything you might imagine: very loud, a tightly packed ballroom, lots of flashing lights and strobes, Stacia dancing naked, strong smells of joss sticks and dope, strong bass and rock rhythms, lots of strange noises, weird space-rock, great psychedelic light show, booming sinister vocals from Calvert, Lemmy looking cool. This gig had every ingredient a rock 'n' roll gig should, and, as a young kid, I was just blown away and totally hooked on Hawkwind.

As well as being pioneers of space rock, Hawkwind were also associated with bringing political ideology to their music. They were strongly linked with many far-left and anarchist groups, having performed at a number of benefit gigs for several fringe political organisations such as the White Panthers and the Stoke Newington Eight. "The surface layer of Hawkwind's lyrics consisted of hippy-trippy fantasy or sci-fi themes, with an under-lying expression of a desire to over-come oppression, to be free" (Mayo, 2020). Indeed, Lemmy stated in an interview for Classic Rock that, "We definitely had a sense that we were part of a revolutionary movement" (Mayo, 2020). It was as if their music had emerged out of a dissatisfaction for what the peace and love of the late 1960s had done for hippies, and Hawkwind were exploring the possibilities of escaping.

CONCLUSION

The linkages between rock music, folk music, and politics are well known. Several of the artists listed here are renowned for their political stances and the way in which they use their lyrics to relay strong political messages to their audiences. Attending a performance by such a figure is, in itself, making a political statement. The vast majority of the audience will share the (usually left-wing) political views of the performer. The songs become anthems which the audience sing along to. For many years in the late 1960s and into the early 1970s, we all believed that music could make real political change, and to some extent this was true. Along with political rallies in America, it was the strong youth movement which led to the end of the Vietnam War. So, in some small way, each of these political artists did manage to create change through their lyrics, their music, and also through the support of their audiences.

It was the Band Aid single "Do They Know It's Christmas?" and the massive concert Live Aid which began the use of music as a catalyst for real political change through the raising of money for charitable purposes. Whether this led to real change in terms of the countries and communities involved is questionable. Live Aid certainly resulted in a lot of publicity and raised much funding, but how much of it actually led to making an impact on starving communities in Ethiopia is debatable. Nonetheless, for those of us taking part in the event in Wembley Stadium, it did feel that we were making real change.

There were other movements which combined politics and music including Rock against Racism, a series of concerts and festivals which took a stand against racism, and Red Wedge, the left-wing movement which was aligned to socialist political parties.

In the 1970s, many of the festivals were themselves taking a political stance. The Windsor Free Festival is one such example. The Windsor Free Festival was held in Windsor Great Park from 1972 to 1974. It was organised by a group of hippies from London, and was the forerunner of the Free Festival movement and later events like the Stonehenge Festival. The festival was set to run for ten days in 1974, starting over the bank holiday weekend, and continuing to the following weekend. Some friends were intending to go to Reading, across to Windsor, and then finish the festival week with a free Hyde Park event, starring Roger McGuinn, Roy Harper, and Julie Felix. I popped across to Windsor for a visit, and went home between the weekends. I don't recall which bands I saw but do remember the great friendly atmosphere at the festival. The 1974 Windsor Free Festival was the largest, and also the most eventful, festival as a result of the police reaction to the gathering. On the Wednesday morning the police raided the festival and broke it up, amid reports of police brutality. In 1975 an alternative event took place at Watchfield, which I also attended, again after the Reading festival. It wasn't a particularly well-attended event, and had lost some of the spirit of the previous year's festival at Windsor. Those days of the free festival and its ideals seem so long ago, and so different to the events we have now, which have become much more middle of the road, and corporate. We lost something along the way. In those days a group of hippies believed that they were building an alternative society, and I guess some of them did, and are still living it through the new age traveller's movement, which is the descendant of those events in the 1970s.

The link between music and politics remains strong. Since music began it has been used as a political statement and this will continue. What is questionable is the real, tangible, and sustained impact that this makes.

In terms of performance the link between the audience, the performer, and the songs is strengthened by a joint political stance. The audience feel that they are at one with the performer; they share political views and, in doing so, a bond is formed between performer and the audience. This strengthens the authentic feel and nature of the performance.

Chapter Nine

Art-rock

Here I first reviewed the literature on performance art including Johnson (2015) who provided an oral history of performance art; Jones (2018) who discussed improvisation as art-rock; and Goldberg (2001) who provided a comprehensive history of art as performance. I also reviewed the literature on Kate Bush (Thomson, 2015), Yoko Ono (Clayson, Jungr & Johnson, 2004), and David Bowie (Waldrep, 2016). I then selected ten performances relating to art-rock and analysed these. Table 9.1 lists the artists covered within the chapter.

Table 9.1. Artists Analysed in This Chapter

Artist	Genre	Date of Performance
Yoko Ono	Art-rock	2000s
Bjork	Art-rock	2010s
David Bowie Tribute	Art-rock	2020s
War of the Worlds	Rock Theatre	2000s
Kate Bush	Art-rock	1980s
Massive Attack	Dance	2010s
Roxy Music	Art-rock	1970s
Brian Eno	Art-rock	2010s
Talking Heads	Art-rock	1980s
Genesis	Progressive	1970s

YOKO ONO, THE BLUECOAT, LIVERPOOL, 4 APRIL 2008

As a musician, artist, filmmaker, and activist, Yoko Ono has, throughout her fifty-year career, blurred the boundaries of perception and explored the ways fundamental human truths and values can be communicated. Although firstly setting out to establish a music career, "in the 1960s, Ono became increasingly involved in conceptual art, especially in performance as an occasional member of Fluxus, an art group inspired by neo-dadaism and the avant-garde" (Rowland, 2017). After moving to London, Ono gave her first paid performance at the Bluecoat in 1967 (Biggs and Belchem, 2020). When the Bluecoat was refurbished in 2008, Yoko returned to the new performance space to celebrate the reopening of the venue. Tickets for the one-hour live event sold out in minutes, and Yoko agreed to a live feed going into the Bluecoat hub and a big screen in the city centre.

Marie and I arrived in plenty of time for the event, and joined the queue to enter the performance space, which has a capacity of 116. It was clear from discussions in the queue that Yoko fans had travelled from all over the world for the chance to attend. We were each handed an "Imagine Peace" badge and a small Onochord torch as we entered. The white torch was marked "Onochord Liverpool y.o. 2008." Marie and I sat in the front row and waited for Yoko to arrive.

Soon Yoko entered the room and stood in front of a large screen showing footage of her 1967 Bluecoat performance where she requested the audience wrap her from head to foot in bandages. "I'm 75 and I'm alive and very thankful to be here every day, and to still be in love with life, and with you," she told us. Yoko then left the room for a short period and returned wrapped in bandages, picking up from where she left off in 1967. She sat in a chair and invited us to unwrap her. A few of us did so; I still have the bandages that Marie and I removed from her legs.

At one point during the performance, she sat at the chair and silently crocheted. Footage of John and Yoko from the "bed-in" days followed; she later danced and rolled on the floor omitting her characteristic screaming vocalisations to the video for her song "Walking on Thin Ice" and showed a short documentary on her 2004 work Onochord. At that point we got to use the small torches that we had been given when we came in. We were instructed to flash the torch towards Yoko three times to signify the three words "I LOVE YOU."

Although much has been written about Ono's contribution to experimental and conceptual art, her musical output is often seen as a separate part of her work. However, after experiencing this performance, it struck me how interwoven Ono's music and art appear to be. Her extreme, sometimes unnerving vocals as well as her purposefully provocative musical arrangements seem to transcend usual musical conventions and occupy an artistic space all of their own. Indeed, Brown considers Ono's vocals to be "politically charged instances of abject sonic art" in which "the scream functions as an act of sonic abjection, and brings to the fore a marginalised body, negotiating and defying its own liminal boarders" (Brown, 2012). This message was not only expressed musically, but also through Ono's physical movement. This, along with the audience's participation and the performance as a whole, all came together to create the artistic experience.

Yoko had one of her famous white chess sets beside her throughout the performance. This anti-war statement features white chess pieces on a totally white board; it was originally made for Ono's exhibition at Indica Gallery, London, in 1966. At one point in the performance, she threw the board to the ground, scattering the pieces all over the floor.

To close the performance Yoko put on a top hat and asked us all to come down to the front and dance with her to a remix of "Give Peace a Chance." At one point Marie was holding hands with Yoko, dancing and twirling round. When we started to dance with her, she gave Marie the chess board. We also managed to pick up a few of the pieces. They make a great reminder of the event.

On our way out, we were handed a booklet entitled "13 days do-it-yourself dance festival," which is a series of instructions and pictures as to how we might perform our own personal dance in our "mind" and that "each member of the dance, thus, will communicate with the other members by mental telepathy." An incredible, amazing performance, which we will remember forever.

BJORK, MANCHESTER FESTIVAL, CAMPFIELD MARKET, 10 JULY 2011

The Biophilia project was set up in 2011 by Bjork, the city of Reykjavik, and the University of Iceland. The project aimed to "inspire children to explore their own creativity, while learning about music, nature and science through new technologies" (Biophilia Educational Project, 2019). As part of this, Bjork released the "biophilia" album, the music on which was based around the structures and patterns within nature. Plate tectonics, genetics, and human biorhythms are all explored through sound. A suite of apps was also released which enabled users to manipulate the album tracks and re-interpret the music to create their own compositions based around nature. To showcase the album, and its connected project, Bjork announced a three week residency at the Manchester International Festival where she would be joined by a twenty-four piece Icelandic choir.

Campfield Market Hall is an old cattle market in the centre of Manchester. Laura and I arrived in good time for the performance and took our places in the excited mass of fans who were queuing outside. Once we had entered the venue, we began to realise what an unusual experience this was going to be. The seats were positioned in tiers around the edges of the hall, creating a space in the centre where the performance took place.

As soon as the show began, it was evident that we were witnessing a spectacular piece of theatre unfold before us. The choir in their gaudy blue and gold costumes, the specially commissioned musical instruments, and four giant harps which use the earth's gravitational pull to create musical patterns. The music was ethereal, experimental, and unlike anything I had heard before.

Bjork herself wore a huge orange wig, blue face paint, and massive platform shoes. Her legendary unique vocal expression was yet another instrument, exploring the concepts of the blending of nature and technology. Her wild, seemingly organic outbursts had a raw naturalistic quality to them and, merging with the pure sound of the coral vocals provided by the choir, they provided a stark contrast to the heavily produced beats which featured in many of the tracks.

A series of apps had been released prior to the gig which enabled the audience to further explore the music and curate the sounds. "The whole thing has clearly been designed to make music more malleable and interactive" (Petridis, 2011). Indeed, the multimedia event seemed to explore from so many different angles the concept of nature, its merging with technology, and the impact humans can have upon this. The music was almost secondary to the message itself. "It represents, not merely an attempt to "define humanity's relationship with sound and the universe" but also to "pioneer a new format that will smash industry conventions" (Petridis, 2011).

Indeed, the gig was very different to anything I'd experienced before, and I felt like I'd been involved in a groundbreaking piece of experimental conceptual art. "This is a very 21st century take on the possibilities of pop . . . a real adventure into the beyond" (Robb, 2011).

DAVID BOWIE: A CELEBRATION, ORCHESTRATED BY MIKE GARSON, STREAMING EVENT, 10 JANUARY 2021

Almost fifty years after first seeing Bowie on the Ziggy Stardust tour and five years after Bowie's death, I attended a three-hour extravaganza celebrating David Bowie's birthday. This took place in January 2021 during the Covid pandemic, so it was a streaming event featuring artists from around the world all performing together through the power of modern technology. The whole event was orchestrated and planned by Mike Garson, David Bowie's piano player from around 1973 and then throughout his career. The artists ranged from those whose names I recognised: Duran Duran, Macy Gray, Boy George, Rick Wakeman, Ian Hunter, Ian Astbury, Joe Elliot, Adam Lambert, and Peter Frampton and many others who were less familiar to me (probably because they are more recent and up to date than my old guy musical tastes and knowledge). We were also promised a band consisting of musicians who accompanied David Bowie throughout his career: Earl Slick, Carlos Alomar, Tony Visconti, Tony Levin, and many others.

In 2016 the David Bowie Interart, text, and media conference "called for an examination of David Bowie's Oeuvre and its global legacies" (Mendes and Perrott, 2019). Mendes and Parrott examined the evolution of David Bowie's art, and how his output "from Starman to Blackstar and beyond" has influence, inspired, and united people. As well as celebrating his birthday, this streaming event perfectly captured the breadth of Bowie's contribution to music, lyrics, video, costume, and art as a whole.

The event itself exceeded all of my expectations. It really made the most of modern technology, seamlessly drawing together artists from all over the world; some live, some I suspect recorded, all on different screens yet all playing together. Mike Garson took us through the whole event, introducing each artist and the song and played piano on all but one (I will explain this later) of the songs.

The concert started with Duran Duran playing "Five Years," the opening track of *Ziggy Stardust* and one of my favourite Bowie songs. I suspect this choice of opener paid tribute to the fact that Bowie sadly passed away almost five years to the day, a few days after his birthday. Now I had lost touch with Duran Duran. It is many years since I have seen them and I used to be a fan in the 80s, back in the day. I was pleasantly surprised how well they delivered this classic track; Simon Le Bon almost spitting out the vocals. A great opener. But there was more to follow. An electric version of "Moonage Daydream," followed by Billy Corgan of the Smashing Pumpkins meandering around the screen in his own TV, lost in a "Space Oddity." An excellent version of "The Man Who Sold the World." Gary Barlow punching above his weight throughout "Fame." And so, it went on. Bowie classic after classic, mixed with some less familiar tunes, Mike Garson constantly present on a grand piano. Macy Gray popped up on a screen to the left singing one of my Bowie favourites "Changes," doing it full justice. A tribute to Mick Ronson and his wonderful version of "Slaughter on 10th Avenue" performed by Kevin Armstrong, bringing back memories of seeing Ronson perform it on his solo tour, in Newcastle City Hall many years ago. Bowie fan, and Def Leopard front man, Joe Elliott sang "Ziggy Stardust" paying tribute to a hero of his youth, as he often does. Ricky Gervais popped up for a moment to introduce "Little Fat Man," harking back to Bowie's performance of that song on his TV sitcom *Extras*.

Actor Gary Oldman performed a highly emotional version of "I Can't Read," soon followed by a great rocking version of "Suffragette City" performed by none other than Peter Frampton. Ian Astbury of the Cult performed "Lazarus," and then Mike Garson handed over his piano stool to Rick Wakeman who appeared in a virtual box delivering the introduction and wonderful background to "Life on Mars" as he did on the original version so many years ago; the song being performed by new voice Youngblood. Boy George delivered a highly theatrical performance of a trio of classics: "Lady Grilling Soul," "Time," and "Aladdin Sane." Then my hero Ian Hunter appeared to the left of the screen and performed his tribute to Bowie "Dandy," followed by "All the Young Dudes" (of course). Current Queen front man and star in his own right, Adam Lambert, performed an appropriately dramatic version of "Starman." I can't claim to recognise the name Bernard Fowler, but I did recognise the man as a longtime singer for the Rolling Stones. He performed a number of songs during the show and closed the event with a powerful rendition of "Heroes." A fitting end to an incredible event. One which finally realised the potential of streaming and modern technology. An excellent tribute to a genius who I feel so privileged to have seen in performance several times.

WAR OF THE WORLDS, NEWCASTLE ARENA, 27 APRIL 2006

Jeff Wayne's Musical Version of The War of the Worlds was originally released in 1978. It was inspired by and based upon an HG Wells novel and is a combination of prog, space rock, and classical and musical theatre, whilst drawing upon literary influences.

When it was announced that, for the first time, the classic *War of the Worlds* album was to be performed as a full-scale musical production, I couldn't resist getting tickets as I was curious to see how this musical extravaganza could be transformed from a concept album into a live theatrical piece. My anticipation grew as it was announced that Jeff Wayne would be conducting the orchestra and that Moody Blues front-man Justin Hayward would also feature. Richard Burton was also to reprise his role as "The Journalist through the wonders of technology." Jonathan Parke, Pink Floyd's legendary set designer, had been recruited to bring the story to life, and, overall, I was intrigued to experience what was shaping up to be a spectacular event.

The show featured an all-star cast: A "virtual" Richard Burton: a large bust of the Journalist with a projected image; Justin Hayward; Alexis James; Chris Thompson; Russell Watson; Tara Blaise; and Rachael Beck (all on spoken words and vocals). The band included: Jeff Wayne (conductor), Chris Spedding (guitar), Herbie Flowers (bass), Tom Woodstock (guitars, keyboards),

Laurie Wisefield (guitars, mandolin), Accy Yeats (drums), Julia Thornton (percussion, harp, keyboards), Steve Turner, Neil Angilley, and Kennedy Aitchison (keyboards) (Smith, 2015).

The concert was very much a musical as much as it was a rock performance. It integrated music, dance, theatre, spoken word, and technology to create a full theatrical experience. What interested me, however, was the audience that had gathered together in the vast Newcastle Arena to witness the show. Many long-haired old rockers such as myself were clearly in attendance and I wondered how many of us were accustomed to experiencing live music in this way.

The multi-arts production was so removed from the standard "rock" gig experience. With the narrative framing of the original text, the costumes, set, technology, movement, and musical orchestration, the show elevated the original concept album to become something else. According to Cameron and Gillespie, theatre, as a mixed art medium, is less about the artistic genre itself but moreover about the way the piece is experienced. They denote theatre as the "home of the now," whereby the collective art forms merge together to illicit an audience response (Cameron and Gillespie, 1999). Due to the theatrics before us, the music was able to take on a new meaning and create a new level of emersion, which, for me, listening to the album alone could not achieve. In this way, the music was transformed and manifested into a piece of art. It was a hugely enjoyable experience; very spectacular, although a little "lost" in the vastness of an arena setting. A very different experience which I was pleased to attend.

KATE BUSH, SUNDERLAND EMPIRE 12 APRIL 1979, AND HAMMERSMITH APOLLO, LONDON, 3 SEPTEMBER 2014

I nearly didn't go to this gig, but I am so glad I did. Marie and I had tickets to see Thin Lizzy at Newcastle City Hall on the same night. I'd already bought the Thin Lizzy tickets before Kate's gig was announced. I was quite a fan of Lizzy, and went to every tour; however, I also quite fancied seeing what this strange new artist was like. So, we decided to forgo the Lizzy concert (I can't remember what I did with the tickets, I may have sold them or given them away) and to go see Kate Bush. (In fact, Lizzy were playing two nights, and in the end, I managed to get a ticket for the alternate night and saw Lizzy one night and Kate Bush the next.)

I queued for tickets at the Empire the day they went on sale. There was quite a queue when I arrived and by the time I reached the box office all I could get were a couple of seats to the rear of the circle. But never mind, we were in. The show itself was quite different from a normal rock show. It was very theatrical, with dancers and Kate herself doing a lot of dancing. The set featured songs from her first two LPs, and the hits to date. The sound was impeccable and the performance faultless. She succeeded in bringing the concept to the stage, and blended pop/music, dance, and theatre perfectly, encompassing all of these genres and yet transcending them at the same time to create almost a piece of performance art. It seemed that the cultural context of the late 1979s had somehow influenced this young woman to bring together a set of ideas which were manifested and expressed through this experimental and unusual performance. Withers explored how Bush's music comes alive, and indeed only "exists at the inter-relation of popular culture, theory, art, the avant-garde and history" (Withers, 2010). As her music appears to have been created in response to a set of ideas and transcends musical conventions, for me, it can be experienced as a piece of art in its own right.

I never believed in my wildest dreams that I would ever see Kate Bush live in concert again. I felt lucky to have seen her during her one and only tour when it called at Sunderland Empire, and I was totally amazed when, after a thirty-five-year hiatus from the stage, she announced her return, which seemed to come completely out of the blue in early 2014. Marie (like me an old trooper from the Empire concert) came along with Laura, David, Shauna, and me to the concert.

From the moment Kate walked barefoot onto the stage, the crowd showed how much she had been missed. Fans had travelled from every corner of the globe to witness and be part of the second coming, "Before the Dawn," and they made sure that Kate knew how much they loved her, giving her standing ovations at the end of each of the first few songs.

The first things I noticed was how strong her voice was, how well she looked, how confident she appeared, and how much she smiled. She seemed genuinely pleased to be there performing, and to see everyone.

The first set of six songs was the closest that the concert got to a "gig" with Kate performing a selection of songs from her career, including "Hounds of Love," "Running Up That Hill," and "King of the Mountain." Before the next segment we were given an unexpected interval, while a technical fault was sorted out, which added to the drama of the evening. By 9 p.m., fault rectified, we were all back in our seats to witness "The Ninth Wave," which told the story of a lady (Kate) lost at sea after her ship crashed. She fades in and out of life, fighting with the waves and evil skeleton fish, who fight to drag her under. She has an out-of-body experience as, ghostlike, she returns home to observe her husband and son (played by Kate's real son Bertie) in their living room watching TV and having supper (toad in the hole: good choice). The coast guard drag her from the sea, only to lose her to the fish skeletons again. A helicopter hovered above us all, lights shining and swirling around the venue. The evil fish held Kate aloft and carried her through the aisle and out a side entrance.

Ultimately, she was dragged out alive, and the evil fish lost her, back to the earth and her life. All of this was staged in the most professional, artistic, and engaging way that you could imagine. Simply breathtaking.

After another interval we were treated to a performance of "A Sky of Honey," from *Aerial*. This sequence also had strong links to earth and the environment. Kate played the part of a birdlike woman who observes the actions of a 19th-century painter (played by Bertie) who was painting a scene of the sky and a strange quirky mannequin who followed her around throughout the piece. The performance featured several birds; a white dove, a rooster, a seagull, and an evil black raven who attacked Kate, transforming her arm into a black wing. The story climaxed with Kate duelling with her guitarists who wore evil beak masks. Dark, moody, scary. The place went crazy, everyone on their feet. Kate was beaming. For the encore she returned to sit alone at her grand piano and sing "Among Angels." The band then returned for a joyous "Cloudbusting" with everyone singing along.

We left the Apollo at 11:20 p.m. The woman sitting to my right looked at me and simply said, "Wow!" Laura proclaimed it the best concert she had ever seen. A very emotional experience in so many ways, lots of tears-in-the-eyes moments. Indeed, Kate Allen wrote for *Disorder*, "Before the Dawn rates pretty damn highly in my own record of emotional experiences, as it is exactly that, not a gig, not a show, not a musical but an 'experience' in every sense" (Allen, 2014b). Kate Bush might just be the greatest creative rock artist that the UK has produced.

MASSIVE ATTACK VERSUS ADAM CURTIS, MANCHESTER INTERNATIONAL FESTIVAL, 7 JULY 2013

This was a very different sort of performance. Adam Curtis is a film and documentary maker, whose work explores politics and philosophy. For this event, commissioned by the Manchester International Festival, he worked with Bristol trip hop legends Massive Attack to produce an experience which explored power and politics and their impact on all of us. Adam called the performance "a Gilm"— "a new way of integrating a gig with a film that has a powerful overall narrative and emotional individual stories" (Curtis, 2013). Indeed, the show was devised in order to convey concepts and ideas through a multimedia experience. "The show will be a bit of a total experience. You will be surrounded by all kinds of images and sounds. But it is also about ideas. It tells a story about how a new system of power has risen up in the modern world to manage and control us. A rigid and static system that has found in those images and sounds a way of enveloping us in a thin two-dimensional version of the past" (Curtis, 2013).

David came up from London especially for the event, and we drove down from home via Leeds, where we picked up Laura who had been attending a friend's birthday barbecue celebration. The venue for the event was the Mayfield Depot, Manchester, which is a disused and somewhat spooky old building, right next to Piccadilly station. We arrived at the venue at 8:15 p.m. and waited in anticipation for the start, which came at 9 p.m. prompt, when we were directed along with 1,500 others into a dark space completely surrounded by giant screens on three sides. The screens then showed Curtis's new documentary *Everything Is Going According to Plan*, while Massive Attack played at the end of the room, from behind a translucent screen.

The film took us through a story of how politics, the advent of computers and the proliferation of data, war, and the financial crisis have all set out to control and plan our destiny and how ultimately "The Plan" has failed. This was achieved through a mash-up of news images and some quite bizarre selections of scenes from Bambi, Mary Poppins, and Jane Fonda's workout-video. Massive Attack's soundtrack ranged from their own doomy, deep bass-laden soundscapes, which rocked and vibrated the very foundations of the space, to a series of quite off-the-wall covers performed by guest vocalists and longtime collaborators Elizabeth Frazer (formerly of the Cocteau Twins) and reggae singer Horace Andy. These covers included Nirvana's "Where Did You Sleep Last Night," Burt Bacharach's "The Look of Love" and "Baby It's You," the Archies' "Sugar Sugar," and Barbra Streisand's "My Coloring Book." The highlight for me was Elisabeth Frazer's performances of "The Look of Love," and "My Coloring Book"; the latter is one of my favourite songs. Elizabeth stood centre stage behind a screen; a giant image of her own face projecting over her, softly wringing the emotion out of each word, in that haunting ethereal voice.

The "Gilm" concluded with an upbeat message, reaffirming that we were in control of our own destiny and that we could change the world. The final slogan displayed on the screens told us to "Now Find Your Own Way Home." We were directed out of the building in a quite different direction to the one in which we entered; guided only by one extremely bright searchlight. As we passed through the derelict building, we were watched over by a guard with an Alsatian dog; the dog barked loudly at us. "The organisers of the Manchester international festival love to re-invent space, especially if it is derelict and post-industrial" (Dickinson, 2013). All quite strange. Did it work? Yes, in part. It was certainly a unique and impressive experience. I felt that some of the images were a little too bizarre, and some a little too obvious, as were some of the slogans. But I'm pleased I attended.

ROXY MUSIC, THE LINCOLN FESTIVAL, 27 MAY 1972, AND NEWCASTLE CITY HALL, 27 AND 28 OCTOBER 1974

I first saw a new and relatively unknown Roxy Music at the Lincoln Festival on 27 May 1972. This was their first major performance and only the seventh time the band had played together. They appeared early on the Saturday afternoon, sandwiched between sets by Locomotive GT (a Hungarian rock band who were pretty big during the 1970s) and Heads, Hands & Feet. The Roxy lineup at the time was Bryan Ferry (vocals and keyboards), Phil Manzanera (guitar), Andy Mackay (sax and oboe), Paul Thompson (drums), Eno (synths), and Graham Simpson (bass). I recall that there was quite a buzz about the band at the time, largely as a result of their connections with King Crimson. Bryan Ferry had auditioned as lead singer for King Crimson, and impressed Robert Fripp and Pete Sinfield, although they felt that his voice was not suitable for Crimson. They went on to help Roxy Music obtain a record contract, and Sinfield produced their first, wonderful album (Rees, 1982).

The sound at the festival wasn't great; it was windy, and the mix was poor. But it was obvious even at this early stage in their career that there was something new, different, and unique about this band. The guys all dressed outrageously, and looking at pictures of Roxy taken at the festival you would think they had come from another planet. The music sounded very different to anything else around at the time. Eno's use of synths, Ferry's vocals, and Mackay's oboe all gave Roxy their own distinctive sound.

Roxy Music were recording tracks for their first album at the time of this appearance, and it was well before the release of their first single "Virginia Plain." Roxy provided a short interlude of majestic bright glam/art-rock in what was an excellent lineup, but a very wet, windy, and cold weekend. Looking back, and although I didn't realise it at the time, there were glimpses of the greatness and richness of musical texture which would follow. Foolishly, I saw Roxy Music simply as a quirky weird new band, and because of this I left it a couple of years before I saw them again.

It was 1974 and Roxy Music were on a roll. Things were very different from the last time I saw the fledgling band perform at the Lincoln pop festival jamboree in 1972. In the two years that had passed, Brian Eno had left the band, they had hit the singles charts with "Virginia Plain," "Pyjamarama" (wonderful and one of my favourites), and "Street Life" and were just about to release their fourth album. Eno had been replaced by local hero Eddie Jobson, whose violin virtuosity I had marvelled at when Fat Grapple stormed out local Locarno ballroom, and John Wetton was the new guy on bass, fresh from prog super maestros King Crimson. So, all was good in the Roxy camp, and the band were truly at the height of their powers. There is a view that Roxy was never really Roxy again after the genius that is Eno left the fold, but it doesn't hold water in my book. Yes, Eno was a vital part of the early band, but the 1974 lineup was strong enough to stand on its own, and although Eddie Jobson may not have seemed as enigmatic as his predecessor, his musical skills are without question.

I'd missed a couple of Roxy tours, and realised how foolish I had been, so made sure that I went along this time. They played two sold-out nights at Newcastle City Hall. I went along with a group of mates to the first night, and we were so knocked out by Roxy's performance that a couple of us decided to go along the following night and try to buy tickets outside. We succeeded, and this is one of the few occasions where I went to see a band two nights in a row (and enjoyed both concerts). Amazingly, I was in the same row of the stalls both nights.

Bryan Ferry was at his best, stylish, and cool, although sometimes looking a little nervous and uncomfortable on stage. And Eddie Jobson was simply brilliant. Oh, and the songs: "Mother of Pearl" a beautiful classic, the dark brooding menace of "In Every Dream Home," which we thought to be curious, funny, and shocking all at the same time, and the hits "Street Life" and "Virginia Plain"; the crowd went completely wild! By the last encore of "Do the Strand," the entire City Hall was going absolutely crazy, singing and dancing along.

So, what of the "art-rock" mantle which Roxy Music have had placed upon them throughout their career. "The authentic art-rock impulse is to create an "'educated' sounding music, to 'legitimise' rock 'n' roll" (Wuelfing, 1978). Indeed, Roxy Music have the recognisable conventions of rock and pop, however, they add in aspects of electronic, classical, and jazz, rendering it one step removed from traditional rock 'n' roll. In this sense, it could be argued that their output gives the impression that the music is purposefully crafted to transcend traditional rock or pop conventions.

BRIAN ENO, MOVEMENTS, EDINBURGH INTERNATIONAL FESTIVAL, NATIONAL MUSEUM OF SCOTLAND, 23 AUGUST 2013

Part of the Edinburgh International Festival, Movements was a series of talks and events which was presented in association with National Museums Scotland. The talks explored how artists have kept pace with technology over the centuries and how technology in turn has influenced artists. "An afternoon in conversation with influential, ex-Roxy Music synth player Brian Eno, as he shares his thoughts on the future of music and music production" (Festival Listing, 2013). Eno was to give a lecture-style talk, examining how music technology can be used as a relatively "new art," exploring "How did it evolve?" and "Where might it be going?" (Festival Listing 2013).

Laura and I had a pleasant train journey up to Edinburgh, arriving at Waverley station shortly after noon. The weather was fine for this, our third visit to Scotland in a couple of weeks, and our second to the Edinburgh festival. We were both looking forward to hearing Brian Eno speak. He is a hugely influential figure in popular music, and we figured that it would be interesting to hear his views. I hadn't seen him in any live context since the 1970s and his days with Roxy Music, and a performance with Phil Manzanera and the 801 band at the Reading festival.

The venue for Eno's lecture was the National Museum of Scotland, which is a grand building just off the Royal Mile and a short walk from the station. We had a sandwich lunch at a cafe on Bristol Square before taking our seats in the lecture theatre. The chance of hearing Brian Eno speak does not come very often, and the event had been sold out for some weeks. At 2:30 p.m. prompt, Eno entered the hall to a round of applause. He stood at a desk strewn with visuals, which he displayed on an overhead projector.

He explained that his talk was to centre around the two concepts of "the composer" and "the audience," how these have developed over time and continue to develop, and how music sits between the two and "sometimes brings them together."

Eno firstly took us through the history of the composer, starting back when music was there simply to enable dance, or as a way of creating noise which would frighten away big cats who had come to prey on ancient man. This progressed to a discussion of early recording media, and how the advent of multitrack enabled music to become an entity in its own right, a piece of aural painting or sculpture, separate from the performance, and existing not in a score, but in the record itself. He used the recording techniques of Les Paul and Mary Ford, and Phil Spector and George Martin as illustrations of this, showing visuals to support his point.

Eno then turned to the subject of the audience, making a distinction between the formal, regimented, and structured way in which an audience of a classical recital behaves, and that of a rock concert, where the audience and the performer come together, sometimes literally, showing a picture of Iggy Pop standing on top of his crowd. He explained how he wanted to use technology to create aural soundscapes, as he has done in his pioneering work in ambient music. He described how, when composing, he focuses on how sounds sit together, complement each other, and create a sonic picture and how "he approaches music from the perspective of a curator, or instillation artist" (Roquet, 2009).

The lecture finished with a short discussion of where music lies now, being created and layered from the recordings of our past, drawing an analogy with the techniques of the animator in film. Time was short, and the lecture was strictly constrained to one hour, which soon passed, with our speaker finishing with a couple of questions from the audience, and a few visuals left unused.

Laura and I caught the 4:30 p.m. train back to Newcastle; we were home around 7 p.m. It was a very interesting and engaging afternoon, which passed all too quickly.

TALKING HEADS, NEWCASTLE POLYTECHNIC, 27 JANUARY 1978, AND NEWCASTLE CITY HALL, 27 NOVEMBER 1979

I first saw Talking Heads at a concert at Newcastle Poly in January 1978. They were touring with Dire Straits as support at the time. Dire Straits were starting to become known as a result of their single "Sultans of Swing" and Talking Heads were the darlings of the US new wave, with rave reports of their concerts in the States coming through the UK music press.

I saw Talking Heads on TV performing "Psycho Killer" on the Old Grey Whistle Test and was hooked. The quirky jabbing rhythms and the strange lyrics (who would write a song about a psycho killer?) intrigued me. By the time they came to play at Newcastle Poly, they were performing songs from their first album and the yet-to-be-released "More Songs About Buildings and Food."

Live Talking Heads were excellent. There was a feel of an art school band about them; very different to the punk of the Ramones or to any of the UK new wave. David Byrne was the eccentric schoolteacher, whose manic stage manner held us all transfixed, and Tina Weymouth bobbed away playing a bass that looked bigger than she did. I remember there being mutters that Dire Straits would outshine them; not so, Talking Heads were great, and the crowd loved them.

"Talking Heads described their act in the analytical and anti-individualistic terms of conceptual art" (Steenstra, 2010). Their lyrical content, structure, and fusing of numerous musical genres ensured that their output was unpredictable, unusual, and multifaceted. "Talking Heads apply a genuinely educated, that is, shrewd, analytic perspective to the execution of purely rock aesthetics: theirs is an act of true refinement" (Wuelfing, 1978). Their music encompasses Motown, soul, and bubble-gum pop, rendered down to their essential components and then with the band's own quirky individuality added to it. It is difficult to experience Talking Heads' music without feeling as though you are experiencing an artistic experiment, disguised as fun, catchy pop.

GENESIS, READING FESTIVAL, 11 AUGUST 1972

I saw Genesis several times in 1971 and 1972. They supported Mott the Hoople at a gig at Sunderland Locarno, and I also saw them as support for Lindisfarne and at the Lincoln and Reading Festivals in 1972. The band were up and coming but they were very much at the top of their game in many ways. During those years they released the classic albums *Nursery Cryme* and *Foxtrot*. Much of the set was drawn from "Nursery Cryme," and I remember those songs best of all. "The Musical Box" and "The Return of the Giant Hogweed" were great stage favourites and would be preceded by long complex stories delivered in an enchanting, spell-binding, and spooky manner by Peter Gabriel.

Peter shaved the front of his head during this period, and also started to experiment with costumes. "His costumes were designed to enhance the fantasy tales" (Welch, 1975). Gabriel used his physical performance to convey the messages, themes, and narratives within the music.

Steve Hackett would be sitting on a stool playing those intricate beautiful melodies, Tony Banks was wringing swirling, brooding sounds from his organ, and Mike Rutherford would be quietly plucking away at his bass. Phil Collins was at the back on drums having recently joined the band, and providing backing vocals, which were actually a very important part of their sound; I didn't realise this until he was to become the front man a few years later. The set would also feature the dramatic and fierce "The Knife" as encore, from their first "real" Genesis album *Trespass*, and later in 1972 new songs "Watcher of the Skies" (Peter would fly onto the stage as a weird bat-like creature) and the epic "Supper's Ready," both from the *Foxtrot* album, were introduced into the set.

The set which sticks in my mind most of all is Reading 1972. Genesis were featured on the Friday night of the festival, on a lineup headed by Curved Air and also featuring Mungo Jerry. It was a warm, calm evening and Genesis came on stage at dusk, just as it was getting dark. Their beautiful textured sound flowed across the field, and we were all silent, entranced by Peter's stories and by his strong presence. "The Musical Box" story was my favourite: Cynthia kills Henry by knocking off his head with a croquet mallet, and then finds his musical box in the attic. It was pure magic, and they were easily the highlight of that night.

During these years, the band were, for me, at their most inventive, their most powerful, and most artistic. Their simplicity, innocence, and playfulness were contrasted by the band's seriousness and dedication. "The beauty of Gabriel's Genesis was that they created a perfect balance between serious rock performance and serious visual art" (Welch, 1975).

CONCLUSION

There are many linkages between art and rock performance. One might argue that every music performance is a piece of art. However, some performers are more recognisable as "artists." They take their performance very seriously as a piece of art and this comes through strongly in the performance itself. Yoko Ono is recognised as both an artist and a musician and often presents pieces of performance art, such as that which I attended in Liverpool.

Art-rock is often equated to progressive rock, the avant-garde, and experimental approaches to rock music. It aspires to elevate rock performance from simple entertainment to a more significant artistic statement. In doing so, art-rock may draw from many different influences including experimental, jazz, folk, and classical music. An art-rock performance is characterised by an audience who sit and listen carefully to the music, rather than dancing to the rhythms.

In conclusion, art-rock is entwined with music performance, particularly in relation to the early 1970s. It is a difficult genre to define, as many would argue that the energy of punk music saw the ending of the genre; however, several punk bands were, themselves, termed art-rock.

Chapter Ten

Authenticity

I reviewed the literature on the role of authenticity in live performance (Tetzlaff, 1994; Albrecht, 2008), illustrating this by considering Bird's (1994) analysis of the authenticity of Bruce Springsteen. I then selected ten relevant performances and analysed these. Table 10.1 lists the artists covered within the chapter.

Table 10.1. Artists Analysed in This Chapter

Artist	Genre	Date of Performance
Bruce Springsteen	Singer/Songwriter	1970s
Bob Marley	Reggae	1970s
Ravi Shankar	World Music	2010s
Nick Cave and the Bad Seeds	Alternative	2010s
Arctic Monkeys	Alternative	2000s
Oasis	Alternative	2000s
Patti Smith	New Wave	1970s
Lynyrd Skynyrd	Southern Rock	1970s
Neil Young	Southern Rock	1970s
U2	Classic Rock	1980s

BRUCE SPRINGSTEEN, HAMMERSMITH ODEON, LONDON, 24 NOVEMBER 1975

I'd read the famous report: "I saw rock and roll's future and its name is Bruce Springsteen," which was originally written by Landau in a 1974 edition of the USA magazine *The Real Paper* (Hann, 2010). I'd also heard the single "Born to Run" booming out of my radio, and my interest peaked. So, when

I read that Springsteen was finally coming to the UK, and was playing a show in London at Hammersmith Odeon on Tuesday, 18 November 1975, I was tempted. Should I go? I wouldn't usually travel to London to see a guy whose songs I didn't know. But there seemed to be something special about this particular guy. The reports I'd read suggested that he was the new Dylan with shades of Elvis thrown in for good measure. I asked around, but none of my friends really knew who Springsteen was or particularly wanted to go to see him. By then the concert was sold out anyway, but a second date had been added on the following Monday, 24 November 1975. I passed on the first gig, but still kept the idea of going to see him at the second concert alive in my mind. Eventually, something convinced me that I had to see this guy and that the gig was going to be something special.

So, on the Monday morning I decided I would make the 500+ mile round trip to London to try to get into the concert. I didn't have a ticket, and I knew demand would be high, but, hey, it wouldn't do any harm to try. I got the bus to town, bought a day return to London, caught a train to Newcastle, and got on the next train to London.

As I walked along the street from the underground, I could see Hammersmith Odeon. Above the doors the sign proclaimed: "Finally London is ready for Bruce Springsteen and the E Street Band." The first thing I noticed was that the posters said that the show didn't start until 9 p.m. The time was around 6 p.m. I'd expected the concert to start at 7:30 p.m. and the late start time worried me. If I did get in, would I make the last train home (which was shortly after midnight). Anyway, I put such concerns to the back of my mind and set about the task of acquiring a ticket. I started to talk to the touts outside the venue. "Oh, going to be tricky. Yeh, I can get you a ticket but it'll cost you" was the answer I got. As the time passed and it got closer to the doors opening around 8 p.m., I was offered a few tickets. The prices ranged from £20 upwards for a seat, which was a heck of a lot of money at the time, and more than I had with me. Finally, one of the touts came up to me. "Are you still looking for a ticket? I have a cheap one here. It's a £1 standing ticket, and you can have it for £10." That was almost all the money I had and would leave me just enough for my train fare back to King's Cross. So, I bought it and entered the venue.

A heavy feeling of great anticipation was in the air. Simon Frith referred to it as "an odd buzz because everyone was expecting something but no one knew what" (Frith, 1975). Springsteen and the E Street Band came on stage at 9 p.m. My ticket allowed me to stand at the back of the stalls which provided a not so bad view of the stage.

It all started with "Thunder Road." Bruce had a woolly hat on his head, a casual shirt, and a pair of jeans. The first thing that struck me was how tight the band was. The sax player, Clarence Clemons, came to the front a lot, re-creating the image from the front cover of *Born to Run*. I didn't know any of the songs, other than "Born to Run," which came quite early in the set, but I'd read enough reviews to recognise some of them, simply by their title. He played some classic covers, including Manfred Mann's "Pretty Flamingo." The main set was quite long, fast paced, and very intense throughout.

"Bruce had a smile of great joy, which you rarely see on a rock-star these days" (Frith, 1975). In fact, perhaps the most captivating part of the performance was nothing to do with the music itself, but moreover it was to do with the manner in which it was performed. Springsteen seemed completely caught within the present moment, putting every ounce of energy he possessed into expressing what needed to be expressed, second to second, minute to minute. "He was just there, winning some, losing some but always in the action . . . Springsteen's secret is his absolute belief in what he's doing" (Frith, 1975).

Indeed, there was an immense feeling that Springsteen was singing about his actual, lived experiences and the performance was thus laden with honesty. In his 2016 autobiography, Springsteen stated, "First, you write for yourself, always, to make sense of experience and the world around you, it's one of the ways I stay sane" (Springsteen, 2016). At times, it felt like he was exorcising some personal demons, singing of his childhood, his sense of not belonging and his hope for a better future. "Our stories, our books, our films are the way we cope with the random trauma inducing chaos of life as it plays" (Springsteen, 2016).

Bruce and the band returned for several encores, which just seemed to go on and on forever. During the encores, Springsteen, took us through his influences, playing classic rock 'n' roll by Elvis and Chuck Berry, and the wonderful Jackie De Shannon song "When You Walk in the Room." Bruce and the band were really into the groove by then, and it was hot, tight, stunning.

I started to worry about missing the train home. I left at 11:30 p.m., just as he was finishing. I ran down the road to the underground station, jumped on a train, and made my train home just in time. It got me back home around 8 a.m., tired, worn out, but with a feeling that I had witnessed something extremely special. As soon as I had a little money, I went out and bought *Born to Run* and played it again and again. I was a convert.

BOB MARLEY AND THE WAILERS, LEEDS UNIVERSITY REFECTORY, 26 JUNE 1976

It was the red-hot summer of 1976 and Bob Marley was big news. "No Woman, No Cry" had hit the charts, and his legendary 1975 show at the

Lyceum was a massive success and had received rave reviews in the rock press. "It was an absolutely transcendent event, one of those rare life-changing shows. I left in such an elevated state I didn't even mind when some guy tried to pick my pocket on the way out" (Murray, 2012).

Leeds University was the nearest gig to the North East of England on Marley's 1976 tour, but it had been sold out for weeks in advance, and I didn't have a ticket. Marie and I decided to drive down to Leeds on the off chance of buying a couple of tickets outside. We arrived early and joined crowds of people sitting on the grass and in the union bar, waiting for the doors to open. I wandered around asking if anyone had any spare tickets and eventually managed to buy a couple from a guy in a nearby pub. I paid a little more than face value.

The Union refectory was completely packed to the walls for the gig. You could barely move, and it was so hot and sweaty in there that night. I wasn't that familiar with Bob Marley's material at the time, but I do remember recognising "I Shot the Sheriff," "No Woman, No Cry," and "Get Up, Stand Up." At this time the Wailers featured Family Man, Junior Marvin, and the I-Threes with Rita Marley. I remember finding it a very different sort of concert to the rock gigs that I was used to at the time. In particular, the music was much quieter, and the reggae beats and rhythms were so relentless, which got everyone dancing. The dreadlocks, the Rastafarian dress, the I-Threes in their robes, and a strong smell of dope in the air: This was all so new to me. A world away from heavy rock.

Bob Marley seemed so natural and unassuming on stage, yet there was an intense, electrifying charisma about him. "Marley, almost literally, lit up the stage" (Murray, 2012). You just knew that he meant every word he sang and the crowd accepted those words as their own. Indeed, Marley's music is more than just output, gigs, and chart positions, "It belongs to a community and it speaks for a community" (Walters, 1974). Its truth is evident in the impact it has on those who receive it.

This gig left a lasting impression on Marie and me, not only because we were lucky enough to experience a musical legend, but also because we were able to see the far-reaching effects a performer can have upon an audience. Marley's political and sociocultural messages seemed as real and important as any spoken by activists, politicians, or world leaders. A very special gig.

RAVI SHANKAR, USHER HALL, EDINBURGH, 22 AUGUST 2011

I fulfilled a longtime ambition when I finally got to see the great Ravi Shankar in concert. Ravi, who was ninety-one years old at the time, was George

Harrison's sitar teacher, an influence on the Beatles and countless other bands, and played at the great 1960s festivals, such as Woodstock and Monterey. This rare UK concert was at the Usher Hall Edinburgh, as part of the Edinburgh International Festival.

The concert started at 8:15 p.m. and finished at around 9:45 p.m., with no intermission. The crowd was a real mixture, comprising people of all ages and backgrounds; everyone keen to see the great man perform. Outside, waiting for the doors to open, I heard voices of many different nationalities; several looking for spare tickets, as this concert had been sold out for some time.

My seat was upstairs in the Upper Circle looking down on the stage. Not a great view, but I could see the entire stage (although my neck was rather stiff the next morning!). Just before 8 p.m. the hall filled and an announcement was made that the concert would begin shortly. You could hear a pin drop in the vast Usher Hall; everyone waiting in anticipation for what promised to be a very special evening.

The stage was set with Indian rugs; the instruments strewn across them and in the centre was a small podium on which Ravi would shortly sit. The scent of incense hung in the air. Just before the performance started, two ladies took their seats in the front row accompanied by a cute little white dog, who also had a seat bang in the middle, right in front of the stage. I wondered if there was any connection with Ravi.

At around 8:15 p.m. the musicians took to the stage, followed by Ravi who looked quite frail, was walking with a stick, and was helped on stage by one of his fellow musicians. The reception from the audience was immense. I don't think I've ever heard an audience clap as loud or as long. The musicians all took their place and Ravi introduced the first raga in a gentle voice.

I'd read some recent reports that suggested that he may have lost some of his musical power in recent years. From where I was sitting his playing was first class; indeed, it was astounding for a man of his years. Ravi and his fellow musicians first played two short ragas, followed by a short piece for Krishna's birthday. Ravi introduced each piece in a gentle voice, which was almost inaudible from my seat upstairs. The final piece was a longer raga which became a jam and showcased each member of the band. Before it started, Ravi introduced his fellow musicians, several of whom had been, or were currently, his students. This piece meandered through various melodies and rhythms, and featured extended percussion and flute interludes from each of the musicians; always returning to Ravi and his sitar. At various points he invited his colleagues to come into the piece with a simple, gentle wave of the hand; with another wave, he would tell them to stop. The piece climaxed with some strong rhythmic sitar.

Shankar's performance, as well as remaining authentic and true to the Indian sitar traditions, also appeared to remain true to the spirit and integrity of the man himself. His personal familiarity to the other musicians, his clear enjoyment in what he was doing, and his organic approach to the performance ensured that "His genius seemed as fresh and innocent as ever" (Hewett, 2011). Although I was experiencing Shankar at the end of his musical career, reviews from the 1960s spoke of the immense personal touch he brought to his performance. "His unique showmanship was not lost as he ecstatically played his soul" (Goldberg, 1969).

Then it was over. Ravi bowed, receiving a standing ovation from the crowd. The little white dog who I had seen join the concert at the beginning of the evening jumped up and joined him on stage. I later learned that the cute dog is Ravi's pet, Suki. Ravi left, and returned again with his musicians to take a final bow. A remarkable evening. As the lady in the seat next to me said at the end, "Amazing. I hope I am like that at 91." I wouldn't disagree with that. As I walked down the stairs and out of the hall, I sensed that we had all experienced something truly unique.

NICK CAVE AND THE BAD SEEDS, EDINBURGH USHER HALL, 1 NOVEMBER 2013

Laura and I crossed the border to Scotland, where we took a step over another border into the darker side of rock, for a night in the company of Nick Cave and his compatriots the Bad Seeds. I had only seen Nick Cave once before, and that was at a solo concert at the Sage Gateshead some years before. This was the first time that Laura had seen him, although she was a fan and familiar with much of his music. We had seats in the upper circle looking directly down on the proceedings, with a good view of the stage and the packed stalls where all the seats had been removed, and fans were crammed around the front, awaiting an audience with Nick.

Nick Cave and the Bad Seeds came on stage shortly before 9 p.m., and were truly amazing. I don't think I've ever seen a performance which maintained such passion, power, and intensity throughout. "There is something about the immediacy of Cave's music that gets inside the individual listener" (Welberry and Dalziell, 2009). Nick was dressed all in black, looking like a cool, young Bela Lugosi, and the songs were all very dark in both mood and lyric. Crazed bearded violinist Warren Ellis tore shreds out of his instrument and was a perfect foil to front-man Cave. Nick prowled around the front of the stage singing and talking directly to the first few rows of fans. The guy seemingly had no fear, and seemed to completely lose himself in the performance. The songs were, at one end of the spectrum, all power chords, manic instrumental breaks, with Cave dancing crazily and haranguing the front rows; to another extreme of dark, sombre, power ballads with Cave at the piano.

Despite drawing heavily on persona, drama, and theatrics, Cave managed to use these elements to connect in what feels like an extremely honest and authentic way. It is as though he was able to express parts of himself by adopting these approaches. "Latching onto a rich scheme of storytelling, arcs of his persona become transparent" (Fadele, 1992). Indeed, his theatrics and dramatic performance "illuminates hither-to hidden depths of the much-revered Australian's hidden character" (Fadele, 1992).

Highlights for me were "Jubilee Street," "Tupelo," "Red Right Hand," "The Mercy Seat," and "Stagger Lee." The main set finished with "Push the Sky Away," but the band returned for an incredible five-song encore including "Deanna," the great "Breathless" (my favourite), and closer "Give Us a Kiss." The show finished just before 11 p.m., and we had an uneventful drive back down the A1; arriving home around 1:45 a.m.

ARCTIC MONKEYS, LANCASHIRE CRICKET GROUND, 28 JULY 2007

The Arctic Monkeys exploded onto the UK music scene in 2006. A group of seventeen-year-old lads from Sheffield, they sang about teenaged Northern life and embraced their schoolboy status, creating a refreshingly authentic antidote to the more commercial acts of the time (Osborne, 2013).

This was to be the Arctic Monkey's big gig. It sold out in an amazing time, with a second night being added immediately to satisfy demand for tickets. The Arctic Monkeys had seemingly come from nowhere and were suddenly massive. Even the way they rose to fame was refreshingly authentic. "Demos entrepreneurially handed out at live gigs, outside venues and on public transport led to frenzied word of mouth across Sheffield" (Stolworthy, 2021). Eventually, word of mouth, coupled with popularity on the online platform "Myspace," led to the band securing a number one spot on the charts with "I Bet You Look Good on the Dancefloor." I hadn't heard anything by them, but David and Laura were fans so I bought tickets as soon as they went on sale. I'm glad I did, as this turned out to be an extremely special gig.

We drove down and arrived just in time to see the Coral. David and I had already seen them supporting the Who at the Albert Hall a year or so before. Their very 1960s-ish blend of jangling guitar, folk-rock, and psych was exactly the sort of thing I liked. They went down well with the crowd, but the sound mix was pretty poor. Supergrass came on and really rocked, providing a bit of a pleasant surprise to me. They were much rockier than I expected and reminded me of Steve Marriott and Humble Pie. Amy Winehouse was just great, as captivating as her legend suggests and also went down well with the crowd.

The Cricket Ground is a massive venue, and it was absolutely packed by the time the Arctic Monkeys took to the stage. The reception was unlike anything I'd seen for some time. The whole crowd sang along with every word, and went absolutely wild, throwing beer (at least, I hope it was beer!). By the day of the gig, Laura had bought the album and I knew some of the songs, particularly "I Bet You Look Good on the Dancefloor," "Mardy Bum," and "When the Sun Goes Down."

Front-man Alex Turner's lyrics speak of feverish nights out, inner-city violence, and the juxtaposing of romance amidst a bleak, Northern landscape. All of this was delivered in the "ordinary speech of Sheffield, as opposed to the 'fake' mid-Atlantic accent of the mainstream" (Beal, 2009). Turner's use of his authentic Sheffield accent adds to the sense that these guys have walked straight out of the high-school gates to be with us. "They seem so unstyled, unpolished and refreshingly uncalculated" (Sharp, 2006).

We all sang along, and had a great time. We stayed the night in a hotel which was walking distance away and drove back in the morning.

OASIS, REEBOK STADIUM, BOLTON, 15 JULY 2000

I came late in terms of getting to see Oasis in concert. They came up during a time that my gig-going was at a low point, and it wasn't until 2000 that I finally got to see them. By then I had missed their massive Knebworth gig, much to my regret, so I was very keen to see what the Gallagher brothers were like live. When they announced their next tour, I bought tickets immediately for their (relatively) hometown gig at Bolton Reebok football stadium.

Marie and I travelled across to Manchester by train, staying at the Midland hotel, and taking the train across to Bolton. We arrived just in time to catch some of the first support act, which was ex-Smiths Johnny Marr's new band the Healers. Next up were Shaun Ryder and Manchester favourites the Happy Mondays. Both went down well with the home crowd and warmed everyone up for the main attraction.

This gig came shortly after the Gallagher brothers had one of their regular and somewhat infamous bust-ups which resulted in Noel walking out of the European leg of the *Standing on The Shoulders of Giants* world tour, and the subsequent cancelling of some French tour dates. The tour continued with a stand-in for Noel, but luckily the brothers had made it up by the time the tour reached the UK.

Oasis opened their set with "Don't Let It Out," and played for around ninety minutes, featuring all of their well-known songs. We were up in the stands to the left of the stage, and, although the sound wasn't great up there, Oasis were still impressive.

For Oasis, "authenticity is achieved by describing things as existing in a real world" (Schulze, 2014). They gave the impression that they were singing about their own lived, working-class male experience, which much of the crowd could identify with. Their connection with their Manchester roots and their honesty regarding their backgrounds made us all feel that they were bringing truth and a sense of honesty to all that they did.

We left during the encores in the hope of getting a head start before the massive crowds rolled out onto the trains. The station was walking distance from the stadium. We got onto the platform without any problems, and stood waiting for the next train. We waited and waited, as more and more people piled onto the platform. Soon the station was completely packed to the extent people were in danger of being pushed onto the tracks. Eventually a train arrived and everyone piled on. I've never been on such a packed train; it was so full you couldn't move at all, with people up on tables and every inch of space taken, to the extent it was dangerous and rather frightening. The short journey from Bolton to Oxford Road seemed to take forever. How we managed to squeeze our way out of the carriage I don't know. Marie lost a shoe in the process and I literally had to pull her out of the carriage.

Travelling back the next morning, Marie with only one shoe, we agreed it had been very bad organisation, which left a bad taste after what was, otherwise a great gig. However, now I am inclined to think, perhaps, this was an authentic end to an Oasis gig.

PATTI SMITH, READING FESTIVAL, 27 AUGUST 1978, NEWCASTLE CITY HALL, 29 AUGUST 1978, AND THE SAGE GATESHEAD, 23 MAY 2007

Patti Smith is a force of nature; outspoken, compelling, authentic, passionate, kooky, arty, funny, challenging, cheeky, and the craziest rock 'n' roll anti-star to arrive on the scene during the late 1970s. She exploded out of the new wave movement, but there was always much more to her than punk rock. Patti wears her rock and pop influences on her sleeve, and her music owes as much to the Who, the Stones, and Dylan as it does to the Pistols and the Ramones.

I first saw her live in 1978, twice in three days; on a Sunday night closing the Reading Rock Festival, and then again on Tuesday at Newcastle City Hall. Patti had just been in the UK singles charts with "Because the Night" which she co-wrote with Bruce Springsteen, and which reached No. 5.

Patti closed the 1978 Reading Festival, headlining the Sunday lineup, which also featured Ian Gillan, Tom Robinson, and Foreigner. She was amazing and had the whole crowd with her as she stormed, screamed, and snarled "Rock 'n' Roll Nigger," tore into "Gloria" and "Because the Night," and performed great covers of the Byrds' "So You Want to Be (A Rock 'n' Roll Star)" and the Who's "My Generation." I managed to collect a "Rock 'n' Roll Nigger" plectrum which Patti threw into the crowd at Reading. I scrabbled around on the ground, in the mud for it, after she threw a handful into the crowd.

Two days later I saw Patti in concert at Newcastle City Hall, and she was equally as electric. Support came from the Pop Group. The set was slightly longer than her Reading performance, and the last song was a wonderful performance of the Stones' "Time Is on My Side."

Through these early performances, Patti Smith brought a raw authenticity and dedication to expressing truth, both on a personal and musical level. Alves explores how Smith was unwilling to settle for adopting the voice of those that had gone before, "it was every generation's role to find their own and not blindly trust and accept the one that had been coercively given to them" (Alves, 2018). Indeed, in her autobiography, Smith speaks of how important expressing her own ideas was to her, stating, "We could only give from the perspective of who we were and what we had" (Smith, 2011). This ethos is evident within Smith's output; even when performing a cover track, she manages to express new meanings and communicate a new energy, setting it apart from the original.

As well as this personal authenticity, Patti Smith also expressed an explicit commitment to the preservation of authentic rock music as a whole. "We imagined ourselves as the sons of liberty with a mission to preserve, protect and project the revolutionary spirit of rock 'n' roll" (Smith, 2011). As she explored in her autobiography, Smith recognised the commercialism and commodification of music which was becoming commonplace in the mid-1970s. "We feared that the music which had given us sustenance was in danger of spiritual starvation. We feared it losing its sense of purpose, we feared it falling into fattened hands, we feared it floundering in a mire of spectacle, finance and vapid technical complexity" (Smith, 2011).

Patti Smith married Fred "Sonic" Smith, former member of the MC5, in 1980. For most of the 1980s she went into semi-retirement from music, living with her family in Michigan. In 1994 Fred Smith tragically died of a heart attack, and soon afterwards Patti decided to move back to New York. Her friends Michael Stipe of R.E.M. and beat poet Allen Ginsberg reportedly urged her to go back on the road.

In 2007 Patti Smith was touring the UK and returned to the North East for a concert at the Sage Gateshead. This was almost thirty years since I last saw her live. My friend John and his family were over from the USA at the time and John and his son Matthew came along to the concert with David and me. John and I had tickets in the front row, and we bought a couple more seats for Matthew and David, who were seated in the circle.

Patti had just released the album *Twelve*, which (as the title suggests) contained twelve tracks, all of which were cover versions, including songs by Bob Dylan, Jefferson Airplane, Jimi Hendrix, and the Rolling Stones. Patti was as wild as ever, and in a particularly chatty mood. She was quite taken by the Sage concert hall; she told us it reminded her of a "big silver peanut," and how she had been walking about the riverside, looking at the "big silver peanut." Patti asked us all to stand up, but a girl down front explained that if we did, we might all be "hoyed oot." It took a little time for others to explain to Patti that "hoyed oot" was Geordie for "thrown out." Patti's reaction: "When you want to do something, make everyone do it so they can't stop you"; several of the audience followed her advice and stood up for the rest of the concert. She was in quite a cheeky mood overall. I went to the gents; when I returned, I had to make my way along the front row right in front of Patti; she quipped: "Did you have a good p**s?." (Moral: Don't sit too close to the front at a Patti Smith concert.)

The set consisted of classic 1970s Patti: "Free Money," "Because the Night," "Gloria," and several covers from *Twelve*: "Changing of the Guards" (Dylan), "Are You Experienced?" (Hendrix), "White Rabbit" (Jefferson Airplane), "Perfect Day" (Lou Reed), "Gimme Shelter" (Stones), "Soul Kitchen" (Doors), "Smells Like Teen Spirit" (Nirvana), and "Helpless" (Neil Young), all given the Patti Smith treatment.

LYNYRD SKYNYRD, NEWCASTLE CITY HALL, 8 FEBRUARY 1977

I saw Lynyrd Skynyrd three times in the 1970s. The first time was at Newcastle City Hall supporting Golden Earring. It was an unlikely pairing of acts even at the time, as Skynyrd were an up-and-coming band, having just released their second album. In fact, many members of the audience left after Skynyrd's set. My friend John recalls: "I can remember the very large Confederate Flag behind the band and for me it was the best gig I saw them play. They were fresh, different and very exciting with an epic version of "Freebird" (Smith, 2013). John and I then saw Skynyrd at Knebworth where they (almost) stole the show from the headliners, the Rolling Stones. They played a lengthy version of "Freebird" that day, with amazing guitar solos, which gained them a lot of friends. It was a red-hot afternoon and Skynyrd came into their own, with their twin guitars dualing across the opposite sides of the Stones tongue stage. This was televised on the Old Grey Whistle Test, and helped propel the band to mega status in the UK.

They were back for their own tour in 1977, which sold out very quickly. Support act was Clover, an American band with a country boogie feel. Skynyrd came over as conquering heroes, and the thing I remember most is that they were incredibly LOUD. It was probably one of the loudest gigs I have ever been to. Oh, and "Freebird" went on forever, and ever, and ever. I thought that the song was never going to end! "They were very loud and very tight, with guitarists Collins and Rossington swapping immaculately enmeshed riffs before screaming out solos that may not have meant much musically, but fitted perfectly in their places within the Lynyrd Skynyrd wall of sound" (De Whalley, 1976).

Skynyrd did not step away from the conventions of traditional Southern rock and lues. Their lyrics often reference the "wispy" and "gambling" stereotypes of the genre, and they had a rawness about them that, despite being incredibly tight, gave the impression that everything could fall apart at any moment. These "generic practices of the band," despite perhaps being intentionally fabricated, "work to position their performance as authentically southern" (Albrecht, 2008). This is to say, in "acting the part of authentic southern rockers," Lynyrd Skynyrd transcended this performance and actually found authenticity in doing so (Albrecht, 2008).

NEIL YOUNG, NEWCASTLE CITY HALL, 9 NOVEMBER 1973, AND EDINBURGH PLAYHOUSE, 3 MARCH 2008

I went along to this concert on spec, hoping to score a ticket outside. The City Hall sometimes used to let fans pay to sit on the choir seats which surround the stage. These seats are on the stage itself, facing the back of the performers. On this occasion, there was quite a queue of ticketless people hoping to see Neil Young, so they decided to let us into the choir seats.

Support came from the Eagles, who were simply on fire. This was the original Eagles lineup of Glenn Frey, Don Henley, Bernie Leadon, and Randy Meisner, at the time of their second album *Desperado*, and their set featured songs from their first two LPs. So that included classics like "Take it Easy,"

"Tequila Sunrise," "Witchy Woman," and "Peaceful Easy Feeling." Stunning. I became an Eagles fan that night and remain one to this day.

Neil Young was touring with backing band the Santa Monica Flyers, who were Billy Talbot (bass), Ralph Molina (drums), Ben Keith (pedal steel), and Nils Lofgren (guitar, piano). Neil is a pretty uncompromising performer and for this tour he decided he would play his forthcoming album *Tonight's the Night* in its entirety, a brave move.

The stage was set out as a beach, complete with sand and a palm tree, and Neil was drinking from a bottle of tequila throughout the show. We were all expecting tracks from *After the Goldrush* and *Harvest* but instead we were treated to a set of unfamiliar tunes, much to the annoyance of many of the audience members. However, despite being unfamiliar with the set, Young's music and performance somehow seemed to connect with the crowd in a way I'd not experienced before.

It was astonishing to experience the connection that a performer could establish with an audience, via a set of songs none of us knew. His lyrics had an honesty to them, and it felt as though they were both personal to Young himself, whilst also speaking to the audience as a whole. The song, "Tonight's the Night" contained the lyric "real as the day was long," this for me summarised Young himself, or, at least, how we all felt about him. "The Romantic ideals of rock music are nicely expressed in Neil Young's song 'Tonight's the Night (Part 1)'" (Auslander, 1998). Indeed, Young's performance served to "summarise the mythology of self-expression central to rock in terms of authenticity" (Auslander, 1998). Personal and full of truth, his music expressed his background and values whilst also communicating something which represented the whole.

After he had finished playing the new songs, Young did play "Cinnamon Girl" with a lengthy, meandering guitar solo, which got a great reception from the crowd, who were pleased to hear something familiar. A great gig, with Neil Young in great form, even if the set wasn't what we had expected or hoped for.

Thirty-five years after I first saw Neil Young in concert, David and I went to see him at Edinburgh Playhouse on a cold winter evening. We drove up through Jedburgh, stopping for a coffee along the way. The Playhouse is a beautiful old theatre and was completely sold out for this concert.

Neil played two sets, and this time he played a lot of old favourites. There was no support act; rather, he was accompanied by an artist who painted as Neil played. "For reasons known only to Young, an artist paints canvases at the rear of the stage and announces songs by placing interpretative pictures on a large easel stage right. The unexplained visual art theme extends to Young's paint-spattered suit" (Petridis, 2008).

The first set was acoustic, during which Young performed old favourites including "Heart of Gold" and "Old Man," much to the delight of the crowd. After the interval, Neil became Mr Rock 'n' Roll and Grunge, and we were treated to an excellent and powerful electric set, with some amazing meandering guitar solos. The encore included "Cinnamon Girl."

The snow was falling as we drove home. This time we followed the A1 through Berwick, which is a slightly longer route, but a safer road, given the winter conditions. A great concert by a legendary artist.

U2, NEWCASTLE, MAYFAIR, 9 OCTOBER 1981

According to Grossburg (1992), whether a music can be considered to be "authentic" or "inauthentic" can be determined by examining the reason for the music's very existence. Truly authentic output is, Grossburg states, the opposite to commercial in that it is driven by truth and sociocultural phenomena, rather than being ego-driven or for monetary gain. U2's stadium-filling rock-star personas, under Grossburg's definition, make for curious candidates for a truly authentic band. Indeed, this gig came a couple of months after we had seen U2 deliver an incendiary performance at the Rock on the Tyne festival at Gateshead Stadium, where Bono clambered up the lighting towers, played the part of the rock star, and generally got everyone onside by employing classic front-man stereotypes. Moore (2002) argues that authenticity is much more subjective, hinging on an audience's interpretation and organic response.

The Mayfair was packed to the rafters. Everyone wanted to see this new band. U2 had just released their second album *October* and the excellent single "Gloria." There was something very different about them; something that it was difficult to get a handle on, or describe in the same terms as any other band of the period. To put it in some sort of context, U2 were coming up alongside the Teardrop Explodes and the Bunnymen, both excellent bands. But there was something almost intangible about U2 that seemed to set them apart. Their music came through new wave, but its roots lay deeply and squarely in the '60s, beat, the Beatles, Stones, soul, religion, spirituality, and, of course, Van Morrison. All of this combined to result in an output that sounded highly original whilst possessing all the familiarity needed to feel at home. "People haven't asked U2 if they're the future of rock. They've told them" (Green, 1982).

What I remember of this gig was a joyous, heady night with Bono singing his heart out for us in a way which felt raw, real, and intimate. The early songs, "Gloria," "I Will Follow," "Fire," and "11 O'Clock Tick Tock," were powerful yet possessed an intense emotion which made the audience believe every word. In a time when synthesisers and electronics were becoming ever-more present within the charts, U2's dependency on guitar-based instrumentation gave the impression that they were rooted within traditional rock conventions and that they were using simple methods to express a message (Moore, 2002).

The U2 who played those club gigs was a raw, hungry, stunning act who were a million miles away from the stadium rock band that they would very soon become. A different time, a different band, a different place. It seems so far away now. But on the night, in the heat and sweat and volume and crush of the Mayfair, U2 were shiny and young and so intense. And Bono ran around that stage seemingly singing for all of us. It felt like the audience had a connection with the band that night and that our feelings were being perfectly represented by the guys on stage.

CONCLUSION

All of the bands and artists listed here share one common theme in terms of their music and their performance. "What you see is what you get" in terms of all these acts. They come over as honest, and portray themselves exactly as they are. Because of this, they command followings who are incredibly loyal and remain with them throughout their careers. The audience feel that they really understand the performer. The performer relays the songs in their own language, using their own accent and words. There is no pretence and the persona of the artist is that of themselves.

Attending a concert by one of these artists is a very special experience. They connect with their audiences in a true and honest way. There is a sense that one is not attending a performance; rather you are seeing the artist for who they are, and as they really are, "laying their souls bare" in front of you. This is a special kind of performance, unlike any other.

Chapter Eleven

Maturity

There is limited literature on the concept of "elderly rock," both in terms of older bands and artists such as the Rolling Stones, the Who, Bob Dylan, the Hollies, and Status Quo, alongside the concept of the elderly rock fan (see, for example, Gibson, 2010). Kotarba (2005) has worked in this area, exploring rock 'n' roll experiences in middle age. Table 11.1 lists the artists covered within the chapter.

Table 11.1. Artists Analysed in This Chapter

Artist	Genre	Date of Performance
Led Zeppelin	Classic Rock	2010s
The Kinks	Classic Rock	2010s
The Hollies	Pop	2010s
The Grateful Dead	Classic Rock	2010s
Black Sabbath	Heavy Metal	2010s
The Who	Classic Rock	2010s
Status Quo	Classic Rock	2010s
60s Gold Tour	Pop Variety Show	2010s
The Rolling Stones	Classic Rock	2010s
Bob Dylan	Singer/Songwriter	2010s

LED ZEPPELIN O2 ARENA LONDON 10 DECEMBER 2007

On 10 December 2007 the (almost) impossible happened and Led Zeppelin reformed and took to the stage at the O2 Arena in London for The Ahmet Ertegun Tribute Concert. This was a benefit concert held in memory of music executive Ahmet Ertegün, who had been involved in breaking Zeppelin in the United States. This was the first full Zeppelin concert since the death of John Bonham in 1980. Bonham's son Jason Bonham took his dad's place at the drum-stool. There had been rumours for some time that Zeppelin might reform, and in September, 2007, Harvey Goldsmith confirmed at a press conference that it was, indeed, going to take place (Calef, 2011). The concert was originally scheduled to take place on 26 November 2007, but was rescheduled when Jimmy Page injured his finger (Calef, 2011).

As soon as I heard about the show, I was determined to do my best to attend. Tickets were made available via a lottery system. I entered my details several times into the website, hoping against the odds that I would be one of the lucky few to be selected. Apparently one million people registered for the 20,000 available tickets, so the odds of success were, to say the least, low. As soon as the results of the lottery were released, I was on every Zeppelin online forum that I could find, and soon realised that I hadn't been successful. Those who had won, were emailed a passcode which enabled them to but two tickets via Ticketmaster. I looked on eBay, and to my dismay, found passcodes on sale. It was clear that some enterprising individuals had managed to make multiple entries (presumably using multiple computers, email addresses and postal addresses) to ensure success. I decided to take the risk and bought two passcodes for $100 each. These enabled me to buy two pairs of tickets. The face value of each ticket was £125 (expensive anyway), which meant I was paying around £150 per ticket (which didn't seem too bad a deal to me). I went straight to Ticketmaster and bought two tickets in my name, and two in my wife Marie's name, using different credit cards. The rules said that one individual could only buy two tickets, and that orders on the same card would be cancelled. The plan was for all four of us: me, Marie, David and Laura to go to the gig. We received our confirmation email immediately, and were told that Marie and I would have to collect our tickets from the O2, along with photographic ID. We were in! Or so I thought. I was so excited, and looking forward to seeing Zeppelin again. Over the next few weeks there was a lot of talk in the press and on the internet about the method of ticket allocation, and the fact that some touts had managed to get hold of tickets. Harvey Goldsmith announced that he would cancel any tickets that had been bought by anyone other than those drawn in the lottery. This resulted in several guys, who had obtained tickets in a similar manner to me, particularly from the USA, threatening legal action. In the end, I'm not sure if any tickets were actually cancelled, but I was pretty stressed out at the time, in case he cancelled our tickets.

On 1 November 2007, it was announced that Page had broken his little finger after a fall in his garden, and the show was postponed to 10 December

2007. Panic! We had trains and hotel rooms booked! We cancelled those and rebooked, which cost us.

We were advised to turn up early to collect our tickets. The O2 opened the day before to issue tickets and wristbands for the show. We went down to London a day early, joined the queue, and collected our tickets and wristbands. It was obvious from talking to people in the queue that many had traveled from all over the world for this historic gig. The United States contingent was particularly strong.

We went along to the O2 on the night of the gig very excited about the prospect of seeing Zeppelin. David and Laura were really looking forward to it as the last time Zeppelin played together it was before they were born. We had seats in two pairs upstairs in the same block, with a reasonable view of the stage. The show opened with a performance by a supergroup consisting of Keith Emerson (ELP), Chris Squire and Alan White (Yes) and Simon Kirke (Free, Bad Co) with the brass section from Bill Wyman's Rhythm Kings. They started with ELP's "Fanfare for the Common Man." The show also featured Bill Wyman's Rhythm Kings, Paul Rodgers, Paolo Nutini, and Foreigner. The Rhythm Kings acted as backing group for Nutini and Rodgers both singing two songs each. Other guests were Maggie Bell and Alvin Lee. Ronnie Wood was billed to perform, and appears in the program and on the t-shirt, but he didn't play. We watched the start of the set, caught Paul Rodgers and Foreigner, but spent much of the time having a look around the arena, taking in the atmosphere. We saw Bob Geldof and Joe Elliott from Def Leppard in the bar. Many other stars attended the gig.

There was a short interval and then we took our seats. You could feel the anticipation in the air. What would they be like? What would they start with? The entrance of Led Zeppelin was preceded by a short film, taken from TV reports of a 1970s US tour. And then there were on stage, and the familiar opening riff of "Good Times, Bad Times" echoed across the massive arena. The sound was a little patchy at first, but that was soon sorted out. The atmosphere was strange; the crowd seemed subdued, as if they were completely awestruck, and couldn't believe what they were experiencing. This developed as the evening progressed, with later songs getting crazy audience receptions. They were everything I could have hoped for. The performance of each band member was stunning, the weeks of rehearsal paid off. Plant sang songs in a lower key, and his scream wasn't as piercing as it had been, but then how could it be? I also reckon that Page fluffed some of the notes at the start of Stairway. But these were minor points. Overall, it was a great performance, and Zeppelin reclaimed their legacy. Highlights for me were "Since I've Been Loving You," "Dazed And Confused," "Stairway To Heaven" (although

I've heard it so many times that the magic it held for me in the 1970s has dimmed), and Kashmir. Encores were "Whole Lotta Love," and "Rock And Roll." I was hoping for a further encore of "Communication Breakdown," which they had apparently rehearsed, but hey you can't have everything. Marie, David, and Laura, all thought it was just great. Probably not the best time I've seen Zeppelin, but a momentous, unforgettable, and emotional event.

DAVE DAVIES (AND RAY!), ISLINGTON ASSEMBLY HALL, LONDON, 18 DECEMBER 2015

As an early Christmas present to myself, I went to see Kinks guitar riff hero Dave Davies in London on a chilly December evening. And what a Christmas present it was. Dave Davies played an astonishing set to his home crowd.

Still recovering from flu, Dave bounded on stage, greeting us, "Hello London! It's good to be back in town!" He ran through a set of Kinks classics, album tracks, and solo songs. Dave's guitar was loud and fuzzy, just as we expected it to be, and his band's versions of Kinks hits "Dead End Street" and (my favourite) "See My Friends" were raw and heavy. Dave's own "Death of a Clown" started pretty ramshackle but finished as a great sing-along. But the best was yet to come, a true Christmas miracle.

For the last song, Dave introduced a "surprise for Christmas" and on walked his brother Ray!!! The two brothers played "You Really Got Me," and the place erupted. I was sitting upstairs and everyone leapt to their feet; singing, clapping, shouting, and going generally wild. The next few minutes became an unbelievable almost surreal dream. "The night's concluding treat, agreed at the last minute, starts with a pause, as Ray keeps his brother waiting. When he looks at him for his 'You Really Got Me' solo, as he did when they recorded it, Dave delivers. 'What a noise' says Ray, 'what a night'" (Hasted, 2015). Ray and Dave shook hands as they left the stage.

This was the Davies brothers first time on stage together for nineteen years, and it was an amazing event to witness; musically, historically, and emotionally. Two brothers, in their hometown, back together on stage, singing the song that started so much. Indeed, this reunion, however brief, transported me back in time to the 1970s and 1980s days of seeing the Kinks. Indeed, Driessen explored how fans "give meaning to pop reunions through the lens of the life course" (2019). Blasting the music from my teenage bedroom and standing in packed crowds, Dave's guitar ringing in my ears; so many memories and moments rolled into little over two minutes of music. The band's breakup and the infamous tensions between the brothers were all deleted in this moment of unity.

As I walked out of the venue onto the street, what we'd witnessed seemed to momentarily unite the crowd and provided a sense of unity. Everyone was looking at each other; grinning, not quite believing what we had all just witnessed. It was perhaps the best Christmas present I'd had since I opened my Johnny Seven in 1966.

THE HOLLIES, 50TH ANNIVERSARY TOUR, SAGE GATESHEAD, 14 APRIL 2012

The Hollies were a benevolent presence throughout my childhood years during the 1960s. Their clean-cut image and catchy songs meant that parents often approved of and enjoyed their music, whilst their quintessential '60s vibe also gave them mass appeal with teens. I used to buy old juke box singles from the pub over the road. "Bus Stop" was one that I played and played time and again on a little child-sized record player. The Hollies may not have had the social (or musical) significance of the Stones, the Beatles, or the Who, but they were a very important part of the 1960s, particularly in the UK.

I'd seen the band many times over the years and with several lineups due to the loss of key members, in particular Graham Nash and Alan Clarke. By 2012, new singer Peter Howarth had been with the band eight years, and was as natural in the lead singer role as anyone could be. So, when their 50th anniversary tour was announced, I was keen to go along and celebrate the band's legacy.

I was in a cheap seat looking down on the stage. As ever the band were 100 percent professional and presented us with an evening of classic 1960s songs. Tony Hicks still looked great and displayed some nifty fret work on his electric sitar during the intro to "The Baby" and some great banjo on the intro to "Stop Stop Stop." Bobby was the elder statesman in the band and kept them all on track from the "engine room" (Peter's term) at the back.

This was another great show from a band who just keep on going. The set had remained largely unchanged for the past few years. However, for this gig, the band had reinterpreted several of the songs, and given them something fresh. "Look Through Any Window" had been completely rearranged. "King Midas in Reverse" was sung by Steve Lauri, rather than Peter. Peter performed "Can't Tell the Bottom from the Top" alone with an acoustic guitar, giving it new life. They had also added a couple of songs which were hits in Scandinavia, namely "Stewball" and "Very Last Day." However, it was the big hits that evoked the strongest reactions from the audience, many of them clapping with delight as soon as they recognised the intro to their favourite song.

Indeed, the Hollies are a band for whom the audience consists of almost exclusively older (over sixty) people. When going to see other 1960s bands such as the Who or the Stones, there are plenty of younger faces mixed in with the ageing crowd. However, the Hollies always attract an older demographic. "Music is an omnipresent component of many people's lives . . . used to set moods, mark milestones and connect to one's personal history" (Harmon and Adams, 2018).

GRATEFUL DEAD, LIVE SCREENING EVENT , "FARE THEE WELL: CELEBRATING 50 YEARS OF GRATEFUL DEAD," EMPIRE CINEMA, NEWCASTLE, 6 JULY 2015

Twenty years after their last concert, the remaining members of the Grateful Dead (Mickey Hart, Bill Kreutzmann, Phil Lesh, and Bob Weir) returned to Soldier Field in Chicago for a historic performance. The four members were joined by Trey Anastasio (guitar), Jeff Chimenti (keyboards), and Bruce Hornsby (piano). The Dead reunited for a series of five concerts (three in Chicago and two in San Francisco where it all started), which was entitled *Fare Thee Well: Celebrating 50 Years of Grateful Dead* and grossed an amazing $52.2 million in ticket sales (Press release, 2015). The Pay to View package, included footage from the band's Levi Stadium San Francisco shows (attended by 151,650 fans) and the Soldier Field Chicago shows (attended by 210,283 people). The collection of live broadcasts now holds the record for the largest syndication of a live music event ever (Waddell, 2015).

The Grateful Dead were, of course, formed in California in 1965 and rose to become one of the best-known bands of the psychedelic movement of the late 1960s. They were inducted into the Rock and Roll Hall of Fame in 1994 and have sold over 35 million albums worldwide. The last time the Dead played live together was in July 1995, just one month before the tragic death of the band's lead guitarist and singer, Jerry Garcia. The demand for the reunion concerts was incredible, and I was delighted that UK fans would have a chance to be part of the event via the live broadcast.

The final Chicago concert was screened at more than 250 cinemas across the UK on the evening of Monday 6 July, the day after the last ever Dead show. It was a delayed screening; a live broadcast was impractical, given the six-hour time difference between the UK and Chicago.

I went with Laura and Dale to watch the film and joined a small group of UK Deadheads who wanted to see the band "live" one more time. I have to admit being unsure what to expect. My only other live encounter with the Dead was when they played Newcastle City Hall in 1972, and I didn't quite get what all the fuss was about. However, I'd come to appreciate the band's legacy and their influence on psychedelic music and the hippy culture. Laura and Dale didn't know much of the band other than their cultural significance.

Despite not being the biggest of fans, we all really enjoyed the movie. The songs, as always in a Dead concert, progressed into extended jams, but were never boring. I even enjoyed the "Drums" solo, which was followed by a lengthy "Space" piece involving trippy electronic sounds and heavy use of theremin. You could feel the love and respect that the fans have for this band, and see how moved Phil Lesh and Bob Weir in particular were by the whole event. If this was really the end, it was a very fitting way to close the final chapter of the career of a band who have meant so much to so many people, and touched fans throughout the world.

As Adams (2000) describes, fans of the Grateful Dead (Deadheads) are not the typical music fan. They adhere to and embrace an ethos similar to that of the 1960s counter-culture. Peaceful living, sharing resources, and free expression are some of the things which Deadheads value (Adams, 2000). These shared value structures create a community and shared identity which is why the concert experience was always central to being a Deadhead. Even fifty years on, those who have been personally influenced by the Deadhead subculture still wish to feel a sense of community and unity which the concerts provided for so many.

BLACK SABBATH, SHEFFIELD ARENA, 14 DECEMBER 2013

My friend Norm and I went to see those mighty metal pioneers Black Sabbath in concert at Sheffield Arena. It had been over thirty years since I had last seen Sabbath, so we were really looking forward to revisiting our youth and reminding ourselves who the true gods of metal were.

We left around 4 p.m. and drove down to Sheffield arriving just after 6 p.m. There was time for a bite to eat at one of the pubs over the road from the arena, before we walked over to the venue. We passed on the attractive but quite pricey merchandise and caught the support act, who were a young new UK band called Uncle Acid and the Dead Beats. Uncle Acid and the Dead Beats had been described as "the original Alice Cooper band jamming in a cell with early Black Sabbath and the Stooges" (and that summed them up pretty well (Metal Blade Records, 2013). Their heavy, dark riffs filled the hall and prepared the crowd for the main act.

The crowd was a mix of heavy rock and metal fans of all ages; old-timers like us, and young metalheads, everyone knows how important Sabbath are in the history of heavy metal and classic rock. Right on time at 8:30 p.m.,

Black Sabbath took to the stage. We had standing tickets and made our way as close to the front as we could get. We knew what to expect, Norm had been watching a DVD of Sabbath on tour in Australia earlier this year, so we were anticipating a set full of classics. And that's exactly what we got; Ozzy and the guys took us right back to their first album, and played all those great 1970s metal anthems, with a few songs thrown in from their new album *13*.

The crowd were all completely committed and immersed in the experience. Bennet describes how "the re-connecting with one's youth both liberates the individual from the present whilst allowing for the acceptance of one's current situation" (Bennett, 2013). Indeed, Bennett argues that there is a healthiness to, from time to time, reconnecting with the past as it allows one to strengthen identity whilst also appreciating the present. Certainly, the older members of the audience that night were connecting with a past self in a very real, immediate way.

The packed arena was up and ready for a night of classic heavy metal. From the first chords of opening song "War Pigs," everyone had their hands in the air, waving back at Ozzy who goaded us to "Go F***ing Crazy!" The sound was clear, loud, and crisp, and the playing excellent; all four band members were rocking, giving it full throttle and volume throughout the entire set. I had feared that they might not have been able to cut it anymore, but they delivered 100 percent and then some.

Ozzy looked pretty fit, and his voice was in much better shape that I had hoped or expected. The guy still had stamina and kept the fast pace going all night. Tony Iommi's guitar playing switched between exquisite dark, doomy riffs and impressive solos, and Geezer Butler stood solid, pounding thunderous classic metal rhythms from his bass. It was sad that Bill Ward wasn't with them on the tour, but explosive new dynamo drummer Tommy Clufetos did an excellent job, full of energy and power. The stage set was impressive with large screens showing a mix of live videos of the band, and images of darkness, doom, war, and blasphemy underlining that we were witnessing *the* classic dark heavy metal band. The show was almost exactly two hours, and included "Snowblind," "Black Sabbath," "N.I.B.," "Fairies Wear Boots," and "Iron Man." The encore just had to be "Paranoid." Stunning, powerful stuff. Sabbath showed us just what heavy metal is and can be, and for me that night they reclaimed their crown as the hardest, darkest rock band on the planet. Sometimes the old guys are still the best.

We left the Motorpoint Arena at 10:30, drove up the MI, A1, and the A19 and were back home safe just before 12:30 a.m., our ears still ringing, and thoughts of a classic rock band running through our heads, some forty-plus years since we first saw and heard them.

THE WHO, WEMBLEY ARENA, 13 FEBRUARY 2016

The Who returned to their home turf to play a one-off gig at Wembley Arena. Roger Daltrey had been suffering from viral meningitis, which resulted in the postponement of the last leg of their American tour, and this gig was slotted in by way of a warm-up before the band returned to the United States to play the rearranged dates. Roger looked and sounded well, although he did tell us that he wasn't 100 percent and that his "legs weren't fully there." Well, it didn't show. This was another classic Who performance, easily on par with, if not surpassing, their Hyde Park show of the previous summer.

A sold-out crowd of locals and die-hard Who fans from across Europe gave the band the rousing London welcome they deserved. The Who Hits 50! tour was a celebration of the amazing legacy of a legendary band who have given us so much over the years. This was my twenty-first (I think) Who live experience, and the third time I'd seen them on that tour, having caught the first leg at Newcastle Arena in late 2014 and the Hyde Park gig the previous summer. The set was largely the same, although it had become slightly shorter with openers "I Can't Explain" and "Substitute" being dropped, as had their early attempt at a mini opera "A Quick One (While He's Away)." We were treated to the inclusion of the instrumental "The Rock" as part of a trio of songs from *Quadrophenia*.

The evening started with a slideshow which took us through the history of the band, and featured many great images of the late Keith Moon and John Entwistle. This tour was a celebration of their legacy and contribution to music, as well as a run through of some of the Who's greatest songs. The band walked on stage and launched straight into "Who Are You?" and away we went on another amazing journey through so many classic tunes; a history of this extraordinary band, and also of our own lives and memories.

The giant screen behind the stage displayed powerful full-face images of Roger, Pete, Keith, and John, along with clips of the Who in the 1960s and the 1970s and clips from *Quadrophenia*. The sound was crisp; I was sitting halfway back on the terrace to the left of the stage, and every note was very clear. The first part of the set featured early classics: "The Seeker," "Pictures of Lily," "The Kids Are Alright," "My Generation," and my personal favourite "I Can See for Miles." Then we moved swiftly to the '70s and the haunting "Behind Blue Eyes" followed by "Bargain" from "Who's Next," "Join Together," and "You Better You Bet." The aforementioned segment from *Quadrophenia* followed. "Eminence Front" is not my favourite track, so I took the opportunity to have a walk around the arena, finding a spot downstairs on the floor towards the back. I spent the rest of evening there, enjoying the band and observing the crowd singing along, dancing, and generally going wild.

The songs from *Tommy* followed, culminating in a powerful crowd sing-along to "Listening to You," which always gets me. I knew we were on the home stretch. Roger's voice was holding out fine, and Pete was full of power and angst, twirling and twirling his arm, and squeezing great solos out of his Fender Stratocaster. The familiar minimalist synthesiser intro signalled "Baba O'Reilly," which then led into closing song "Won't Get Fooled Again," as raw and relevant as ever. Pure class. Pete introduced the band, and they left the stage at around 10:30 p.m. I took the two-minute walk across the road to the Wembley Hilton. Pete said at the end, "Hope to see you again." Yes, indeed, hope so.

STATUS QUO, NEWCASTLE CITY HALL, 6 DECEMBER 2017

I have been a long-term Status Quo fan, ever since I saw them for the first time in 1971. I must have seen them over forty times since then, maybe even over fifty; I have lost count. For me, the band's success centred on the chemistry and relationship between singer/guitarist Francis Rossi and singer/rhythm guitarist Rick Parfitt. "Rick and his fellow singer/guitarist Francis Rossi made up the band's creative and between them set the band's matey, wise-cracking tone" (Press Association, 2016). After Rick's death in 2016, I thought I couldn't bring myself to go to see Status Quo again. I missed Rick. In fact, I missed Rick to the extent that I thought Status Quo shouldn't continue when he passed away. However, a year after his death, there I was in the City Hall waiting to see what the new band was like.

Francis told us that the *Last of the Electrics* tour, the last tour with Rick, would be just that; the last electric rock Status Quo tour. In fact, this show was originally announced as an acoustic tour, *Aquostic*. Somewhere along the line, Francis decided to go back to the rock show. Now I was partly looking forward to the acoustic concert, but I was also secretly pleased that this was going to be a rock tour. Anyway, as I said, there I was, a little against my better judgement, sitting in my chair at the end of the row waiting for my first dose of the new Status Quo.

The band were heralded onto stage with the usual drone, which led into those opening chords of "Caroline," which always hit me emotionally and signify the beginning of yet another evening spent with my old Status Quo friends. I was glad to hear new guitarist, Richie Malone, did justice to Rick's power chords; however, they took on a new resonance, signifying that one of my Quo pals, Rick, was not there that night.

The set was a mixture of old favourites such as "Little Lady" and "Softer Ride," as well as newer "Creeping, Up on You" and "The Oriental." The usual Status Quo medley of hits contained some other old favourites "Down the Dust Pipe" and "Railroad" and was swiftly followed by the loud, driving chords of "Down Down," which always signify that the show is drawing to a close. They ended, as they always do, with "Rockin' All over the World." The encore began with the classic "Don't Waste My Time" from the equally classic album *Piledriver*, followed by (the little too middle-of-the-road/poppy for me) "Burning Bridges" and they finally ended with, as always, "Bye Bye Johnny."

Well, all things considered, the evening was actually pretty good, and I found myself still enjoying it all despite my misgivings. So, Status Quo were back, and, you know, they were actually pretty good. I even re-joined the fan club. So, in the lyrics of "Beginning of the End," "Happy days are here again."

1960s GOLD TOUR, THE SAGE GATESHEAD, 8 NOVEMBER 2011

I can't resist classic 1960s bands and, somehow, the prospect of a showcase-style concert, featuring a number of bands from my childhood really caught my attention. This particular show featured Gerry Marsden, the Searchers, the Fortunes, and Chip Hawkes. I'd bought two cheap tickets up in the gallery looking down onto the stage many months in advance for the show. However, when it came to the night of the concert and after a very hectic day at work, I was feeling exhausted and was in two minds as to whether to go. I was also still feeling tired after seeing Roy Harper that weekend in London. However, David said he'd come along with me, so off we went to the Sage.

My prime reason for buying the tickets was to see the Fortunes, as I'd seen the other bands on the bill. When we arrived, the Fortunes were on stage. They performed a pretty slick set of their hits such as "You've Got Your Troubles" and "Storm in Teacup." The band has been touring consistently since the 1960s, the lineup having changed along the way, with the last of the original band members, Rod Allen, sadly passing away in 2008.

It was interesting to me how a band without any original members could be embraced as being, still, the same band that it was all those years ago. The Fortunes were accepted and treated as if they were the authentic article, however, part of me wondered what it is that makes a band a band, and whether the legacy and band's history were enough to carry its spirit forward. According to Kotarba (2015), nostalgia can forgive and overlook many things. For instance, the songs and the fact that there has been a progression and lineage to the Fortune's is enough to keep fans connecting with their work. "Music itself can connect an individual to a specific moment in their life and regardless of whether this music is true to the original, it is the particular song, melody or lyrics which acts as a bridge between an individual and the past" (Kotarba, 2015).

Our compere for the night (yes, this was a proper, variety style show) then introduced the Searchers. I'd seen the Searchers on a number of occasions, the last being around ten years or so before. They always put on a professional show, and this was no exception with the hits "Needles and Pins," "Don't Throw Your Love Away," and "What Have They Done to the Rain" still sounding great. Guitarist John McNally was seventy that year and singer Frank Allen couldn't have been far behind him (yet, they still clearly enjoy playing and showed no sign of slowing down).

David and I were both tired and beat a retreat home during the intermission. I remember thinking . . . I'm getting too old for this!

THE ROLLING STONES, HYDE PARK, 13 JULY 2013

When I walked out of the O2 in London in August 2007 after seeing the Rolling Stones at the end of the *Bigger Bang* tour, I really thought I had seen them for the last time. Even I, as a lifelong Stones fan, couldn't have imagined that they would be back five years later and that they would deliver a series of concerts which would easily match and, in some ways eclipse, their concert tours of the 1970s and 1980s. But as David and I walked out of Hyde Park, I felt I had seen them do just that.

In whatever way you measure it the *50 and Counting* tour was a massive success and the Stones legacy remained intact, nay, enhanced, by the stunning performances that Jagger and Co. delivered. I had the privilege of attending three shows on the tour: the opening night at the O2 in November, their overwhelmingly successful Pyramid stage debut at Glastonbury a couple of weeks prior to this gig, and then the last night of the tour in London's Hyde Park, their hometown and the setting for their iconic show of 1969.

I took the train down to London on Saturday afternoon and met David at Marble Arch at 6 p.m. I was staying at the Cumberland hotel just over the road. We had a drink in the hotel bar and then wandered over to the park. Jake Bugg was on stage as we made our way in through the crowds. The weather was hot, almost unbearably so; in fact, this was the hottest day of the year so far. I'd been invited by Barclaycard to try out their new contactless wristband, which I had loaded with £20 to spend in the park. We spotted the Barclaycard Unwind stand and wandered over to ask which food outlets accepted payment through my wristband, and how we could access the Unwind bar. The lady assured us that most food stalls took it and directed us towards the bar, which was behind the stage. Now our tickets were cheap (£100!) standard General Access, which didn't actually allow access to the bar or the areas close to the stage. Still, we followed her directions, and walked through a couple of gates without being challenged and ended up in the backstage bar and with access to the Tier 2 area close to the stage. Result! We had a burger and a coke each which just about used up the money on my wristband and found a spot to watch the Stones.

One thing struck me about the crowd. I would say the majority were in their twenties or thirties. Sure there were some old guys like me but not too many. And everyone knew all the songs and sang along and danced. Hogarty explores the importance retro culture has within post-2000s youth culture. "Retro culture is the result of an inseparable mix of cultural and technological changes" (Hogarty, 2016). With many bands such as White Stripes and the Kings of Leon citing the Stones as an influence, many younger people have come to their music. The digital availability of listening to music from the past has meant that younger audiences have been able to easily access the Stones' output and appreciate the impact they have had upon their own cultural icons. This was much more a Stones crowd than at Glastonbury and you could feel the difference. The sound, the visuals, and the atmosphere were all much better. No guest, but what we did get were "Ruby Tuesday" and "Emotional Rescue," both of which I hadn't seen played for some time. For me the highlight of the tour had become "Paint It Black" along with "Gimme Shelter" and "Sympathy for the Devil"; but "Ruby Tuesday" was equally stunning with the whole place singing along.

You just couldn't fault the band. It felt as though they really were at the top of their game; Jagger seemed so fit and so confident; Keith came across as so cool and characterful; Ronnie more than makes up for any of Keith's shortcomings and shines through as the musical backbone of the band along with Charlie who was, well, just Charlie and who actually said "Hello" to the crowd. Oh, and I can't forget to mention Mick Taylor who must have felt like the luckiest guy in the world and who pushed the band to greater heights in "Midnight Rambler."

As David and I left the park, the riff from "Satisfaction" still ringing in our ears, my wondering started again. Could this be the last time? This time it felt like it wouldn't be.

BOB DYLAN, BLACKPOOL OPERA, HOUSE 24 NOVEMBER 2013

This was my first visit to Blackpool, and it was for a pretty special occasion. Laura and I were going to see the one and only Bob Dylan in concert at the

Blackpool Opera House. This was my sixteenth Bob Dylan concert experience, and Laura's second. For the first time, I'd struck really lucky and managed to score front row seats. I bought the tickets the minute that they went on sale, and was amazed to find that we were sitting right down the front.

We set off for Blackpool around 3 p.m. and arrived just before 6 p.m., after a nice drive over the A66 and down the M6. I could see the Blackpool tower lit up from miles away as we drove in. The Opera House was quite easy to locate, being part of the Winter Gardens Complex, right in the centre of town. We ran into some old friends, had a chat about Dylan, and there was just time for a quick Italian meal before show time. We also spent a little time hunting for a stick of Blackpool rock to take back for Marie, but everything was closed on a Sunday night, so we sadly failed in that task.

Dylan was on a short tour of the UK, calling at Glasgow, Blackpool, and the Albert Hall; playing three nights at each venue. This was his first visit to Blackpool, and it seemed a little strange, but very welcome choice. "There is something quite perfect about Dylan playing Blackpool . . . framing the gig with its beautiful Victoriana, the venue and indeed the town itself lends a perfect backdrop to events like this" (Scott, 2013). There is a feeling of old grandeur about Blackpool, a mix of greatness, tradition, and the past, yet a validity within the present; all of which sits well with the legend that is Dylan. I imagined him wandering the streets and arcades after sound-check. I wonder if he did . . . ?

We were attending the final night of Dylan's three consecutive shows in the venue. The Opera House is a lovely ornate hall, which holds just short on 3,000 people, and reminded me of the Odeon cinemas I would visit as a kid. It's a small intimate venue, compared to the arenas which Dylan normally played when he visited the UK. In recent concerts, Dylan had been playing a lot of tracks from his latest album, *Tempest*, with a few classics thrown in; so, Laura and I knew what to expect.

The audience itself was mainly grey-haired, older fans such as myself, although there were a few younger faces. "It was one of those nights where the word, 'legend' was muttered regularly by an audience of ageing disciples in awe of Dylan" (Scott, 2013). It was clear even before he'd set foot on the stage that being here meant so much to so many people. "Stars always represent the ideals of individualism and democracy" and Dylan himself has, for many, come to symbolise a vast transition of cultural, political, and social structures, which, for many people attending the concert, still holds deep significance (Marshall, 2007). Indeed, aside from his musical legacy, Dylan is a figurehead of change, changes which many of the audience members would have lived through.

Dylan and his band came on stage at 7:30 p.m. prompt without any introduction. The opening song was "Things Have Changed," a song from the film *Wonder Boys*, which was released as a single in 2000. It was clear from the start that Bob was on good form and in good voice, and the sound was crisp and clear from where we sat (there had been reports of poor sound on the first night in Blackpool). It was great to have such a close and unobstructed view of Bob and his band. Dylan alternated between standing at the mike centre stage (no guitar this tour), and playing a small grand piano which was to stage right. His band were excellent and featured three guitarists: Stu on acoustic rhythm, Charlie on electric lead, and Donnie on pedal steel, mandolin, banjo, and violin. On the last couple of occasions I'd seen Bob Dylan in concert, his voice had sounded stronger than it had for many years. He seemed to have settled into a deep, snarling raspy groove, not unlike Tom Waits. This gave the songs a dark, bluesy feel. There was more emotion in his voice, and it appears that he means every phrase.

The set was, as expected, drawn largely from *Tempest*. I had the album, and had played it a number of times, but the songs still weren't yet familiar to me. However, even lesser-known songs still sounded good, as did old favourites "She Belongs to Me," "Tangled up in Blue," and "Simple Twist of Fate." The encore was a great version of "All Along the Watchtower" with a slower, moodier arrangement than the usual rockier version that Dylan had been playing around that time, and a new song "Roll on John," which was about John Lennon. This was a surprise, as the last song had been "Blowing in the Wind" on other nights of the tour.

The crowd cheered loudly when he started "Roll on John"; it's a crowd favourite already and the end of each verse was the cue for another cheer. Bob spoke to the crowd only once, to announce the intermission. He seemed in a good mood and quite animated at times, with some staccato leg movements while he was at the mike, and some little twists while at the piano. A great performance by a legend that just continues to please. The show finished around 9:45 p.m., and we were home shortly before 1 a.m.

CONCLUSION

And so, my journey comes to an end. Of course, it will never really come to an end; at least not while there is breath within me and I am well enough to travel to concerts.

This final set of narrative accounts covers bands and artists who I have stuck with throughout my life. The Rolling Stones and the Who are both particularly, and equally, important to me. I was lucky enough to witness performances by these bands in my youth. The performances left such an indelible mark upon me that I continue to worship these bands to this day. The Rolling Stones are, of course, legendary, and I really do believe that they deserve the title "The Greatest Rock 'n' Roll Band in the World." I also believe that, like me, they will continue with music as long as it is physically possible; that is why Jagger and Richards survive and are well enough to perform. I really don't think they will ever announce a farewell show or concert tour. They will simply go on and on as long as they are able.

Now, the Who are very different. They comprise only two original members now, Pete Townshend and Roger Daltrey, and yet their performances feature previous members Keith Moon and John Entwistle. Keith and John appear on the screen as a tribute, but also as an integral part of the performance. Somehow, the music, the performance, the image, and the soul of the band has succeeded in transcending the membership. The strong mod ethos of the band remains, as does their tremendous back catalogue of rock and pop anthems. Of course, the band is not the same and never will be, however, their performances remain powerful, authentic, and true to the soul of the Who.

Other bands, such as the Hollies and Status Quo, have also seen key members leave, or pass on. However, again in part a result of the strength of their back catalogue, the bands live on and audiences still go to see them to hear their favourite songs performed once again.

Some bands, such as 1960s band the Fortunes, have no original members, raising the question "When is a band no longer a band?" I guess the answer is as long as people will go to see them and want to hear their music performed live.

If there is one band that I have followed consistently over the past forty-plus years, it is the Groundhogs. The first time I saw the Groundhogs was at Newcastle City Hall in February 1971, when they were support act for the Rolling Stones. This was, of course, the classic power trio lineup of McPhee on guitar, Pete Cruikshank on bass, and Ken Pustelnik on drums. I didn't know who was supporting the Stones until I got into the hall, and they introduced them as they came on stage. So, it was a nice surprise to find out I was about to witness my first Groundhogs gig. This was just around the time that they released *Split*, and their (very short) set comprised a few songs from that and *Thank Christ for the Bomb*. The Groundhogs set was particularly short that night, as there were two performances of the Rolling Stones show, the first being from 6:30 to 8:30 p.m., which didn't allow the support act to play for much more than half an hour. The Leeds University gig of the tour was recorded and released as the *Live at Leeds* EP, which shows the set as being: "Cherry Red," "Garden," "Split Part One," "Groundhogs Blues," and "Eccentric Man." That night I became a lifelong Groundhogs fan. Their music was a unique mix of blues and rock, and they were truly at the height of their powers at the time. I saw this original classic lineup four more times over the next year or so; at Newcastle City Hall, Sunderland Bay Hotel, Newcastle Mayfair, and Sunderland Top Rank.

Over the next fifty years or so, I must have seen the Groundhogs more than fifty times. Thinking about it, they cross several themes of this book. I have seen them at many venues including concert halls, public houses, nightclubs, and working men's clubs over the years; they span the venues theme. They are also truly iconic to me; indeed, Tony McPhee is a lifelong hero and an icon in my eyes. They also touch on maturity. The Groundhogs continued to play until quite recently. Sadly, Tony McPhee is now not so well, and gigs have been few and far between. They are a very special band to me and deserve a special mention. Along with Status Quo, they are probably the band that I have seen the most times, which speaks for itself.

As I get older, the chances to see such mature rock bands become fewer and fewer. I feel that I must grasp each opportunity as it comes, as it may be the last. I was discussing this with my friend John, who now lives in the United States, the other day. He certainly will now drive hundreds of miles to see classic bands such as Uriah Heep and Ten Years After, as he feels that he should take the opportunity while he can.

Another aspect of maturity is that many of the fans now have the disposable income to travel and see bands again. Some of them are returning to see their heroes again after many years. We all had families, commitments, and mortgages to pay. Now, in our mature years, these commitments are gone and we can return to investing in seeing our heroes again and even educating our children about the music of our youth.

Conclusion

I set out initially to answer my two research questions:

- What constitutes a "good" live performance?
- What are the crucial elements of a live performance?

However, having considered my narrative accounts and my ten themes, I now realise that rock performance is much more multifaceted and complex than I had first imagined. Many different influences add to the rich texture of rock performance. These include, among others, the venue, the audience itself, the artist, the interactions and relationship between the audience and the performer, the technologies surrounding the performance, the lighting, the theatricals, the individual and who accompanies them to the performance, the excitement of buying tickets and travelling to the venue, the mood of the attendee on that particular evening and the allegiance of the attendee to the artist or band. All of these contribute to a lesser or greater extent to the experience of attending a rock performance. What is a great rock show to one person may be viewed very differently by another.

One thing that I have not covered, until now, is the importance of one's first rock performance experience. The first concert I attended was by the Bonzo Dog Band, Roy Harper, Yes, and Mad Dog at Sunderland Empire Theatre on 8 March 1969. I was twelve years old. First gigs are especially important (Sylvan, 2002). They can shape one's musical taste and set allegiances for life. For me, this gig set me on an unavoidable path to becoming obsessed with seeing bands and with rock music in general, and gave me a lifelong interest in Yes and Roy Harper, aligning my "self" with these artists (McCloud, 2003). I can still remember aspects of this gig more than fifty years later as I write this. I sat fascinated at the performers on stage and entranced by the loud music. In fact, the volume was a particularly important part of the experience for me, in a similar way that McKinnon (2010) discusses the importance of loud volume to heavy metal fans and during heavy rock concerts.

The bands seemed very loud to me; I was frightened that my hearing would be damaged, something which McKinnon (2010) also alludes to. I experienced something that one might term as "euphoria," and sitting in the front row in a hall full of rock fans I felt I was part of a common experience, almost religious in its nature (Galbraith, 2014). In that moment, during my first concert, I was enjoying a spiritual experience (Inglis, 2017; Sylvan, 2002) which I was to return to many times throughout my life.

Another aspect of this book has been the importance of my blog, and writing about rock music and performance. Without the narrative accounts, I would not have been able to analyse my concert experiences. In order to truly understand the phenomenon which is rock performance, it is vital that rock fans make a written record of their experiences. Only by doing so, will we be able to understand rock performance. Twelve years ago, I started my blog to catalogue my concert experiences (Smith, 2015a). I started to blog each day to catalogue my concert experiences. As quite a private person, it was somewhat unlike me to reveal my concert experiences to the world, however I felt an emotional and creative need to do so (Fullwood et al., 2015). It is important to link the emotional and personal to the accounts of rock performances.

My analysis also drew out the following themes:

- Personal context. The narrative accounts revealed how important my own personal context was to the concert experience; who I went with, how old I was at the time, how I travelled to and from the concert, and the social and political context in which the performance was set. Concerts are very personal experiences and how we view each performance is very subjective. Are we with friends who we are comfortable with? Have we had a good day at work, or argued with our partner? How much have we had to drink? All of these, and many other, factors affect our experience of the rock performance. The totality of the performance is much broader than what takes place in the venue; it is everything which surrounds that.
- Rock concert as "church." Several authors (Cohen, 2016; Harmon, 2014; Pattie, 2007) have written about rock concerts having the status of religious experiences, with the masses travelling to worship their "gods." Many rock fans talk about rock music becoming their "religion," and whether they are serious or not, it really does become a religion for them. They follow their idols in the same way that others follow religious icons; the venue becomes the church, with the audience taking the part of the congregation. This mirrors the same sort of devotion which one encounters and experi-

ences in churches; for example, in those where singing is an integral part of the religious experience, such as in gospel choirs within churches. To those of us who have our idols, these religious experiences are very real and have deep and prolonged meaning, which carries on long after the performance itself has concluded. We carry the memory, and the feeling, of the performance with us for many months, or years to come. It lingers in our memories and we treasure the experience, returning to it several times. Time will, without doubt, alter our memories; these may become stronger and may begin to twist the reality of the performance, or they may dwindle with time, until we get to the point where we can no longer distinguish true memory from a false, imagined memory of how we think the performance was. I have compared my accounts with those of my family and friends who accompanied me to some of the concerts and often our memories of what happened are very different.

- Epiphany. Several writers have written about how they experienced a personal "epiphany" at a rock concert. Morrisey felt that nothing was ever the same once he had seen the Sex Pistols at Manchester Lesser Free Trade Hall (Morrissey, 2013). Others have written of rock concerts as life-changing experiences; Peter Hook also wrote of how his life changed when he first attended the same Sex Pistols concert (Albiez, 2006). In my own case, the closest I got to such an experience was experiencing Bruce Springsteen in concert for the first time in London in 1976 and seeing the Sex Pistols in Whitby in the same year. In both cases, I had a sense that I was observing something very special, which transformed my outlook on music for ever. Some of this was, undoubtedly, brought about by the publicity I had read about the artist prior to the concert. I went along, expecting to see something different, exciting, and almost "life changing." In both cases I was not disappointed. Other instances where I felt something special was happening were at major events such as the Live Aid concert in Wembley Stadium in 1985. My strongest memory is of walking out of the stadium, still singing "Feed the World"; there was a shared feeling that we had experienced something special and in our own small way made a difference to the world. And finally, the Led Zeppelin reunion concert in the O2 Arena, London. Here, we all felt privileged at attending such a special, exclusive event.

And so, I come to the end of my writings. This book has taken Laura and I many hours, indeed many years, to compile. It began as a labour of love and continues to be so. I set out many years ago when I first started writing my blog to catalogue my experiences, and then began to question "what makes a really good rock performance?" And so, I started a journey through my concert experiences looking for the answer. Along the way, I suffered a life-changing accident which has left me paralysed from the neck down in a wheelchair, still loving music and still going to concerts, although the logistics and practicalities of this have become much more difficult and complex. As I come to the end, I realise that rock performance is such a complex and personal experience that it is not possible to perform a complete and thorough analysis of the phenomenon. Rather, one can explore themes, such as I have done in this book, or using a schema such as that provided in the excellent works of Auslander; see for example Auslander (2008).

Perhaps, that is how it was always meant to be. Perhaps, to understand the complexities of the rock performance phenomenon would somehow distract from the experience. Perhaps, that is one of the reasons why I am drawn to the magic of rock music, particularly in its live form. I am looking for the Holy Grail; that magic performance that will stay with me forever. And one day, perhaps I will find it.

I hope you have enjoyed reading my experiences of rock concerts, and what they mean to me. I certainly have enjoyed writing about them. This takes me to the end of a project which has taken many years to complete.

References

Adams, R. G. (2000). *Deadheads Social Science: You Ain't Gonna Learn What You Don't Wanna Know.* Lanham, MD: Rowman & Littlefield.

Albiez, S. (2006). "Print the truth, not the legend: Sex Pistols, Lesser Free Trade Hall, 4 June 1976" In Ian Inglis (ed.) *Performance and Popular Music: History, Place and Time.* Abingdon: Routledge, 92–106.

Albrecht, M. M. (2008). "Acting naturally unnaturally: The performative nature of authenticity in contemporary popular music." *Text and Performance Quarterly*, 28(4), 379–395.

Allen, K. (2014a). "Behind the aura: The risky business of Lady Gaga." Rock's Backpages, Planet Notion.

Allen, K. (2014b). "Kate Bush: *Before the Dawn*, Hammersmith Apollo, London." Disorder. Available from https://www.rocksbackpages.com/Library/Article/kate-bush-ibefore-the-dawni-hammersmith-apollo-london. Accessed 14 January 2021.

Altham, K. (1973). "Deep Purple: Who do Purple think they are?" *New Musical Express.* (1973). Available from http://www.rocksbackpages.com/Library/Article/deep-purple-who-do-purple-think-they-are. Accessed 2nd of September 2019.

Alves, T.M.D.S.V. (2017–2018). Patti Smith: Female neo-beat Sensibility and the development of punk. Master's thesis, University of Nottingham.

Anderton, C. (2011). "Music festival sponsorship: Between commerce and carnival." *Arts Marketing: An International Journal*, 1(2), 145–158.

Anderton, C. (2018). *Music Festivals in the UK: Beyond the Carnivalesque.* London: Routledge.

Ando, H., Cousins, R., & Young, C. (2014, January). "Achieving saturation in thematic analysis: Development and refinement of a codebook." *Comprehensive Psychology.*

Arvidsson, A. (2013). *Political Rock.* Edited by Mark Pedelty & Kristine Weglarz. Farnham: Ashgate.

Aubrey, C., Shearlaw, J., & Eavis, M. (2005). *Glastonbury: An Oral History of the Music, Mud & Magic.* London: Ebury Press.

Auslander, P. (1998). "Seeing is believing: Live performance and the discourse of authenticity in rock culture." *Literature and Psychology*, 44 (4), 1.

Auslander, P. (2004). "Performance analysis and popular music: A manifesto." *Contemporary Theatre Review*, 14(1), 1–13.

Auslander, P. (2008). *Liveness: Performance in a Mediatized Culture*. London: Routledge.

Auslander, P. (2009). "Musical persona: The physical performance of popular music." In D. Scott (ed.) *The Ashgate Research Companion to Popular Musicology*. London: Routledge, 303–316.

Auslander, P. (2016). "Twenty-first-century girl: Lady Gaga, performance art, and glam." In Ian Chapman & Henry Johnson (eds.) *Global Glam and Popular Music*. London: Routledge, 190–204.

Bannister, F. (2003). *There Must Be a Better Way*. Cambridge: Bath Books.

Barbra Streisand, website. (2020). Biography. Available from https://barbrastreisand.com/biography/. Accessed 5 November 2020.

Barton, G. (1975). "Kraftwerk: Mayfair Ballroom, Newcastle." Rock's Backpages, Sounds.

Barton L. (2004, July 16). "Laura Barton goes on the trail of the 'guerrilla gig.'" *The Guardian*.

Battersby, T. (2018). "The Buxton Rock Festivals. UK Rock Festivals." Available from http://www.ukrockfestivals.com/buxton-73.html. Accessed 8 December 2021.

Baumeister, R. F., & Newman, L. S. (1994). "How stories make sense of personal experiences: Motives that shape autobiographical narratives." *Personality and Social Psychology Bulletin*, 20(6), 676–690.

Baxter-Moore, N. (2016). "The ties that bind: Springsteen fans reflect on the live concert experience." *Rock Music Studies*, 3(1), 80–104.

Bayton, M. (1992). "Out on the margins: Feminism and the study of popular music." *Women: A Cultural Review*, 3(1), 51–59.

BBC 6 Music Site. (2020). The 6 Music Festival. Available from https://www.bbc.co.uk/programmes/b03nj13d. Accessed 3 December 2020.

BBC News. (2018). "Maryport Blues Cancelation: Devastating." BBC News. Available from https://www.bbc.co.uk/news/uk-england-cumbria-44809915. Accessed 3 December 2020.

Beal, J. C. (2009). "'You're not from New York City, you're from Rotherham': Dialect and identity in British indie music." *Journal of English Linguistics*, 37(3), 223–240.

Bego, M. (2001). *Cher: If You Believe*. Lanham, MD: Taylor Trade Publications.

Belfast Review. (2017). *Belfast Telegraph*. Available from http://www.peggyseeger.com/raves/quotes/belfast-telegraph/. Accessed 20 May 2021.

Bell, M. (1976). "Kiss: Destroyer" Rock's Backpages, *New Musical Express*. https://www.nme.com

Bell, E. S. (2008). *Theories of Performance*. Thousand Oaks, CA: Sage.

Bennett, A. (2017). *Remembering Woodstock*. London: Routledge.

Bennett, A. (2013). *Music, Style and Aging: Growing Old Disgracefully?* Philadelphia, PA: Temple University Press.

Bickerdike, J. O. (2015). *The Secular Religion of Fandom: Pop Culture Pilgrim.* London: Sage.

Biggs, B., & Belchem, J. (2020). *Bluecoat, Liverpool: The UK's first arts centre.* Oxford, England: Oxford University Press.

Bingley Hall, website. (2020). Staffordshire County Show Ground. Available from https://www.staffscountyshowground.co.uk/hire-of-facilities/exhibition-halls/bingley-hall/. Accessed 10 November 2020.

Biophilia Education Project. (2019). About the Biophilia Education Project. Available from https://biophiliaeducational.org/about-biophilia-educational-project/. Accessed 12 January 2021.

Bird, E. (1994). ""Is that Me, Baby?': Image, Authenticity, and the Career of Bruce Springsteen." *American Studies*, 35(2), 39–57.

Bist, D., & Smith, P. (2021). "Music and spirituality: Reflections on the role of music and the natural environment in healing." *Journal for the Study of Spirituality*, 11(1), 75–86.

Black, J. (1999). *Loony Institution: Screaming Lord Such.* Austin, TX: Mojo.

Blair, A. (2016). "Marc Bolan, David Bowie and the Counter-Hegemonic Persona: Authenticities, Ephemeral Identities and the Fantastical Other." *MEDIANZ: Media Studies Journal of Aotearoa of New Zealand*, 15(1), 167–186.

Boucher, C. (2010). "Captain Beefheart Obituary." *The Guardian.* https://www.theguardian.com/music/2010/dec/18/captain-beefheart-don-van-liet-obituary.

Brocken, M. (2017). *The British Folk Revival: 1944–2002.* London: Routledge.

Brown, S. (2012). "Scream from the Heart: Yoko Ono's Rock 'n' Roll Revolution." *La Revue des Musiques Populaires.* Available from https://www.cairn-int.info/revue-volume-2012-2-page-107.htm?contenu=resume. Accessed 14 January 2021.

Butcher J (2012). "North punks Harry Hack and The Big G to release debut CD of 70s demos." *Evening Chronicle*, Newcastle 18 November 2012.

Calef, S. (ed.). (2011). *Led Zeppelin and Philosophy: All Will Be Revealed.* Vol. 44. Chicago: Open Court.

Cameron, K. & Gillespie, P. (1999). *The Enjoyment of the Theatre.* Boston: Allyn & Bacon.

Cannon, G. (1969) "The Rolling Stones, King Crimson, Family: Hyde Park, London." Rock's Backpages, New Society. http://www.rocksbackpages.com/Library/Article/the-rolling-stones-king-crimson-family-hyde-park-london. Accessed 30 October 2019.

Caroline. Posting on my Blog, 30 January, 2018. https://vintagerock.wordpress.com/2012/10/09/bob-dylan-earls-court-london-sat-17-june-1978/. Accessed 28 October 2019.

Charlesworth, C. (1973). "Slade, Sensational Alex Harvey Band: Earls Court, London." *Melody Maker* magazine.

Charlesworth, C. (1975). "The Who: Bingley Hall, Stafford." *Melody Maker* magazine.

Charlesworth, C. (2006). *Come on Feel the Noise: The Story of Slade.* London: Carlton Books LTD

Charlesworth, C (2014). "ABBA: Live at Wembley Arena." Rock's Backpages, Just Backdated.

Charone, B. (1975). "The Who's Bingley Bang." Rock's Backpages, Sounds.

Charone, B. (1976). "Rolling Stones: We're Nearly Famous." Rock's Backpages, Sounds.

Clayson, A., Jungr, B., & Johnson, R. (2004). *Woman: The Incredible Life of Yoko Ono*. Chrome Dreams.

Clifton, S. (2014). "Spinal cord injury and the joy of work." *Scandinavian Journal of Disability Research*, 16(4), 377–390.

Cobley, P. (1999). "Leave the Capitol." In R. Sabin (ed.) *Punk Rock: So, What The Cultural Legacy of Punk*. London: Routledge, 170–185.

Cochrane, T. (2010). "Using the persona to express complex emotions in music." *Music Analysis*, 29(1–3), 264–275.

Cohen, J. D. (2016). "Rock as Religion." *Intermountain West Journal of Religious Studies*, 7(1), 3.

Cohen, S. (2007). "The Clash Take on the World: Transnational Perspectives on the Only Band that Matter." Bloomsbury 3PL, 1 June 2017.

Colegrave, S., & Sullivan, C. (2001). *Punk: The Definitive Record of a Revolution*. New York: Thunder's Mouth Press.

Collins English Dictionary Online. (2019). https://www.collinsdictionary.com/dictionary/english. Accessed 3rd of September 2019.

Coon, C. (1982; 1988). *The New Wave Punk Rock Explosion*. London: Omnibus Press.

Craig, E. (2008). *On the Art of the Theatre*. New York: Routledge.

Crossley, N. (2009). "The man whose web expanded: Network dynamics in Manchester's post/punk music scene 1976–1980." *Poetics*, 37(1), 24–49.

Curtis, A. (2013). "Massive Attack V Adam Curtis." BBC Blogs. Available from https://www.bbc.co.uk/blogs/adamcurtis/entries/f431c7d1-3da0-3c56-bc67-fbc3bca2debc. Accessed 19 January 2021.

Damaso, J., & Cotter, C. (2007). UrbanDictionary.com. *English Today*, 23(2), 19.

Davidson, D. (2001). *Subjective, intersubjective, objective.* Volume 3. Oxford: Oxford University Press.

De Fina, A., & Georgakopoulou, A. (2019). *The handbook of narrative analysis.* New York: Wiley-Blackwell.

De Whalley, C. (1976). "Lynyrd Skynyrd: Hammersmith Odeon, London." *New Musical Express*. https://www.nme.com.

Delplanque P. (2010). "Rock Garden recollections." *Middlesbrough Gazette*, September 16.

Devereux, E., & Dillane, A. (2015). *David Bowie: Critical Perspectives*. New York: Routledge.

Dickinson, B. (2013). "Manchester International Festival: Do It 2013." *Art Monthly*. Available from search.proquest.com/openview/7aa08269db8a6d38f92904d3ec36f59/1?pq-origsite=gscholar&cbl=106011. Accessed 19 January 2021.

Doherty, H. (1976). "Queen: Hyde Park, London." Melody Maker Kiki Dee, Queen. Rock's Backpages. http://www.rocksbackpages.com/Library/Article/queen-hyde-park-london. Accessed 14 October 2019.

Dome, M. (2015) "Bees, Biting and Pig Heads: A History of the Monsters of Rock." *Louder Sound*. Available from https://www.loudersound.com/features/bees-biting-and-pig-s-heads-the-history-of-monsters-of-rock. Accessed 3 December 2020.

Dreier, P. (2011). "The Political Bob Dylan." *Dissent*. Available at https://www.dissentmagazine.org/online_articles/the-political-bob-dylan.

Driessen, S. (2019). "Celebrating Nostalgia or Critiquing Naivety: Reading Pop Music Reunions through the Discourses of Fan Life Course." *Journal of Fandom Studies*, 7(2), 133–150.

Dunn, S. Harkema, R., & McFadyen, S. (2014). *Super Duper Alice Cooper*. Documentary. Eagle Rock Entertainment.

Edgar, R., Fairclough-Isaacs, K., Halligan, B., & Spelman, N. (eds.) (2016). *The Arena Concert: Music, Media and Mass Entertainment*. New York: Bloomsbury.

Edwards J. T. (1984). "Rock 'n' roll, the gig, and time: An investigation of live communication as guerrilla rhetoric." Diss. Southern Illinois University at Carbondale.

Eldridge, R. (1970). "Screaming Lord Sutch: Heavy Friends Help the Lord's Come-Back." *Melody Maker* magazine.

Ellis, C., Adams, T. E., & Bochner, A. P. (2011). "Autoethnography: An overview." *Historical Social Research*, 273–290.

Eno, B. (2013). "Movements." Lecture at the Edinburgh Festival, Edinburgh.

Fadele, D. (1992). "Nick Cave and the Bad Seeds: Brixton Academy, London." *New Musical Express*. https://www.nme.com.

Feezell, J. T. (2017). "It's Not Only Rock and Roll: The Influence of Music Preferences on Political Attitudes." In Uche Onyebadi (ed.) *Music as a Platform for Political Communication*. Hershey, PA: IGI Global, 167–186.

Festival Listing (2013). "Movements, Brian Eno." Available from https://edinburghfestival.list.co.uk/event/346968-movements-brian-eno/. Accessed 12 January 2021.

Finnegan, R. (2003). "Music, experience, and the anthropology of emotion." In Martin Clayton, Trevor Herbert & Richard Middleton (eds.) *The cultural study of music: A critical introduction*. New York: Taylor and Francis, 181–192.

Fiske, J. (1992). "The cultural economy of fandom." In Lisa A. Lewis (ed.) *The adoring audience: Fan culture and popular media*. New York: Routledge, 30–49.

Fitzsimons, R. (2013). *I'm an Upstart: The Decca Wade Story*. Cottingham, UK: Ardra Press.

Flinn, J., and Frew, M. (2014). "Glastonbury: Managing the mystification of festivity." *Leisure Studies*, 33(4), 418–433.

Flett, K. (2004). "Cher's Farewell Tour: Glasgow SECC." *The Observer*.

Fonarow, W. (2013). *Empire of Dirt: The Aesthetics and Rituals of British Indie Music*. Middletown, CT: Wesleyan University Press.

Friedlander, P. (2018). *Rock and roll: A social history*. New York: Routledge.

Freedman, J. (2017). *Peggy Seeger: A Life of Music, Love and Politics*. Champaign: University of Illinois Press.

Frith, S. (1975). "Casing the Promised Land: Bruce Springsteen at Hammersmith Odeon." Rock's Backpages, Cream.

Frith, S. (1998). *Performing rites: On the value of popular music*. Cambridge, MA: Harvard University Press.

Frith, S. (2011). "Do-it-yourself! How 1950s youth culture changed the British live music business; how the British live music business shaped 1960s youth culture." Lecture at University of Sunderland.

Fullwood, C., Nicholls, W., & Makichi, R. (2015). "We've got something for everyone: How individual differences predict different blogging motivations." *New Media & Society*, 17(9), 1583–1600.

Fulton, J., Kuit, J., Sanders, G., & Smith, P. (2013). *The Professional Doctorate*. New York: Palgrave.

Galbraith, D. (2014). "Meeting God in the Sound." In Mike Grimshaw (ed.) *The Counter-Narratives of Radical Theology and Popular Music*. New York: Palgrave Macmillan.

Gambaccini, P. (1973). "Paul McCartney and Wings: New Theatre, Oxford." *Rolling Stone*.

Gans, D. (1984). "Twisted Sister: Twisted Logic (I'd Say Severely Bent)." Rock's Backpages, Record.

Garnett, R. (1999). "Too Low to be Low: Art Pop and the Sex Pistols." In R. Sabin (ed.) *Punk Rock: So What? The Cultural Legacy of Punk*. London: Routledge, 17–30.

Garratt, S. (1982). *The Bay City Rollers: Androgynous Heartthrobs*. Washington, DC: Collusion.

Geldof, R. (1985). Interview with *Melody Maker* magazine.

Gennaro, R & Harrison, C. (2016). *The Who and Philosophy*. Lanham, MD: Lexington.

Gianoulis, T. (2002). "Boy George: George O'Dowd." *GLBTQ Archives*. http://www.glbtqarchive.com

Gibbs, G. (1988). *Learning by Doing: A Guide to Teaching and Learning Methods*. Further Education Unit. Oxford Polytechnic: Oxford.

Gibson, L. (2010). "'You're never too old to Rock 'n' roll': Music and Aging." *Popular Anthropology Magazine*, 1(1), 28.

Gig Programme. (1981). John Martyn: Glorious Fool Tour.

Gill, A. (1997). *Kraftwerk*. Austin, TX: Mojo.

Gill, A. and Penman, I. (1979). "Joy Division, Pill Et Al: Futurama 1979 Festival: Set the Controls for the Squalor of Leeds." *New Musical Express*. https://www.nme.com.

Goldberg, D. (1969). "Ravi Shankar: Fillmore East," New York. *Billboard*. Available from https://www.rocksbackpages.com/Library/Article/ravi-shankar-fillmore-east-new-york-ny. Accessed 9 February 2021.

Goldberg, R. (2001). *Performance art: From futurism to the present*. London: Thames.

Grant, J. (2015). "Live Aid/8: perpetuating the superiority myth." *Critical Arts*, 29(3), 310–326.

Gray, J., Sandvoss, C., & Harrington, C. L. (eds.). (2017). *Fandom: Identities and communities in a mediated world*. New York: New York University Press.

Green, J. (1982). "'U2: Pluck of the Irish.' Trouser Press U2." *Rock's Backpages*. http://www.rocksbackpages.com/Library/Article/u2-pluck-of-the-irish. Accessed 2nd of September 2019.

Green, J. & Barker, G. (1999). *A riot of our own: Night and day with the Clash.* New York: Macmillan.

Grossburg, L. (1992). *Is There a Fan in the House.* New York: Routledge.

Guerra, P., & Bennett, A. (2015). "Never mind the Pistols? The legacy and authenticity of the Sex Pistols in Portugal." *Popular Music and Society*, 38(4), 500–521.

Guest, C. (2016). *Becoming Feminist: Narratives and Memories.* New York: Springer.

Gunn, J. (1999). "Gothic music and the inevitability of genre." *Popular Music & Society*, 23(1), 31–50.

Hann, M. (2010). "Bruce Springsteen and the Most Important Gig Review in History." *The Guardian.* Available from https://www.theguardian.com/music/2011/jun/12/bruce-springsteen-gig-review. Accessed 2 February 2021.

Harmon, J. (2014). "The Itchy Glowbo Blues." *New England Review*, 35(1), 63–77.

Harmon, J., & Adams, R G. (2018). "Building a Life Note by Note: Music and the Life Course." *World Leisure Journal.* New York: Taylor Francis.

Harris, C., (2020). "The JSD Band." ALLMUSIC. https://www.allmusic.com/artist/jsd-band-mn0002287940/biography. Accessed 5 January 2020.

Hewett, I. (2011). "Ravi Shankar: Edinburgh Usher Hall." *The Telegraph.* Available from https://www.telegraph.co.uk/culture/theatre/edinburgh-festival-reviews/8720557/Edinburgh-Festival-2011-Ravi-Shankar-Usher-Hall-review.html Accessed 9 February 2021.

Hasted, N. (2009). "Dr Feelgood: Oil City Rockers." Rock's Backpages, Uncut.

Hasted, N. (2015). "Dave Davies, Islington Assembly Hall: What a Night." *The Independent.* Available from https://www.independent.co.uk/arts-entertainment/music/music-magazine/live-music/live-reviews/dave-davies-islington-assembly-hall-gig-review-what-night-a6782051.html. Accessed 23 February 2021.

Hilburn, R. (2009). "Beyond ABBA's guilty pleasure." *Los Angeles Times.* Available from https://www.latimes.com/archives/la-xpm-2009-mar-24-et-backtracking24-story.html. Accessed 20 October 2020.

Hill, S. (2017). "When deep soul met the love crowd Otis Redding: Monterey Pop Festival, June 17, 1967." In Ian Inglis (ed.) *Performance and Popular Music.* New York: Routledge, 28–48.

Himmelsbach, E. (1999). Cher: Live at Arrowhead Pond, Anaheim, California, August 20 1999. *Rolling Stone.*

Hogarty, J. (2016). *Popular Music and Retro Culture in the Digital Era.* New York: Routledge.

Holder, N. (1999). *Noddy Holder: Who's Crazy Now?* London: Ebury Press.

Holmes, K. (2017). "Remembering Led Zeppelin's Legendary 1975 Earls Court Live Shows." Available at https://www.rockarchive.com/news/2017/led-zeppelin-earls-court-1975. Accessed 3 November 2020.

Horn, K. (2010). "Camping with the stars: Queer performativity, pop intertextuality, and camp in the pop art of Lady Gaga." *Current Objectives of Postgraduate American Studies*, 11.

Hoskyns, B. (1981). "Fantasy Castle: Monsters of Rock." *New Musical Express.* https://www.nme.com.

Hull, R. A. (1976). "Flamin' Groovies: Shake Some Action (Bomp!)." Rock's Backpages, Creem.

Hunter, R. Posting on my blog, 2 January, 2016. https://vintagerockwordpress.com/2012/10/09/bob-dylan-earls-court-london-sat-17-june-1978/. Accessed 28 October 2019.

Husserl, E. (1970). *The crisis of European sciences and transcendental phenomenology: An introduction to phenomenological philosophy.* Evanston, IL: Northwestern University Press.

Hutchinson, A. (2020). "When Michael Jackson celebrated his 30th birthday at Leeds Roundhay Park." *Yorkshire Post.* Available at https://www.yorkshireeveningpost.co.uk/heritage-and-retro/retro/when-michael-jackson-celebrated-his-birthday-leeds-roundhay-park-2951904. Accessed 23 October 2020.

Ingham, J. (1976). "T-Rex: The London Lyceum." Rock's Backpages, Sounds.

Ingham, J. (1976). "The Sex Pistols are four months old. . . ." Rock's Backpages, Sounds.

Inglis, I. (ed.). (2017). *Performance and popular music: history, place and time.* New York: Routledge.

Janowski, M. J. (2013). "Those who slay together, stay together: a thematic analysis of concert fan narratives and the I-57 youth punk music scene." Thesis. Charleston: Eastern Illinois University.

Jasper, M. (2011). *Professional development, reflection and decision-making for nurses.* Vol. 17. New York: John Wiley & Sons.

Johnson, D. (2015). *The Art of Living: An Oral History of Performance.* New York: Macmillan International Higher Education.

Jones, A. M. (2018). "Experimentation, performance, improvisation." In Andrew Meirion Jones & Andrew Cochrane (eds.) *The Archaeology of Art: Materials, practices, affects.* New York: Routledge, 44–56.

Journal, The. (2011). "Reuniting the wild women of punk rock." Newcastle, 23 February.

Kent, N. (1973). "Alice Cooper: Billion Dollar Babies." *New Musical Express.* https://www.nme.com.

Kent, N. (1976). "The Rolling Stones: The Rock 'N' Roll Circus Hits Town." Rock's Backpages. http://www.rocksbackpages.com/Library/Article/the-rolling-stones-the-rock-n-roll-circus-hits-town. Accessed 30 October 2019.

Kent, N. (1977). "Never Mind the Sex Pistols, Here Comes the Wrath of Sid!" *New Musical Express.* https://www.nme.com.

Kinney, F. (2014). "The Libertines at Alexandra Palace: Live Review, Louder than War." https://louderthanwar.com/the-libertines-alexandra-palace-london-live-review/.

Kiss Fan Shop. http://www.kissfanshop.de/KissTours/1983USA.htm.

Kotarba, J. A. (2005). "Rock 'n' roll experiences in middle age." *American Behavioural Scientist*, 48(11), 1524–1537.

Kotarba, J. A. (2015). "Talking about My Generation: A Sociology of Baby Boomer Music Fans." *Symbolic Interaction*, 38(2), 312–314.

Kronenburg, R. (2012) *Live Architecture: Venues, Stages and Arenas for Popular Music.* New York: Routledge.

Lacasse, S. (2005). "Persona, emotions and technology: the phonographic staging of the popular music voice." *Charm Symposium* 2, 17–18.

Laing, D. (1978). "Interpreting punk rock." *Marxism Today*, 22(4), 123–124.

Laing, D. (2015). *One chord wonders: Power and meaning in punk rock.* Oakland, CA: Pm Press.

Laing, J. & Mair, J. (2015). Music Festivals and Social Inclusion. *Leisure Sciences*, 4.

Leonard, M. & Strachan, R. (2010). *The Beat Goes On: Liverpool, Popular Music and the Changing City.* Liverpool, UK: Liverpool University Press.

Lewis, L. A. (2002). The adoring audience: Fan culture and popular media. New York: Routledge.

Liverpool Echo. (2008). "Echo Liverpool Arena Opening Extravaganza." Available from https://www.accliverpool.com/media-centre/latest-news/2008/echo-arena-liverpool-opening-extravaganza/. Accessed 5 November 2020.

Lopez, C., & Leenders, M. (2019). "Building a local identity through sellout crowds: The impact of brand popularity, brand similarity, and brand diversity at music festivals." *Journal of Strategic Marketing*, 27(5), 435–450.

Lydon, J. (2014). *Anger Is an Energy: My Life Uncensored.* London: Simon Schuester.

Lynskey, D. (2014). "Pete Seeger: The Man Who Brought Politics to Music." *The Guardian.*

Madonna Tribe. (2004). "Idol: Adored by the Tribe." Available at http://www.madonnatribe.com/idol_03/manchester.htm. Accessed 23 October 2020.

Makowski, P. (1975). "Led Zeppelin: Earls Court, London." Rock's Backpages. http://www.rocksbackpages.com/Library/Article/led-zeppelin-earls-court-london. Accessed 27 August 2019.

Marcus, G. (2009). *Lipstick Traces: A Secret History of the 20th Century.* Cambridge, MA: Harvard University Press.

Marr, J. (2014). P. Smith Blog. Available at https://myvintagerock.com/2014/03/30/red-wedge-tour-newcastle-city-hall-31st-january-1986/.

Marshall, L. (2007). *Bob Dylan: The Never-Ending Star.* New York: Polity Press.

Marshall, M. & Iddon, M. (2014) *Lady Gaga and popular music: Performing Gender, Fashion and Culture.* New York: Routledge.

Marshall, P. D. (2014). "Seriality and persona." *M/C Journal: A Journal of Media and Culture*, 17(3), 1–10.

Mayo, B. (2020). "A Tale of Domestic Terrorism, a BBC Ban, and the End of Hawkwind's Pop Career." Classic Rock. Available at https://www.loudersound.com/features/a-tale-of-domestic-terrorism-a-bbc-ban-and-the-end-of-hawkwinds-pop-career.

McCloud, S. (2003). "Popular culture fandoms, the boundaries of religious studies, and the project of the self." *Culture and Religion*, 4(2), 187–206.

McKinnon, C. A. (2010). "Louder than hell: Power, volume and the brain." In Rosemary Hill & Karl Spracklen (eds.) *Heavy Fundametalisms: Music, Metal and Politics.* Netherlands: Brill, 111–126.

Medhurst, A. (1999). "What Did I Get? Punk, Memory, and Autobiography." In R. Sabin (ed.) *Punk Rock: So What?: The Cultural Legacy of Punk.* London: Routledge, 219–231.

Mendes, A.C. & Perrott, L. (2019). "Navigating with the Blackstar: The Mediality of David Bowie." *Celebrity Studies*, 10(1), 4–13.

Metal Blade Records. (2013). "Uncle Acid and the Deadbeats: Biography." Available from https://www.metalblade.com/uncleacid/bio.php. Accessed 25 March 2021.

Moore, A. (2002). "Authenticity as Authentication." *Popular Music*, 21(2).

Morrissey. (1986). Interview with *New Musical Express*. https://www.nme.com.

Morrissey, Steven Patrick. (2013). *Morrissey: Autobiography*. New York: Penguin.

Murray, C. (1977). "The Stiff Tour: Stiffs, Drugs and Rock 'n' Roll." The Man Band Archive. http://www.manband-archive.com.

Murray, C. (2012). "Bob Marley: The Lost Profit." Rock's Backpages, The Word.

Naylor, T. (2020). "Music Venues Are Where British Culture Is Born: It's Our Duty to Keep Them Alive." *The Guardian*. Available from https://www.theguardian.com/commentisfree/2020/may/30/music-venues-british-culture-taskforce. Accessed 3 November 2020.

Needs, K. (2007). "20 Minutes to 20 Year: The Banshees Tail." Record Collector

Neill, A. & Kent, M. (2007). *Anyway Anyhow Anywhere: The Complete Chronicles of the Who 1958/1978*. London: Virgin Books.

North Tyneside Council, website. (2019). "The Buddle Arts Centre." Available from https://my.northtyneside.gov.uk/news/23560/proposals-historic-building-formerly-used-sting-unveiled. Accessed 10 November 2020.

Northern Echo. https://www.thenorthernecho.co.uk/news/7133968.eltons-king-of-the-castle/. Accessed 4th of September 2019.

O2 Arena, website. (2020). "About the O2." Available from https://www.theo2.co.uk/about-us. Accessed 5 November 2020.

O'Brien, L. (2018). *Madonna: Like an Icon*. New York: Random House.

Osborne, B. (2013). *Arctic Monkeys: Whatever People Say They Are, That's What They're Not*. Baltimore, MD: Omnibus Press.

Osgerby, B. (1999). "Chewing Out a Rhythm on My Bubble Gum: The Teenage Aesthetic and Genealogies of American Punk." In R. Sabin (ed.) *Punk Rock: So What? The Cultural Legacy of Punk*. New York: Routledge, 154–169.

Oswell, D. (2006). "When images matter: Internet child pornography, forms of observation and an ethics of the virtual." *Information, Communication & Society*, 9(2), 244–265.

Palsgraf, A. (2015). Posting on my Blog, 25 July. https://vintagerock.wordpress.com/2012/10/09/bob-dylan-earls-court-london-sat-17-june-1978/. Accessed 28 October 2019.

Pattie, D. (2007). *Rock music in performance*. New York: Palgrave Macmillan.

Peel, J. (2019). Wiki. https://peel.fandom.com/wiki/My_Top_TEn_Transcript. Accessed 14 October 2019.

Petridis, A. (2008). "Neil Young: Hammersmith Apollo, London." *The Guardian*. Available from https://www.theguardian.com/music/2008/mar/07/popandrock.neilyoung. Accessed 2 February 2021.

Petridis, A. (2011). "Bjork: Biophilia." *The Guardian*. Available from https://www.theguardian.com/music/2011/oct/06/bjork-biophilia-cd-review. Accessed 12 January 2021.

Poolan, T. (2014). Peter Smith personal blog of rock concerts attended. https://vintagerock.wordpress.com/2012/07/16/the-clash-newcastle-polytechnic-oct-28-1977-and-dec-2-1978/. Accessed 31 March 2016.

Press Association. (2016). "Status Quo's Rick Parfitt Was 'Archetypal Rock Star' Says Bandmate." *The Guardian.*

Press Release. (2015). "Fair Thee Well: Celebrating 50 Years of Grateful Dead." Available from https://media.rhino.com/press-release/fare-thee-well-celebrating-50-years-grateful-dead. Accessed 25 February 2021.

Price, S. (2004). "The Who: Royal Albert Hall, London." Rock's Backpages. http://www.rocksbackpages.com/Library/Article/the-who-royal-albert-hall-london. Accessed 2nd of September 2019.

Programme. (1976). KISS Alive. Tour Programme.

Punk77, website. http://punk77.co.uk/.

Punky Gibbon, website. http://punkygibbon.co.uk/bands/a/angelicupstarts_interview.html. Accessed 30 December 2013.

Raby Castle, website. https://www.raby.co.uk/raby-castle/. Accessed 4th of September 2019.

Rachel, D. (2016). *Walls Come Tumbling Down: The Music and Politics of Rock against Racism, Two-Tone and Red Wedge.* New York: Pan MacMillan.

Ratner, C. (2002). "Subjectivity and objectivity in qualitative methodology." In Forum Qualitative Sozialforschung/Forum: Qualitative Social Research 3(3).

Redcar Jazz Club, website. http://www.redcarjazzclub.com/index.html. Accessed 30 December 2013.

Redstar73. (2006). fanzine. Accessed 23 June.

Rees, D. (1982). *Bryan Ferry and Roxy Music.* North Yorkshire, UK: Proteus Publishing, LTD.

Richards, S. (2019). "Crass: 'Suddenly We Were Being Courted by the KGB." Uncut.

Robb, J. (2006). *Punk rock: An oral history.* New York: Random House.

Robb, J. (2011). "Bjork: Manchester International Festival." Louder than War. Available from https://louderthanwar.com/bjork-manchester-international-festivallive-review/. Accessed 12 January 2021.

Robinson, R. (2015). *Music Festivals and the Politics of Participation.* Farnham, UK: Ashgate Publishing.

Rogers, J. (2008). "The Spice Girls: Never Mind the Bum Notes." New Statesman. https://www.newstatesman.com/culture.

Roquet, P. (2009). "Ambient Landscapes from Brian Eno to Tetsu Inoue." *Journal of Popular Music Studies,* 21(4).

Rowland, H. (2017). "Yoko Ono: The World's Most Famous Unknown Artist." *The Culture Trip.* Available from https://theculturetrip.com/asia/japan/articles/yoko-ono-the-world-s-most-famous-unknown-artist/. Accessed 12 January 2021.

Sabin, R. (ed.). (2002). *Punk Rock: So What? The Cultural Legacy of Punk.* New York: Routledge.

Sage Gateshead, website. (2020). Available at https://sagegateshead.com/your-visit/access-information/facilities/. Accessed 6 November 2020.

Salewicz, C. (1983) "Punk: 1977—Two Sevens Clash." Rock's Backpages, History of Rock.

Savage J. (1981). "Punk Five Years On." *The Face.* https://www.theface.com/culture.

Savage J. (1991). *England's Dreaming: Sex Pistols and Punk Rock*. London: Faber & Faber.

Savage, J. (2009). *The England's Dreaming Tapes*. Minneapolis: University of Minnesota Press.

Savage, J. (2012). *Sex Pistols and Punk, Faber Forty-Fives: 1976*. London: Faber & Faber.

Scarborough Penthouse article, *Scarborough Evening News*, 24 May 2006

Scoppa, B. (1976). "The Rolling Stones: Black and Blue." Rock's Backpages.

Scott, S. (2013). "Bob Dylan, Blackpool: Live Review." Louder Than War. Available from https://louderthanwar.com/bob-dylan-blackpool-live-review/. Accessed 3 February 2021.

Segal, L. (1990). *Slow Motion: Changing Masculinities, Changing Men*. London: Virago.

Schulze, C. (2014). "Identity Performance in British Rock and Indie Music: Authenticity, Stylisation, and Localisation." Thesis, Lund University.

Sharp, J. (2006). "Arctic Monkeys: Whatever People Say I Am That's What I Am Not." Available from https://www.rocksbackpages.com/Library/Article/arctic-monkeys-iwhatever-people-say-i-am-thats-what-im-noti-2. Accessed 2nd of September 2021.

Shuker, R. (2002). *Popular Music: The Key Concepts*. London: Routledge.

Shumway, D. R. (2014). *Rock Star: The Making of Musical Icons from Elvis to Springsteen*. Johns Hopkins University Press.

Simonelli, D. (2012). *Working Class Heroes: Rock Music in British Society in the 1960s and 1970s*. Lanham, MD: Lexington Books

Sinfield, S. (2017). "Staffordshire Live." https://wwwstaffordshire-live.co.uk/news/history/monsters-of-rock-festival-1982-210734. Accessed 3rd of September 2019.

Smith, P. (2013). "Ladies and Gentlemen, the Greatest 'n' Roll Band in the World: Reflections of the Rolling Stones in Concert." In Helmut Staubmann (ed.) *The Rolling Stones: Sociological Perspectives*. Lanham, MD: Lexington Books, 201–222.

Smith, P. (2011). *Just Kids*. London: Bloomsbury.

Smith, P. (2014a). "How Might We Analyse Popular Music Performance?: From the Sex Pistols to the Rolling Stones," presented at the International Festival for Artistic Innovation at Leeds.

Smith, P. (2014b). "The Changing Face of Popular Music Performance." PopLife conference, University of Northampton.

Smith, P. (2015a). "Making Private Experiences Public: Creating a Blog of Rock Performance, presented at Popular Music Fandom and the Public Sphere conference, Chester University.

Smith, P. (2015b). "Holidays in the Sun: The Sex Pistols at the Seaside." *Popular Music and Society*, 1–13.

Smith, P. (2016a). "A Personal History of UK Arena Concerts: Reflections on Gigs over the Past Forty Years." In R. Edgar, K. Fairclough-Isaacs, B. Halligan, & N. Spelman (eds.) *The Arena Concert Music, Media and Mass Entertainment*. London: Bloomsbury.

Smith, P. (2016b). "An analysis of the Who in Concert: 1971 to 2014." In R. Gennaro & C. Harrison (eds.) *The Who and Philosophy*. Lanham, MD: Lexington Books, 209–222.

Smith, P. (2017). "An Analysis of the Clash in Concert: 1977 to 1982." In S. Cohen & Peacock, J. (eds). *The Clash Takes on the World: Transnational Perspectives on the Only Band that Matters.* London: Bloomsbury, 27-44.

Smith, P. (2018). *The Sex Pistols.* Lanham, MD: Rowman & Littlefield.

Smith, P., Lawson, R., Sanders, G., & Shaw, G. (2013). "The Use of Storytelling as a Research Method: The case of the Police Service of England and Wales." Proceedings of the 12th European Conference on Research Methodology for Business and Management Studies, Portugal, July 2013.

Smith P blog (2013). http://vintagerock.wordpress.com. Accessed 30 December 2013.

Smith, P. Blog. (2013). "Lynyrd Skynyrd, Newcastle City Hall 1977." Vintage Rock's Weblog. Available from https://vintagerock.wordpress.com/2013/09/30/lynyrd-skynyrd-newcastle-city-hall-1977-and-a-look-back-to-1974-and-1976/. Accessed 2 October 2021.

Smith, P. Blog. (2014). "The Reading Festival 23/25 August 1974." Vintagerock's Weblog. Available from https://vintagerock.wordpress.com/2014/02/02/the-reading-festival-16th-18th-august-1974/. Accessed 1 December 2020.

Smith, P. Blog. (2015). "War of the Worlds Newcastle Arena 27 April 2006." Vintagerock's Weblog. Available from https://vintagerock.wordpress.com/category/war-of-the-worlds/. Accessed 12 January 2021.

Smith, P. Blog. (2020). "The Vibrators Newcastle Polytechnic, 10 January 1977." Vintage Rock's Weblog. Available from https://vintagerock.wordpress.com/2020/06/11/the-vibrators-newcastle-polytechnic-10-january-1977/. Accessed 11 September 2020.

Songfacts Newsletter. (2020). "Ziggy Stardust." https://www.songfacts.com/facts/david-bowie/ziggy-stardust. Accessed 5 January 2020.

Spelman, N., Fairlough-Isaacs, K., Edgar, R., & Halligan, B. (eds.). (2016). *The Arena Concert: Music, Media, and Mass Entertainment.* London: Bloomsbury.

Springsteen, B. (2016). *Born to Run.* London: Simon & Schuster UK.

Staubmann, H. (ed.). (2013). *The Rolling Stones: Sociological Perspectives.* Lanham, MD: Lexington Books.

Steel, C. (2012). "Local History: Whitley Bay Ice Rink." Roundabout Publications. Available from http://roundaboutpublications.co.uk/feature/features/local-history/local-history-whitley-bay-ice-rink/. Accessed 11 October 2020.

Steenstra, S. (2010). *Song and Circumstance: The Work of David Byrne from Talking Heads to the Present.* London: A&C Black.

Stolworthy, J. (2021). "Arctic Monkeys, 15 Years On: How 'Whatever People Say I Am, That's What I Am Not' Defined a Generation." *The Independent.* Available from https://www.independent.co.uk/arts-entertainment/music/features/arctic-monkeys-whatever-people-say-i-am-anniversary-b1791306.html. Accessed 2nd of September 2021.

Stott, C., & Drury, J. (2004). "The importance of social structure and social interaction in stereotype consensus and content: Is the whole greater than the sum of its parts?" *European Journal of Social Psychology*, 34(1), 11–23.

Street, J. (2003). "'Fight the Power': The Politics of Music and the Music of Politics." *Government and Opposition*, 38(1), 113–130.

Sullivan, C. (1999). "The Bay City Rollers: Standing the Butt Test of Time." *The Guardian*.

Sunderland Echo. (1978). "Rock Fans Wreak Havoc in Empire." Available at http://www.sladescrapbook.com/cuttings-1978.html. Accessed 27 October 2020.

Sussex University, website: http://www.sussex.ac.uk/newsandevents/?id=20669. Accessed 30 December 2013.

Sutcliffe, P. (1978a). "'Blackbushe Festival—Nice to See Ya, Bob." Bob Dylan, Eric Clapton, Graham Parker, Joan Armatrading. Rock's Backpages." http://www.rocksbackpages.com/Library/Article/blackbushe-festival---nice-to-see-ya-bob. Accessed 14 October 2019.

Sutcliffe, P. (1978b). "Angelic Upstarts: Bolingbroke Hall, South Shields." Sounds, 4 March.

Sutcliffe, P. (1979). "Penetration/Punishment of Luxury/Neon: City Hall, Newcastle." Sounds, 6 January.

Swash, R. (2010). "Crass's Political Punk Is as Relevant Now as Ever." *The Guardian*.

Sweeting, A. (1986). "Wham! Wembley Stadium, London." *The Guardian*.

Sweeting, A. (1988). "The Greatest Showman: Michael Jackson, Wembley Stadium, London." *The Guardian*.

Sweeting, A. (2016). "Prince: Obituary." *The Guardian*. Available at https://www.theguardian.com/music/2016/apr/22/prince-obituary. Accessed 23 October 2020.

Sylvan, R. (2002). *Traces of the spirit: The religious dimensions of popular music.* New York University Press.

Tetzlaff, D. (1994). "Music for meaning: Reading the discourse of authenticity in rock." *Journal of Communication Inquiry*, 18(1), 95–117.

Thompson, B. (1998). *Seven Years of Plenty: Handbook of Irrefutable Pop Greatness, 1991–98*. London: Orion.

Thomson, G. (2015). *Under the ivy: the life & music of Kate Bush*. London: Omnibus Press.

Thornton, A. (2013). "How They The Libertines Bound Together: The Story of Pete Doherty and Carl Berat and How They Changed British Music." *Sphere*, 23 May.

Townsend, P. (2012). *Who I Am*. New York: HarperCollins.

Toynbee, J. (2016). *Making Popular Music: Musicians, Creativity and Institutions*. London: Bloomsbury.

Trowell, IM. (2017). "Hard Floors, Harsh Sounds and the Northern Anti-Festival: Futurama 1979 / 1983." *Popular Music History*, Vol. 2.

Turrini, J. M. (2013). "Well I Don't Care About History: Oral History and the Making of Collective Memory in Punk Rock." *Notes*, 70(1), 59–77.

Udo, T. (2017). "Did Punk Kill Prog?" Louder Sound. Available from https://www.loudersound.com/features/did-punk-kill-prog. Accessed 11 October 2020.

UK Rock Festivals Site. (2012). "The Hyde Park Free Festivals." Available from http://www.ukrockfestivals.com/Hyde-park-Festivals.html. Accessed 12 August 2020.

Vallack, J. (2010). "Subtextual phenomenology: A methodology for valid, first-person research." *The Electronic Journal of Business Research Methods*, 8 (2), 109–122.

Van Alst, I. and Van Melik, R. (2012). "City Festivals and Urban Development: Does Place Matter?" *Urban and Regional Studies*, Vol. 5.

Van Ham, L. (2009). "Reading Early Punk as Secularized Sacred Clowning." *Journal of Popular Culture*, 42(2), 318–339.

Waddell, R. (2015). "Grateful Dead Concerts made $52 Million and Set Record for Biggest PPV Event Ever. *Billboard*." Available from https://media.rhino.com/press-release/fare-thee-well-celebrating-50-years-grateful-dead. Accessed 25 February 2021.

Waldrep, S. (2004). *The Aesthetics of Self-Invention: Oscar Wilde to David Bowie*. Minneapolis: University of Minnesota Press.

Waldrep, S. (2016). "David Bowie and the Art of Performance." In Ian Chapman & Henry Johnson (eds.) *Global Glam and Popular Music: Style and Spectacle from the 1970s to the 2000s*. New York: Routledge, 42–54.

Walters, I. (1974). "Bob Marley: Lively Up Yourself. Let it Rock." Available from https://www.rocksbackpages.com/Library/Article/bob-marley-lively-up-yourself. Accessed 2 February 2021.

Welberry, K. and Dalziell, T. (2009). *Cultural Seeds: Essays on the Work of Nick Cave*. London: Ashgate Publishing LTD.

Welch, C. (1975). "Genesis to Revelation." *Melody Maker* magazine.

Welsh, P. (2011). *Kids in the Riot: High and Low with the Libertines*. New York: Omnibus Press.

Whitehead, J. (2014). *Pete Seeger (1919–2014): He Changed the World One Song at a Time*. Charlottesville, VA: The Rutherford Institute.

Whitelam, P. (2018). "The Day that the Beach Boys, Rod Stewart, Roxy Music, Status Quo, Slade and Don McLean performed to 50,000 people in a Muddy Field in Bardney." Lincolnshire Live. Available from https://www.lincolnshirelive.co.uk/news/lincoln-news/day-beach-boys-rod-stewart-1986745. Accessed 3 December 2020.

Witfield, G. (2020). "Elvis Costello at Sunderland Empire: Still Agitating." *Chronicle Live*. Available at https://www.chroniclelive.co.uk/whats-on/music-nightlife-news/review-elvis-costello-sunderland-empire-17859196. Accessed 4 March 2020.

Withers, D. (2010). *Adventures in Kate Bush and Theory*. Bristol, UK: Intellect Books.

Wuelfing, H. (1978). "Talking Heads Approach Art Rock from the Right Direction." *Unicorn Times*. Available from https://www.rocksbackpages.com/Library/Article/talking-heads-approach-art-rock-from-the-right-direction. Accessed 12 January 2021.

Index

ABBA, 6, 13, 72–73
ABC, 116
Adams, R. G., 173
Adams, T. E., 3
The Adoring Audience (Lewis), 71–72
the Adverts, 57
Aladdin Sane, 39
Albert Hall, 26–27
Alexandra Palace, 66–67
Alice Cooper, 12, 40–41, 50
"Alison," 64
Allen, Kate, 143
Allen, Rod, 177
Allman Brothers Band, 107
Altham, K., 28
"Amazing Journey/Sparks/See Me Feel Me," 27
American Life, 76
"Amsterdam," 39
"An Analysis of the Clash in Concert" (Smith), 11
"Anarchy in the UK," 53
Anastasio, Trey, 172
Anderton, C., 109
Ando, H., 15
Andy, Horace, 144
"Andy Warhol," 39
Angelic Upstarts, 55, 60–63
Annan, Kofi, 124

Anvil, 29–30
Arctic Monkeys, 157–58
arenas, 101
Argent, Patrick, 54
Artpop Ball, 42
art-rock, 3, 12, 14, *17*, 150
Arvidsson, A., 14
Ashcroft, Richard, 124
Atomic Rooster, 106
Auslander, P., 1, 13, 19, 50; on live performance, 9–10, 188
authenticity, 3, 12, *17*, 159, 164, 165
"Autobahn," 44
autoethnography, 10, 19
Average White Band, 105

Bacharach, Burt, 5
Bad, 77
Baez, Joan, 127–28
Band Aid, 133
"Bang Bang," 85
Banks, Tony, 149
Barbary Coast Sunderland, 48–49
Barlow, Gary, 139
Barton, Geoff, 44
Bartos, Karl, 44
Battersby, Terry, 108
Baumeister, R. F., 8
Baxter, Alex, 101–2

Baxter-Moore, N., 18
Bay City Rollers, 86–87, 117
BBC 6 Music Festival, 21 February 2015, 114–15
Beach Boys, 105
Beckett, 32
Beckham, David, 124
Bedrock Festival, 60–63
"Believe," 85
Bell, Keith, 62
Bell, Maggie, 105
"Be My Baby," 87
Bennett, A., 174
"Bennie and the Jets," 30
Berry, Chuck, 29–30
Bickerdike, J. O., 14, 71
Big Audio Dynamite, 115
Biophilia project, 137–38
Birmingham Odeon, 47–48
Bjork, 137–38
Black, Jet, 57
Black, Johnny, 49
Black and Blue, 21
Blackbushe Aerodrome, 94–95
"Black Night," 28
Blackpool Opera, 179–80
Black Sabbath, 1, 173–74
Blair, A., 38
Blamire, Rob, 60
Blitzkrieg Bob, 61
"Blitzkrieg Bop," 60
blog, 1–2, 5–9, 186
The Bluecoat, 135–37
Blunstone, Colin, 79
Bob Marley and the Wailers, 153–54
Bochner, A. P., 3
Bolan, Marc, 59
Bolingroke Hall, 60–63
Bonham, Jason, 168
Bonham, John, 25
Bon Jovi, 112
Bono, 122, 165
Bonzo Dog Band, 1, 5, 185
Booker T, 111
"Born to Be Wild," 81

"Born to Run," 151–53
Bowie, David, 5, 12, 24, 38–39, 50, 104, 122–23, 138–40
Bow Wow Wow, 45
Boy George, 45
Bragg, Billy, 125–26
Branson, Richard, 117
Brilleaux, Lee, 52
Brock, Dave, 132
Bromham, Del, 47
Brooks, Elkie, 106
Broughton, Edgar, 113–14, 118, 130–32
"Brown Sugar," 23
Buckley, Tim, 106
Bucolic Frolic, 106–7
Buddle Arts Centre, 97
Bugg, Jake, 178
Bundrick, Rabbit, 26
Burnel, Jean-Jacques, 57
Bush, Kate, 7, 14, 141–43
Buxton Festival, 108–9, 131
Byrne David, 148

Calvert, Robert, 132
Campfield Market, 137–38
cancel culture, 78
"Candle in the Wind," 30–31, 74
Canned Heat, 111
Cannon, G., 23
Captain Beefheart and the Magic Band, 39–40
Captain Sensible, 46
"Carcass," 58–59
"Careless Whisper," 74
Carey, Mariah, 124
Cave, Nick, 12, 156–57
Cecil, Paul, 55
"Changes," 39, 139
Changing Face of Popular Music Performance, 10
Chaplin, Gary, 60
Chapman, Roger, 108
Charlesworth, C., 93
Cher, 85–86
Chimenti, Jeff, 172

"Chiquitita," 73
church, concerts as, 18, 186
"The Circle of Life," 30
civil rights movement, 128
Clapton, Eric, 7
the Clash, 5, 7, 11–12, 54–56, 67–68
The Clash Takes on the World, 11
Clifton, S., 12
Close to the Edge, 92
Clufetos, Tommy, 174
Cobley, P., 46, 56
Cochrane, T., 13
Cocker, Joe, 106
Coldplay, 124
Collins, Phil, 123, 149
Colour by Numbers, 45
Communards, 125–26
communities, 2, 12, *17*, 117–19
Computer World, 44–45
concert halls, 100
Coon, Caroline, 46, 57
Corgan, Billy, 139
Cornwell, Hugh, 57
Costello, Elvis, 63–64
Cottonwood, 113
"Coz I Luv You," 81
Crass, 13, 129–30
Cray, Robert, 111
Cream, 7
"Crocodile Rock," 30
Cruikshank, Pete, 110, 182
Culture Club, 45–46
Curtis, Adam, 143–45
Curved Air, 113, 149–50

Daltrey, Roger, 26, 27, 93, 175, 182
the Damned, 12, 46, 68
"Dancing Queen," 72–73
Dangerous, 78
"Daniel," 30
Daniels, John, 54
"Darling Be Home Soon," 81
Davidson, D., 15
Davies, Dave, 170–71
Davies, Ray, 110, 170–71

"Day in the Life," 80
Dee, Kiki, 117, 123
Deep Purple, 1, 28–29
De Fina, A., 8
Dettmar, Del, 132
Devoto, Howard, 54
Dido, 124
Dire Straits, 148
Doherty, Pete, 124
"Don't Dictate," 61
"Don't Let the Sun Go Down on Me," 30
"Don't Rain on My Parade," 100
Doobie Brothers, 107
the Doors, 29
"Do They Know It's Christmas?," 124, 133
"Down Down," 29
"Do You Really Want to Hurt Me," 45
Dr. Feelgood, 51–52
Duran Duran, 139
Durutti Column, 116
"Duty Free Technology," 60
Dylan, Bob, 5, 8, 13, 32–34, 94–95, 127, 179–80

Earl's Court, 24–26, 32–34, 75–76
Edinburgh Festival, 9
Edinburgh Playhouse, 162–64
Electric Light Orchestra, 113–14
"11 O'Clock Tick Tock," 28
Elliott, Joe, 139
Ellis, C., 3, 10
Emerson, Keith, 169
Empire Cinema, 172–73
energy, 2, 12, *16*, 51, 69
Eno, Brian, 9–12, 146–48
Entwistle, John, 175, 182
epiphany, 4, 18, 187
Ertegün, Ahmet, 167
"Evergreen," 100
Exile on Main Street, 21–22

the Faces, 31–32, 108–9, 118
fandom, 2, 12, 14, *16*, 71

Feezell, J. T., 14
Ferry, Bryan, 146
festivals, 118–19
The Fifth Wall, 4, 11, 67–68
"Fire," 28
"Firestarter," 65
"Firing Squad," 61
first gigs, 185–86
Fiske, J., 14, 71
"5:15," 27
"Five Years," 39, 139
Flamin' Groovies, 46, 59
Flint, Keith, 65–66
Floyd, Jerry, 114
Focus, 105, 113–14
Foreigner, 160
Foreign Skies, 74
Forever, 83
Forsten, Steve, 62
the Fortunes, 177, 182
Fourth Wall, 67–68
Fowler, Bernard, 140
Frazer, Elizabeth, 144
"Freebird," 23, 162
"Free Money," 61
Frehley, Ace, 47
Friedlander, P., 97–98
Frith, Simon, 9, 128, 152
Furnier, Vincent Damian. *See* Alice Cooper
Futurama 2 Festival, 115–17

"Gabba Gabba Hey," 60
Gabriel, Peter, 106, 149–50
Gans, David, 42
Garcia, Jerry, 87, 172–73
Garfunkel, Art, 95–96
Garnett, R., 54
Garrett, Siedah, 75–76
Garson, Mike, 138–40
Gates, Bill, 124
Gee, Lorna, 125
Geldof, Bob, 122, 123
Genesis, 106, 113, 118, 149–50
Georgakopoulou, A., 8

"Get Down and Get With It," 81
"Get Off of My Cloud," 23
Gillan, Ian, 28–29, 160
Gilmour, David, 125
Ginsberg, Allen, 161
Giscombe, Junior, 125–26
Glasgow Apollo, 22
Glasgow Hampden Park, 78–80
Glastonbury Festival, 25-27 June 2010, 109–10
Glitter, Gary, 74, 116–17
"Gloria," 27, 28
Glover, Roger, 28–29
"Go Buddy Go," 57
Golden Earring, 161–62
Goldsmith, Harvey, 168
"Go Now," 79
Good Habit, 113
Gorillaz, 110
Grateful Dead, 87, 172–73
Gray, J., 14, 71
Great Western Express Festival, 1972, 104–6
Green, Jim, 27
Greenfield, Dave, 57
"Grip," 57
Grossburg, L., 164
Groundhogs, 110–11, 182, 183
Grundy, Bill, 53–54
Guest, C., 83
"Gypsies, Tramps & Thieves," 85

Hackett, Steve, 149
Halliwell, Geri, 83
Hammersmith Apollo, 141–43
Handbook of Narrative Analysis (De Fina & Georgakopoulou), 8
"Hang on to Yourself," 38–39
"Happy," 23
the Happy Mondays, 158
Harper, Roy, 1, 5, 97, 100, 185
Harrington, C. L., 14, 71
Harrison, George, 154–55
Harry Hack and the Big G, 61
Harry Potter series, 71

Hart, Mickey, 172
Hawkes, Chip, 177
Hawkwind, 29–30, 52, 132
"Headlines (Friendship Never Ends)," 84–85
Heads, Hands & Feet, 105
the Healers, 158
"Hear Me Callin'," 81
Heavy Metal Kids, 40–41
Heavy Pettin', 48
"Helter Skelter," 59
Henry, Lenny, 124
"Hey Jude," 80
Heyward, Nick, 74
Hicks, Tony, 171
"Highway Star," 28
"Hi Hi Hi," 79
Hill, Dave, 81
Hillage, Steve, 117
Hogarty, J., 179
"Holidays in the Sun" (Smith), 10–11
the Hollies, 14, 171–72, 182
Holton, Gary, 40
"Hong Kong Garden," 59
"Honky Tonk Women," 23
Hook, Peter, 18, 187
Horne, Nicky, 25
Hornsby, Bruce, 172
Hot Chip, 115
Hot Rats, 39
Houdini, 47
Howard, Peter, 61–62
Howarth, Peter, 171
Howlett, Liam, 65
"How might we analyse popular music performance?" (Smith), 10
Hull, R. A., 46
Human League, 59
Humble Pie, 108–9
Hunky Dory, 38
Hunter, Ian, 140
Husserl, E., 12
Hütter, Ralf, 44
Hyde Park, 178–79

Ian Dury and the Blockheads, 63
"I Can't Explain," 27
icons, 2, 12, *16*, 21–35, *22*
"I Don't Want to go to Chelsea," 64
If, 113–14
Ignorant, Steve, 129–30
"I Got You Babe," 85
"I Hate the White Man," 97
Ingham, Jonn, 52–53
"In Like a Shot from My Gun," 81
"In My Time of Dying," 25
International Festival for Artistic Innovation, 10
"I Saw the Light," 23
Isle of Wight Festival, 14
Islington Assembly Hall, 170–71
"I've Just Seen a Face," 80
"I Will Follow," 28

Jackson, Michael, 5, 77–78
Jackson Heights, 106, 113
"Jack the Ripper," 49
Jagger, Mick, 123, 179, 182
Jahn, Mike, 41
the Jam, 57
James, Brian, 46
Jasper, Melanie, 18
Jeeves, Mahatma Kane, 114
Jericho, 113–14
Jobson, Eddie, 146
John, Elton, 30–31, 74, 123, 124
Johnny Otis Show, 113–14
Johnny Thunders and the Heartbreakers, 58
Johnson, Wilko, 52
Jones, Brian, 23
Jones, Kenny, 31
Jones, Mick, 56
JSD Band, 38
"Jumping Jack Flash," 23
"Junior's Wailing," 81

"Karma Chameleon," 45
"Kashmir," 25

Keane, 124
Kelly, Jonathan, 106, 113–14
Kent, N., 22
"The Kids Are All Right," 27
King, Martin Luther, Jr., 128
King, Simon, 132
Kinks, 170–71
Kircher, Pete, 29
Kirke, Simon, 169
Kiss, 47–48, 50
Kissing to be Clever, 45
Knebworth, 14, 21–23
"Knowing Me Knowing You," 73
Kotarba, J. A., 14, 177
Kraftwerk, 44–45
Kreutzmann, Bill, 172
Kronenburg, R., 96

Lacasse, S., 13
"Ladies and Gentlemen, the Greatest Rock 'n' Roll Band in the World" (Smith), 10
Lady Gaga, 42–43
"The Lady Is A Vamp," 85
Lady Starlight, 42
Laine, Denny, 79
Laing, D., 13, 51
Lambert, Adam, 140
Lancashire Cricket Ground, 157–58
Lancaster, Alan, 29
Lane, Ronnie, 31
Lauri, Steve, 171
"Lazy," 28
Lea, Jim, 81
le Bon, Simon, 74
Led Zeppelin, 1, 5, 7, 13, 22, 24–26, 93, 167–70
Lee, Albert, 105
Leeds University Refectory, 153–54
Lemmy, 132
Lennon, John, 136
Lennox, Annie, 124
Leonard, M., 91
Lesh, Phil, 172, 173
"Less Than Zero," 64

"Let's Spend the Night Together," 23
Letts, Don, 114–15
Lewis, L. A., 14, 71
Lewis, Linda, 113–14
the Libertines, 66–67
Lick It Up, 48
Lincoln Festival, 82, 89–91
Lindisfarne, 105, 109
literature, consulting, 13–14
"Little Fat Man," 139
Little Richard, 25, 79
Live 8, 7, 123–25
Live Aid, 7, 12, 34, 122–23, 133
"Live and Let Die," 79
live performance, 35; Auslander on, 9–10, 188; elements of, 3; first gigs, 185–86; quality of, 3; subjectivity of, 186
Liverpool Echo Arena, 97–99
Liverpool Empire, 40–41
Liverpool the Musical, 97–99
Locomotive GT, 105
Londonberry Hotel, 89–91
"Londy Lady," 57
"Long Tall Sally," 79
"Look Wot You Done," 81
Lord, Jon, 28
"The Lord's Prayer," 59
"Love Reign O'er Me," 27
Lowe, Nick, 63
Lucas, Matt, 124
Lydon, Jimmy, 116
Lydon, John. *See* Rotten, Johnny
Lynyrd Skynyrd, 23, 161–62

Maclagan, Ian, 31
Mad Dog, 185
Madonna, 5, 13, 75–76, 124
"Maggie May," 31–32
Magnum, 112
Mahavishnu Orchestra, 106–7
Make Poverty History, 123
"Making Private Experiences Public" (Smith), 10
Makowski, Pete, 26

Malone, Richie, 176
Man, 108, 113–14
Manchester Arena, 75–76, 82–86
Manchester International Festival, 143–45
"The Man Who Sold the World," 139
Marillion, 112
Marley, Bob, 5, 153–54
Marr, Johnny, 126, 158
Marsden, Gerry, 177
Marshall, P. D., 13
Martyn, John, 89–91
"Mary," 49
Maryport Blues Festival, 110–11
Massive Attack, 143–45
Matching Mole, 114
Matlock, Glen, 53
maturity, 3, 12, *17*, 181–83
Maxim, 65–66
"Maybe I'm Amazed," 79
Mayfair, 27–28
"May You Never," 90
MC5, 160–61
McCartney, Linda, 78–80
McCartney, Paul, 78–80, 123, 124, 125
McCullough, Henry, 79
McGee, Alan, 67
McKay, John, 58
McKinnon, C. A., 186
McLaren, Malcolm, 45, 54
McLaughlin, John, 106–7
McLean, Don, 106
McNally, John, 178
McPhee, Tony, 110, 182, 183
McPherson, Gillian, 114
"Me and My Woman," 97
Medhurst, A., 18
Melody Maker, 49
Mensi, 62
Metallica, 112
"Metal Postcard," 58–59
methodological approach, 1–2; limitations of, 18; trialling, 9–12
Michael, George, 74

Middlesborogh Town Hall, 58–59, 63–64
Middlesbrough Rock Garden, 101
"Midnight Rambler," 23
Mik, Dik, 132
Mond, 62
"Money Money Money," 73
Monsters of Rock festival, 7, 29–30
Monty Python's Flying Circus, 105
Moon, Keith, 175, 182
"Moonage Daydream," 39, 139
Moore, A., 164
Morris, Kenny, 58
Morrissey, 18, 126, 187
Morton, Rockette, 39–40
Mott the Hoople, 108–9
Moving Targets, 61
Ms. Dynamite, 124
"Mull of Kintyre," 80
Mungo Jerry, 113, 149–50
"The Murder of Liddle Towers," 62
Murray, Charles, 63–64
Murray, Pauline, 60
Muse, 110
Music, 75
"My Generation," 27

Natural Acoustic Band, 105
Nazareth, 105, 113
Needs, Kris, 58, 59
"Never Give Up on the Good Times," 83
Newcastle Arena, 42–43
Newcastle City Hall: Bowie at, 38–39; Captain Beefheart and the Magic Band at, 39–40; Costello, Elvis at, 63–64; Culture Club at, 45–46; Dr. Feelgood at, 51–52; Kiss at, 47–48; Kraftwerk at, 44–45; Led Zeppelin at, 24–26; Lynyrd Skynyrd at, 161–62; McCartney, Paul at, 78–80; Queen at, 34; the Ramones at, 59–60; Red Wedge Tour at, 125–27; Roxy Music at, 145–46; Seger, Pete at, 128; Smith, Patti at, 159–61;

Status Quo at, 176–77; the Stranglers at, 56–58; Talking Heads at, 148–49; Yes at, 91–92; Young, Neil, 162–64; Young, Neil at, 162–64
Newcastle Mayfair, 41–42, 44–45
Newcastle Polytechnic, 63–64, 94–95, 148
Newcastle Telewest Arena, 127
Newcastle University, 54–56
Newman, L. S., 8
the Nice, 106
Nick Cave and the Bad Seeds, 156–57
Nieve, Steve, 64
1960s Gold Tour, 177–78
Noble, Joe, 53
Notsensibles, 116
"No Woman No Cry," 153–54

O2 Arena, 7, 76–77, 82–85, 99–100, 167–70
Oasis, 5, 158–59
O'Connor, Hazel, 116
October, 27
O'Dowd, George. *See* Boy George
Old Grey Whistle Test, 148
Oldman, Gary, 140
"Old Red Wine," 26, 27
Ono, Yoko, 12, 14
Osbourne, Ozzy, 174

Page, Jimmy, 25, 168–69
Paice, Ian, 28
Palladino, Pino, 26
Palmer, Robert, 106
"Paranoid," 174
Parfitt, Rick, 29
Paris, Mica, 111
"Peaches," 57
Peel, John, 32, 114, 118, 131
Penetration, 60–63
persona, 2, 12, *16*, 37, *37*, 50
personal context, 186
"A Personal History of UK Arena Concerts" (Smith), 11
the Persuasions, 105

"Pinball Wizard," 27
Pink Floyd, 124–25
Pitt, Brad, 124
Planet Earth, 76
Plant, Robert, 25, 169–70
"Police Oppression," 62
politics, 3, 12, 14, *17*
Polytechnic Wearmouth Hall, 48–49
Ponty, Jean Luc, 106
Powell, Don, 81
"Power to the People," 99
Prefab Sprout, 126
the Prefects, 56
Price, S., 26
Prince, 5, 13, 76–77
the Prodigy, 65–66
Psychedelic Furs, 116
Public Music Fandom and the Public Sphere conference, 10
punk, 55, 57–58, 61, 68, 69
Pustelnik, Ken, 110, 182

Quadrophenia, 175–76
Queen, 5, 34, 117, 119, 122
"Queen Bitch," 38–39
Quintessence, 114

Raby Castle, 30–31
Radio-Activity, 44
Rainbow, 96–97
the Ramones, 59–60
Ratner, C., 3, 18
Rat Scabies, 68
Ratt, 112
Rattus Norvegicus, 57
Ray of Light, 75
Razorlight, 124
Reading Festival, 112–14, 149–50, 159–61
Reading Rock Festival, 7, 14, 89–91
"Real Good-Looking Boy," 26
Redcar Coatham Bowl, 46
"Red Shoes," 64
Red Wedge Tour, 125–27
reflection, 10, 19

religion, 186–87
R.E.M., 124, 161
"Remember," 87
Rezillos, 60
Richards, Keith, 179, 182
Ringo Starr, 97–99
"Rip It Up," 25
"Roadhouse Blues," 29
Robinson, Tom, 160
Rock against Racism, 133
"Rock and Roll," 25
"Rocket Man," 30
"Rocking All over the World," 29
Rocking the Castle Festival, 111–12
"Rock 'n' Roll Suicide," 39
RocksBackPages, 15
the Rolling Stones, 1, 5, 7, 13, 21–23, 119, 178–79, 182
"Roll Over Lay Down," 29
Ronson, Mick, 139
Rossi, Francis, 29
Rotten, Johnny, 53, 54, 68
"Roundabout," 92
Roundhay Park, 77–78
Roxy Music, 105, 145–46
Royal Albert Hall, 7
Royal Blood, 115
Rundgren, Todd, 23
Rutherford, Mike, 149
Ryder, Shaun, 158

Sabin, R., 13, 51
Safe as Milk, 39
Sage Gateshead, 91, 114–15, 127–29, 159–61, 171–72, 177–78; Baez, Joan at, 127–28; BBC 6 Music Festival, 21 February 2015, 114–15; the Hollies at, 171–72; 1960s Gold Tour, 177–78; Smith, Patti at, 159–61
Sandvoss, C., 14, 71
"Satisfaction," 23
"Saturday Night," 87
Saxon, 29–30
"Say You Don't Mind," 79
Scarborough Penthouse, 52–54

Schneider, Florian, 44
"School's Out," 40, 50
Schwarz, Brinsley, 79
Scissor Sisters, 124
Scoppa, B., 21
The Scream, 58
Screaming Lord Sutch, 48–49
Screamin' Jay Hawkins, 49
"Sea and Sand," 27
the Searchers, 177
Sebastian, John, 81
Seeger, Peggy, 129
Seeger, Pete, 13, 128
Seiwell, Denny, 79
Sensational Alex Harvey Band, 106–7
Severin, Steve, 58, 68
the Sex Pistols, 5, 10–12, 18, 22, 52–54, 55, 68, 187
The Sex Pistols (Smith), 11
Shake Some Action, 46
Sha Na Na, 106
"Shang-a-Lang," 86
Shankar, Ravi, 5, 154–56
shared identities, 96
"Sheena is a Punk Rocker," 60
Sheffield Arena, 173–74
Shuker, R., 74
Shumway, D. R., 21
"Sick Again," 25
"Silent Community," 61
Simkins, Merv, 56
Simmons, Gene, 47
Simon, Paul, 95–96
Simon and Garfunkel, 95–96
Simply Red, 116
Sinfield, S., 29–30
Siouxsie and the Banshees, 58–59, 68
Slade, 80–82, 101
"Slaughter on 10th Avenue," 139
the Slits, 115
Smallman, Gary, 60
"Small Town Small Mind," 62
Smeaton, Bob, 24
Smith, Fred, 160–61
Smith, P., 4, 10–11

Smith, Patti, 13, 61, 159–61
the Smiths, 126
"Smoke on the Water," 28
Snider, Dee, 41–42
Snoop Dogg, 124
Snow Patrol, 124
Solid Air, 90, 91
Solid Gold Cadillac, 113–14
"Someone Saved My Life Tonight," 30
"Song for Bob Dylan," 38–39
"Space Oddity," 38, 139
Spencer Davis Group, 105
Spice Girls, 82–85, 87
"Spice Up Your Life," 83, 84
Spiceworld, 83
Spiteri, Sharleen, 80
Spizz Oil, 59
Split, 182
SPOTS tour, Sex Pistols, 11, 54
Springsteen, Bruce, 5, 13, 151–53, 187
"Squeeze Box," 92–93
Squire, Chris, 169
Stackridge, 114
stadiums, 101
Stafford Bingley Hall, 72–73, 92–93
"Stairway to Heaven," 25
Stanley, Paul, 47
Starkey, Zak, 26
"Starman," 38, 39
Status Quo, 8, 14, 29–30, 81, 106, 114, 118, 122, 176–77, 182, 183
"Stay With Me," 31
Steamhammer, 81, 113
"Step to Me," 83
Stereophonics, 124
Stewart, Dave, 98–99
Stewart, Rod, 31, 118
Sting, 124
Stipe, Michael, 161
Strachan, R., 91
"Strange Kind of Woman," 28
the Stranglers, 56–58
the Strawbs, 105
Stray, 47, 114
"Street Fighting Man," 23

Street Legal, 32
Streisand, Barbra, 6, 99–100
String Driven Thing, 114
Strummer, Joe, 56, 68
"Student Power," 55, 62
Style Council, 125–26
"Substitute," 27, 93
"Suffragette City," 39
"Summerlove Sensation," 87
Sunderland Empires, 5, 63–64, 141–43
Sunderland Locarno, 31–32, 80–82, 86–87, 131
Sunderland Top Rank, 31–32, 38, 50
Supercharge, 117
"The Supermen," 38–39
Sutcliffe, Phil, 61, 63
Sutherland Brothers, 114
Swinging Laurels, 45

Tales from Topographic Oceans, 91–92
Talking Heads, 148–49
"Tangerine," 25
Taylor, Mick, 179
Teardrop Explodes, 27
Teenage Cancer Trust, 26
Tempest, 180–81
Tempest, Kate, 114–15
Temple, Julian, 52
Ten Years After, 81, 114, 183
Thatcher, Margaret, 125
thematic analysis, 12–13
"Things Have Changed," 181
Thin Lizzy, 104, 141
Thin White Duke. *See* Bowie, David
Thomas, Pete, 64
Thompson, B., 65
Thompson, Danny, 90
"Thunder Road," 152–53
ticket stubs, 7
"Time (Clock of the Heart)," 45
"Tiny Dancer," 30
Tommy, 92–93, 176
"Tom Tiddler's Ground," 97
Townshend, Pete, 26–27, 93, 175, 182

Townshend, Simon, 26
"Trampled Underfoot," 25
Travis, 124
T Rex, 58–59
Trout Mask Replica, 39
Turner, Alex, 158
Turner, Nik, 132
Turrini, J. M., 18
"20th Century Boy," 58–59
Twisted Sister, 41–42
"2 Become 1," 85

U2, 27–28, 122, 124, 164–65
UB40, 124
Uncle Acid and the Dead Beats, 173
Ure, Midge, 122, 123
Uriah Heep, 29–30, 183
Usher Hall, 154–56

Vallack, J., 1, 10, 12, 19
Vance, Tommy, 29
Van Ham, L., 46
Vanium, Dave, 46
Van Vliet, Don, 40
Velvet Revolver, 124
venues, 2, 12, *16*, 100–102
the Vibrators, 94–95
Vinegar Joe, 106, 114
vintagerock.wordpress.com. *See* blog
"Vogue," 76

Wade, Decca, 62
"Waiting for the Man," 39
Wakeman, Rick, 140
"Walking on Thin Ice," 136
Walliams, David, 124
"Wannabe," 83
Ward, Bill, 174
War of the Worlds, 140–41
"War Pigs," 174
"Watching the Detectives," 64
"Waterloo," 73
Waters, Roger, 125
Watkinson, Matt, 54
Watts, Charlie, 179

Wayne, Jeff, 140–41
"The Way We Were," 100
Weir, Bob, 172, 173
Welsh, P., 67
Wembley Arena, 175–76
Wembley Stadium, 73–75, 95–96
West, Mae, 42
Wetton, John, 146
"We Vibrate," 94
Weymouth, Tina, 148
Wham!, 73–75
"What Are You Doing the Rest of Your Life?," 100
"Whatever You Want," 29
White, Alan, 169
White Horse Inn, 52–54
"White Light/White Heat," 39
Whitley Bay Ice Rink, 96–97
the Who, 1, 5, 7, 13, 14, 26–27, 92–93, 122–25, 175–76, 182
The Who and Philosophy, 11
"Who Are You," 27
Who Do We Think We Are, 28
Wilde, Kim, 77
Williams, Robbie, 124
"Willie the Pimp," 39
Windsor Free Festival, 133
Wings, 78–80
Wishbone Ash, 105
Wizzard, 114
Woldu, Birhan, 124
Wolff, John, 93
"Woman from Tokyo," 28
Wonder, Stevie, 110
"Won't Get Fooled Again," 27, 93
Wood, Ronnie, 31, 169, 179
Woodstock, 14
WordPress, 8–9
Wreckless Eric, 63
Wyman, Bill, 169

X-Ray Spex, 57

Yes, 1, 5, 91–92, 185
Yoko Ono, 135–37

"You Can't Always Get What You Want," 23
"You Don't Bring Me Flowers," 100
Young, Neil, 162–64

Zappa, Frank, 39, 106
Ziggy Stardust. *See* Bowie, David
"Ziggy Stardust," 38, 139
ZZ Top, 7, 112

About the Authors

Peter Smith is emeritus professor at the University of Sunderland, UK. He is a prolific author, academic, and researcher, having written over three hundred books, book chapters, and academic papers. He has presented at conferences throughout the world, and written on a range of topics including computer science, artificial intelligence, engineering, management, education, and music. He is the author of the book *Sex Pistols: Pride of Punk*, published by Tempo Books. He is a renowned academic having supervised and examined over one hundred PhD candidates. He is an obsessive concertgoer, having attended over 2,000 concerts since the late 1960s. He maintains a blog of his concert experiences on https://vintagerock.wordpress.com/. You can read more about Peter on his Wikipedia page: https://en.wikipedia.org/wiki/Peter_Smith_(computer_scientist).

Laura Smith, Peter's daughter, is a sociologist, teacher, and musician. She is a classically trained singer, qualified vocal tutor, and a regular concertgoer along with her father. She is a writer and mother to two young children. She also provides the haunting vocal soundscape to renowned folk-roots world music band, the Shining Levels.

www.ingramcontent.com/pod-product-compliance
Lightning Source LLC
Chambersburg PA
CBHW061713300426
44115CB00014B/2663